PRAIRIE
DEFENDER

PRAIRIE DEFENDER

The Murder Trials of Abraham Lincoln

GEORGE R. DEKLE, SR.

Southern Illinois University Press   *Carbondale*

Southern Illinois University Press
WWW.SIUPRESS.COM

20 19 18 17   4 3 2 1

Jacket illustration: ambrotype of Lincoln, taken the year before he tried the Patterson case (cropped). PHOTOGRAPH COURTESY OF THE LIBRARY OF CONGRESS.

Frontispiece: ambrotype of Lincoln, taken the day of his successful defense of William Duff Armstrong (unretouched). FROM THE ARCHIVES AND SPECIAL COLLECTIONS, UNIVERSITY OF NEBRASKA–LINCOLN LIBRARIES.

Library of Congress Cataloging-in-Publication Data
Names: Dekle, George R., 1948– author.
Title: Prairie defender : the murder trials of Abraham Lincoln /
George R. Dekle, Sr.
Description: Carbondale : Southern Illinois University Press, 2017. |
Includes bibliographical references and index.
Identifiers: LCCN 2016042467 | ISBN 9780809335978 (hardback) |
ISBN 9780809335985 (e-book)
Subjects: LCSH: Lincoln, Abraham, 1809–1865—Career in law. | Criminal
defense lawyers—Illinois—Biography. | Trials (Murder)—Illinois—History—
19th century. | BISAC: HISTORY / United States / 19th Century. | BIOGRAPHY &
AUTOBIOGRAPHY / Lawyers & Judges. | LAW / Criminal Law / General. | LAW /
Trial Practice. | BIOGRAPHY & AUTOBIOGRAPHY / Presidents & Heads of State.
Classification: LCC KF368.L52 D45 2017 | DDC 345.773/02523—dc23
LC record available at https://lccn.loc.gov/2016042467

Printed on recycled paper. ♲

This paper meets the requirements of ANSI/NISO Z39.48-1992 (Permanence of Paper) ∞

To my wife, Lane, who has patiently stood by me and supported me through thick and thin, including the writing and publication of six previous books

History is not history unless it is the truth.

—*Abraham Lincoln*

Contents

Illustrations

Acknowledgments

JOHN DONNE WROTE THAT "NO MAN IS AN ISLAND, ENTIRE OF ITSELF," AND those words are certainly true of any project that a person undertakes. This book benefited from the input and assistance of many different individuals, and any attempt to name all of them will certainly be plagued by omissions. Nevertheless, I shall undertake to name and thank as many as I can.

Sylvia Frank Rodrigue, executive editor of Civil War and Abraham Lincoln books at Southern Illinois University Press, guided me through the submissions process with many helpful suggestions and critiques. Copy editor Joyce Bond caught many errors and corrected my sometimes unorthodox grammar. Duffy Soto, at Hunter Printing in Lake City, Florida, helped with the illustrations, as did Delaine Spradley Photography and Design, also of Lake City. Travis H. D. Lewin, professor of law emeritus at Syracuse University, provided assistance with research into the Patterson case. Guy C. Fraker, author of *Lincoln's Ladder to the Presidency: The Eighth Judicial Circuit*, gave me background material on the Eighth Judicial Circuit of Illinois. Pamela's Music, curator of the Springer Sisters Museum (found online at http://www .pamelasmusic.co.uk/Museum1.htm), and Michael Shaubs, author of "Mountain Men and Life in the Rocky Mountain West" (http://www.mman.us/index .htm), aided my research into antique weapons.

Many staff members at various museums and libraries assisted me with locating various documents, references, and photographs. Those helpful individuals include Anke Voss, Urbana Free Library; Cheryl Schnirring, Abraham Lincoln Presidential Library; Debbie Ham, the Papers of Abraham Lincoln; Glenna Schroeder-Lein, Abraham Lincoln Presidential Library; Jeanette Cowden, Looking for Lincoln Heritage Association; Joshua Caster, University of Nebraska, Lincoln Libraries; Keith Bruns, Hancock County Historical Society volunteer; Kelly Clausing, the Papers of Abraham Lincoln; and Roberta Fairburn, Abraham Lincoln Presidential Library.

Finally, my wife, Lane, patiently proofread and reproofread the manuscript each time I asked and made excellent suggestions for improvement. Each of the named individuals has helped make this a far better work than it would otherwise have been. Any fault the reader may find with the book should be attributed solely to the author.

PRAIRIE
DEFENDER

Introduction: The Legend of Lincoln the Lawyer

WHEN ABRAHAM LINCOLN RECEIVED THE REPUBLICAN NOMINATION FOR the presidency of the United States, his supporters talked more about the few years of his youth spent splitting logs as a common laborer than they did the twenty-five years he spent splitting hairs as a counselor at law. The one mention they made of his career as a lawyer was to tell the story of *People v. Armstrong*, a case where he defended the son of a penniless widow against a charge of murder and got him acquitted by the brilliant use of an almanac. In the years following his assassination, Lincoln's biographers wrote hundreds of volumes extolling his virtues but virtually ignoring his law practice.

When his biographers took notice of his law practice, they painted it in glowing colors. Unlike the typical lawyer, they insisted, Lincoln never read a law book through in his entire life, never researched a case, did not know or rely on legal technicalities, and relied more on horse sense and folksy charm than on lawyerly skills to win cases.[1] He was portrayed as always championing the underdog and battling on the side of the angels in the war between good and evil. His unswerving honesty prevented him from ever defending anyone he knew or suspected to be wrong, and his desire for justice always overcame his selfish love of victory.[2] In short, he refused to use technicalities, declined to defend unjust causes, and always performed poorly when he found himself on the wrong side of a case.[3] The catalog of Lincoln's reputed virtues as a lawyer comes supported by a host of anecdotes. Probably the most well attested of his legendary virtues is his reputed inability to argue effectively for a guilty defendant.[4] The stories supportive of these virtues were originally told in the decades immediately following Lincoln's death, when hardly anyone had a harsh word for the martyred president, and they form a type of literature that some have labeled "Lincolnolatry."[5]

The opposite of "Lincolnolatry" is "Lincolnoclasm." Lincolnolators believe Lincoln always addressed the merits of a case and never raised technical defenses, would not defend a guilty client, would admit fault when his client was wrong, and never used any "lawyerly" tricks. Lincolnoclasts claim Lincoln was a third-rate lawyer of questionable ethics who was not above hoodwinking judges, making specious jury arguments, fabricating evidence, improperly playing on the emotions of his audience, and otherwise using any available method to win at all costs.[6] The earliest practitioner of Lincolnoclasm was Edgar Lee Masters, who seemingly took great pleasure in cataloging all of Lincoln's real and imagined faults as a lawyer. His critique of Lincoln was so vitriolic that a bill was introduced in Congress to ban his book, *Lincoln the Man*, from the mail as "obscene, lewd, lascivious, filthy, and indecent."[7]

One thing that both Lincolnolators and Lincolnoclasts seem to agree on is Lincoln's performance as a criminal lawyer. There appears to be a firmly entrenched belief that Lincoln hated criminal cases and was a poor criminal lawyer and an especially poor prosecutor, because he lacked either the talent or the necessary "intellectual unscrupulousness" to practice criminal law.[8] According to the Lincolnolators, "If Lincoln appeared in a criminal case at all, it was invariably in defending some poor unfortunate who was unable to hire an attorney, and Lincoln, out of the goodness of his great and sympathetic heart, came to the rescue."[9]

The belief that Lincoln was not a good criminal lawyer has gained traction since the online publication of *The Law Practice of Abraham Lincoln*, edited by Martha L. Benner, Cullom Davis, and colleagues. Historians using this resource have studied the pleadings and papers placed online and have tabulated the various types of cases represented. By a simple count of cases, Lincoln does not appear to have had much of a criminal practice. Records of only 292 criminal cases handled by Lincoln have been found, making up 5.9 percent of the total number of his known cases,[10] and only a few of those were murder cases. By one historian's count, Lincoln tried seventeen murder cases and lost ten of them.[11] By another's count, Lincoln had twenty-six murder cases, just 9 percent of his total number of criminal cases, with a record of ten convictions, eight acquittals, six dismissals, and one plea of guilty.[12]

The scholarly consensus seems to be that Lincoln was first and foremost a politician,[13] but his political career is not the focus of this book. Because I aim to test the validity of the commonly held beliefs about Lincoln's criminal law practice, I will mention his life outside the courtroom only as it had an effect on his performance inside the courtroom. This almost exclusive focus on his legal career, especially his criminal law career, is justified if one is to fully understand the complex man who guided our nation through the Civil War. Such a study can show how Lincoln's experience as a criminal lawyer helped prepare him for the important role he played as he led our nation through that conflict.

Lincoln was not the only Civil War leader to benefit from having practiced law. Among his colleagues were many lawyers who distinguished themselves as general officers during the Civil War, and they all practiced criminal law.[14] An examination of Lincoln's criminal law practice will reveal the qualities that he and his colleagues transferred from the field of oratorical combat to the field of mortal combat—analytical ability, decisiveness, adaptability to a rapidly changing tactical environment, and skill in communicating clearly and unequivocally—all of which are desirable in both field commanders and their commander in chief.

In his role as commander in chief, Lincoln made use of his lawyerly skills in a disagreement with General George B. McClellan. At the beginning of the war, the largest army in the world was encamped around Washington under the command of McClellan, who did not seem to be too eager to do anything with it. Lincoln wanted an immediate direct attack on Richmond, the Confederate capital, which lay almost due south of Washington. McClellan favored slow preparation for a roundabout attack that would transport the army by sea to a peninsula on the southeast of Richmond, from which he would launch his attack. Lincoln wanted to jab; McClellan wanted to throw a roundhouse punch. On February 3, 1862, Lincoln wrote McClellan a letter that demonstrated his analytical ability, communication skill, and facility as a cross-examiner.

My dear Sir: You and I have distinct, and different plans for a movement of the Army of the Potomac—yours to be down the Chesapeake, up the Rappahannock to Urbana, and across land to the terminus of the Railroad on the York River—, mine to move directly to a point on the Railroad South West of Manassas.

If you will give me satisfactory answers to the following questions, I shall gladly yield my plan to yours.

1st. Does not your plan involve a greatly larger expenditure of time, and money than mine?

2nd. Wherein is a victory more certain by your plan than mine?

3rd. Wherein is a victory more valuable by your plan than mine?

4th. In fact, would it not be less valuable, in this, that it would break no great line of the enemie's communications, while mine would?

5th. In case of disaster, would not a safe retreat be more difficult by your plan than by mine?[15]

Lincoln's reasoning was sound—the only way McClellan could give a cogent direct answer was to agree with him—and these arguments should have persuaded an objective listener. McClellan, however, was not an objective listener, and he had no intention of agreeing with Lincoln. He dashed off an unresponsive, intemperate letter to Lincoln defending his position,[16] and Lincoln yielded the point to him. The result was the disastrous Peninsula Campaign, which ended in strategic defeat with the Seven Days Battles.

In summary, this book analyzes the validity of the conventional wisdom that criminal law was only a minor part of Lincoln's practice, he was a mediocre defense attorney, and he was a poor prosecutor, and it sheds light on how his criminal law practice helped him develop some of the skills that he put to good use as president. This is accomplished in the main by a chronological survey of his homicide cases. Although an elaborate mythology has grown up about the details of most of Lincoln's murder cases, this book separates the wheat of fact from the chaff of fiction. It then critiques the performance of Lincoln as a criminal trial lawyer, as well as of his associates and adversaries. Through this process, the book reveals that Lincoln was neither the cardboard saint of the Lincolnolators nor the stock villain of the Lincolnoclasts. It also demonstrates that many times the truth about Lincoln's cases is both stranger and more interesting than the legend.

1.

PEOPLE versus HENRY B. TRUETT, October 13, 1838

THE LATE 1830S SAW A CHANGING OF THE GUARD IN THE ILLINOIS DEMO-cratic Party. William L. May, who had been a congressman since December 1, 1834, seemed to be in firm control. He had the ear of President Martin Van Buren and could dictate who got which government appointments in the recently formed state. A new star was rising in the Democratic firmament, however. Stephen A. Douglas had already flexed his political muscle as a member of the state legislature when, dissatisfied with a decision of the four-member Supreme Court, he sponsored a bill to increase the number of judges to nine and got himself appointed to one of the new seats. In a few short years, Judge Douglas, as he was ever after called, set his sights on a larger prize. He resigned his judgeship, went into a law partnership with John D. Urquhart, and began campaigning for May's seat in Congress.

At the 1837 Democratic convention in Peoria, Douglas wrested control from May and replaced him as the Democratic nominee for Congress. Douglas did this in part by making a political football of a patronage appointment secured by May for his son-in-law, Henry B. Truett, as the register of the Land Office in Galena. Truett was hotheaded and easy to dislike, and the convention passed a resolution calling on the president to remove Truett from office. One of the delegates to that convention was Dr. Jacob M. Early, who served as a member of the committee appointed to draft resolutions.[1] Early would wind up paying for his part in the resolution against Truett with his life.

The thirty-six-year-old Early was a native Virginian who settled in Sangamon County in 1831. He served three enlistments in the Black Hawk War—one as a private, one as a regimental surgeon, and one as the captain of a company of "spies" (really, scouts). One of the "spies" who served under Early was a tall, lanky frontiersman named Abraham Lincoln. After the Black Hawk War, Early became a popular, prominent citizen of Sangamon County despite his volatile temper. A jack-of-all-trades, he was a physician, a Methodist minister, a railroad contractor, and an ensign in a militia artillery unit. Early lived five miles outside Springfield, but his work with the railroad brought him almost daily into the capital. Sometimes at the end of the day, instead of making the five-mile trek over poorly maintained roads back to his home, he stayed in Colonel James Spottswood's hotel. It was in the parlor of this hotel that Early lost his life.

The week of March 5, 1838, promised to be a busy one in Springfield. That Monday was the opening day of the first term of the Sangamon County Circuit Court, and litigants from far and wide had come to town to settle their grievances. Henry B. Truett, one of those litigants, made the 230-mile trip from Galena to prosecute a lawsuit against Wharton Ransdell for $1,371.88. In this suit, Truett had as his attorney an up-and-coming young lawyer named Abraham Lincoln.[2] The case did not get resolved during that term of court because Truett found himself embroiled in litigation for something much more valuable than a sum of money—his very life.

Truett arrived in Springfield on March 4, 1838, and checked into Colonel Spottswood's crowded hotel. While traveling from Galena to Springfield, Truett had been armed with a pocket pistol, which he carried in his overcoat. Contemporary news accounts do not tell us what kind of pistol he had, but we can infer that he carried a small, single-shot, muzzle-loading, percussion cap pocket pistol. A gunsmith by the name of Henry Deringer had been manufacturing such guns since the 1820s. When he checked into the hotel, Truett hung his overcoat on a coatrack in the hallway, and there it stayed during Truett's sojourn in the hotel. When court was in session in Springfield, hotel space was at a premium, with guests sleeping two to a bed and four or five to a room. Sometimes they even slept on the floor in the common room. Spottswood's son Henry had lost his bed to a paying customer and was sleeping on the floor in the common room. He grabbed Truett's overcoat for use as a pillow but found it lumpy—it still had Truett's pistol in the pocket. Young Spottswood used the overcoat as a pillow for two nights, each morning returning it to the coatrack.

At the end of the Wednesday court session, Truett returned to the hotel for supper. Jacob M. Early was also a supper guest at the hotel that night. After supper, a dozen or so men congregated in the common room to talk and warm themselves by the fire. The group included Early; John S. Roberts and James F. Reed, both railroad contractors; and General William D. Ewing, a lawyer who was a mover and shaker in Democratic politics. Truett later joined the group, sitting on the settee by the fireplace. Early sat at a small table reading the *Sangamo Journal*. As the evening progressed, men left the sitting room until there were but five left—Truett, Early, Ewing, Roberts, and Reed.

Pocket pistol similar to the one used by Henry B. Truett. The pistol in the photograph was used by John Wilkes Booth to assassinate Lincoln. PHOTO-GRAPH COURTESY OF THE LIBRARY OF CONGRESS.

Truett approached Ewing and asked to discuss some business with him, and the two retired to the hallway. After their discussion, Ewing left the hotel and Truett returned to the common room, passing the coatrack holding his overcoat as he went. Truett resumed his place on the settee and began staring so intently at Early that Reed noticed his expression. We cannot know what caused the change in Truett's demeanor, but it is reasonable to assume that at least part of his conversation with Ewing concerned the authorship of the resolution calling for his ouster as register of the Land Office.[3]

Roberts departed from the common room, leaving Early, Truett, and Reed as the only occupants. Early, oblivious to Truett's hostile look, finished his paper and moved to the settee beside Truett to warm himself at the fire. Truett, a much smaller man than Early, stood and faced the doctor and asked, "Did you write the resolution which disapproved my appointment as Register of Lands?" Early ignored the question. Truett repeated the question and added, "I have been told that you were."

Early asked, "Who told you that? If you will identify your informant, I will be glad to answer your question."

"I am not at liberty to say," replied the truculent Truett.

"As you will not tell me the identity of your informant," replied Early, "I will not tell you whether I was the author of the resolution. Tell me who accused me, and I will tell you whether the accusation is true." Early had served as one of the five members of the resolution committee at the convention, and it was safe to assume that he at least had a hand in the drafting of the resolution. The resolution, however, was merely one of a number of resolutions passed at the convention, and it had been approved by a majority vote of all the delegates.

"You're a damned scoundrel!" replied Truett. Early did not take kindly to this insult, and James Reed sensed that the situation might soon get out of hand. He stepped forward between the two men and tried to make peace. Truett seemed to cool off.

"Haven't we been friends for a long time?" Truett asked. Early replied that they had.

"Weren't we friends when I left for Galena?" Truett asked.

"Yes," replied Early.

"Then why won't you tell me whether you wrote the resolution?"

"Tell me who told you that I did, and I will say whether he is correct or incorrect."

"You're a damned scoundrel! A damned rascal!" Truett replied. "But if you didn't write the resolution, my insults do not apply to you." At this time, John Roberts came back into the room. Roberts walked to a corner of the room distant from the confrontation and began to take his boots off. It was around 8 P.M., and he was preparing to go to bed. Early told Truett that he wanted no trouble with him, but there was a limit to the amount of abuse he would take.

Truett had not yet run out of insults. He called Early a "damned liar," a "damned hypocrite," and a "damned coward." At this point two things happened, but there is dispute as to which happened first. Early stood and picked up a chair, and Truett drew his pocket pistol. They stood facing each other with the chair between them, and Truett continued his verbal abuse. As the two men began to circle each other, Early lifted the chair. It is unclear whether he intended to strike with it or simply use it as a shield. Truett shifted his position—was it to get a clear shot at Early, or was it to avoid the chair? When Early, whose attention was riveted on Truett, bumped into the settee, Truett fired. The two men were three feet apart when Truett pulled the trigger.

The bullet struck Early's left side in the lower part of his rib cage, passed through the lower part of his stomach and liver, and came to rest against his right side immediately above his hip bone. A modern-day medical examiner would describe the path of the bullet as left to right, side to side, and slightly downward. Truett dropped his pistol and ran from the hotel.[4]

News of the shooting spread like wildfire. The community was up in arms, with talk of lynching. Sheriff Garret Elkin swore in additional deputies to deal with the crisis, and they arrested Truett without bloodshed. Meanwhile, Jacob M. Early had not died. He languished for three days before giving up the ghost and made a deathbed statement concerning the incident. Ironically, the jury that eventually tried the case heard the testimony of Early by way of his deathbed statement, but Truett did not testify because the common law prohibited defendants in criminal cases from testifying in their own behalf.[5]

The prosecution of Henry B. Truett began to go off the rails with the deathbed statement. The legal term for a deathbed statement is "dying declaration," and not just any deathbed statement is admissible in evidence. At the time of the trial, Illinois law gave the following definition: "Dying declarations are, therefore, such as are made by the party, relating to the facts of the injury of which he afterwards dies, under the fixed belief and moral conviction that his death is impending and certain to follow."[6] Four conditions must exist for a dying declaration to be admissible in evidence: (1) the prosecution must be for unlawful homicide; (2) the declarant must know that he is dying; (3) the statement must relate to the cause of his death; and (4) the declarant must die.

It makes no difference in the eyes of the law who heard the dying declaration, but it certainly can make a difference in the eyes of the jury hearing the case. Prosecutors want as good a witness as possible to testify to the dying declaration. Law enforcement officers are sometimes ignorant of the nuances of legal requirements, and unless the officer is very good, there is always a chance that delegating such a chore to him could result in disaster. John D. Urquhart, the state's attorney for Sangamon County, decided to take Early's statement. Obviously he felt that he would be the one most likely to ensure that all the requisites of a dying declaration were fulfilled and that he would have enough credibility to convince the jury of the declaration's validity. Because a lawyer should not testify in a case he is trying, Urquhart was disqualified from prosecuting the case.

Having made one mistake in taking the dying declaration himself, Urquhart compounded the error by suggesting the wrong person as his stand-in. At Urquhart's request, Judge Jesse B. Thomas appointed Stephen A. Douglas as state's attorney pro tem to handle the prosecution. At first blush, this might seem like a good choice. Douglas was Urquhart's law partner and had also served a term as state's attorney. But the negatives far outweighed the positives. Even under the best of circumstances, the prosecution would have political overtones—Douglas was the leader of the political faction opposed to May, and Truett was a May man. Early, on the other hand, had been a loyal Douglas man. These are definitely facts a defense attorney could work with.

May immediately employed the foremost lawyer in the state, Stephen T. Logan, to defend his son-in-law. Logan had earned his license to practice in Kentucky in 1820 at age twenty and twelve years later moved to Illinois, where he continued his practice. Although he was appointed to the bench, he quit after two years because he could make far more money in private practice. Logan was renowned for his penetrating intellect, attention to detail, and skill as a trial lawyer. Over the course of his career, he mentored three governors, four U.S. senators, and one president of the United States. It is near certain that Lincoln owed much of his success as a trial lawyer to the tutelage he received from Logan. At the time of the Truett trial, however, the Logan-Lincoln partnership was years in the future.

Logan's partner at the time was Edward D. Baker, also a formidable criminal defense attorney. Baker had earned his license to practice law in 1830 and soon gained fame as a powerful orator. He honed those oratorical skills as a part-time preacher in the Disciples of Christ. Baker had a military bent, serving in the Black Hawk War, the Mexican-American War, and the Civil War. Although Baker was elected to the Senate in the same election cycle that elevated Lincoln to the presidency, he volunteered for service in the Union army as a colonel. He declined an appointment as major general and eventually died of wounds sustained in the Battle of Ball's Bluff—the only sitting senator ever killed in battle.

Edward D. Baker. One of Illinois' most prominent lawyers and a close friend of Lincoln. PHOTOGRAPH COURTESY OF THE LIBRARY OF CONGRESS.

State's attorneys in antebellum Illinois were usually young and inexperienced, a fact that contributed to a custom of hiring experienced private lawyers to assist in prosecutions. Sometimes the victim's family and the defendant raced to seek out and hire the most experienced criminal trial lawyers. Logan, familiar with the practice, hired the best lawyers he could to assist him in the defense—Cyrus Walker and John T. Stuart. Stuart had as a junior partner a young man whom he had met while soldiering in the Black Hawk War. Stuart had taken a liking to the man and encouraged him to study law, lending him law books that he read and studied until at last he was able to gain admission to the Illinois bar. That young man was Abraham Lincoln.

Of Walker it was said, "When [he] was thoroughly aroused, and in dead earnest, with a determination to win the verdict from the jury, he was as terrible as an army with banners."[7] Six feet tall in his stocking feet and strikingly handsome, Stuart had a reputation as one of the ablest jury lawyers in the state, especially in slander cases. Oddly enough, in this theater of the war within the Illinois Democratic Party, all the defense attorneys were Whigs.

The grand jury returned a true bill of indictment for murder against Truett; he was remanded to custody without bond, and the case was set over to the July term of court. On Thursday, July 5, 1838, Truett was brought before the court and arraigned. He entered a plea of not guilty and received a copy of the indictment, a list of the state's witnesses, and a list of the grand jurors, and Douglas sought to set the case for trial later that week. The defense demurred and asked for a continuance to the October term of the court to allow time to procure defense witnesses. Douglas objected, no doubt arguing that the defense team had been given plenty of time to procure witnesses in the four months since Truett's arrest. Judge Thomas took the matter under advisement until Friday morning. The next day, after studying the affidavit for continuance, he ordered the prosecution to show cause why the case should not be continued. Douglas asked for time to make his response, and Judge Thomas gave him until Saturday.

On Saturday, Douglas filed his pleading, pointing out that the defense's mere allegation that it needed time to procure more witnesses was insufficient. The defense attorneys not only had to say they wanted more time, but they also had to allege what they hoped to gain by the additional time. This meant they would have to show what they hoped to prove by the absent witnesses. Judge Thomas denied the motion for continuance with leave to file an amended affidavit setting out the necessary allegations.

This was a minor victory for Douglas. The defense quite naturally did not want to tip its hand by setting out its strategy in advance of trial. The defense team much preferred to ambush the state's attorney with the testimony, but if it really wanted that continuance, it was going to have to show its cards. After a council of war, the five lawyers decided that the continuance was important enough to reveal their defense. All these machinations had frittered away the entire week, and the case was set over to the following Monday, July 9.

That Monday the defense lawyers showed their cards. They wanted a doctor or doctors who would testify that the nature of Early's wound clearly indicated that he was holding the chair over his head to strike when Truett shot him in self-defense. Judge Thomas continued the case from day to day, expecting the defense to procure the witnesses and get it tried that term. Often judges and lawyers have very different timetables for the disposition of cases. This was one of those occasions. Although Douglas and Judge Thomas were determined to try the case in the July term, the defense was just as determined to hold it over until October. The term expired on July 11 without the defense producing the anticipated witnesses. Judge Thomas continued the case and required all the witnesses, including State's Attorney Urquhart, to post $1,000 appearance bonds.

Given the identity of the medical experts eventually procured, one has to wonder how big a problem it would have been to procure them for the July term of court. The first witness, Dr. E. H. Merryman, was a longtime resident of Sangamon County who was such close friends with Lincoln that he later served as Lincoln's second for a proposed duel with a fellow lawyer named James Shields, who served as a general in both the Mexican-American War and the Civil War.[8] The second medical expert, Dr. William S. Wallace, had been a resident of Springfield since 1836 and was soon to become Lincoln's brother-in-law.

Despite knowing the evidence the defense was mustering, the prosecution again fumbled the ball by doing nothing to recruit witnesses to contradict it. When the October term arrived, the defense had lined up two medical experts to testify that the nature of Early's wound clearly indicated that he was holding the chair over his head to strike when he was shot. The prosecution had no expert witnesses to counteract that testimony. Douglas was probably so busy trying to keep his seat in Congress that he neglected to find an expert. By the time the October term rolled around, however, Douglas was a private citizen and John T. Stuart was a congressman-elect, having defeated Douglas by the resounding margin of thirty-six votes out of more than thirty-six thousand cast.

The trial commenced on Tuesday, October 9, 1838, in a little store on Hoffman's Row that doubled as a courtroom during terms of court. Stuart and

Lincoln had their law office on the second floor of Hoffman's Row immediately above the courtroom. They even had a trapdoor in their floor that could be opened to communicate with the store. According to legend, Lincoln once used that trapdoor to save his fellow Whig, Edward D. Baker, who was making a speech that angered a Democratic audience. Lincoln had been listening to the speech through the trapdoor when disorder broke out, and the audience threatened to mob the speaker. Lincoln dropped through the trapdoor, took up a position in front of the speaker, and reportedly said, "Gentlemen, let us not disgrace the age and country in which we live. This is a land where freedom of speech is guaranteed. Mr. Baker has a right to speak, and ought to be permitted to do so. I am here to protect him, and no man shall take him from this stand if I can prevent it." He then assumed such a menacing posture that the crowd lost its zeal for the attack, and Baker was able to finish his speech.[9]

According to Illinois law at the time, twenty-four "talesmen," or potential jurors, were summoned to appear on the first day of court, and these men would serve as the pool from which all petit juries would be drawn that week.[10] It took no crystal ball to predict that this was going to be a pitifully small group from which to draw a jury in such a high-profile case. If a jury cannot be drawn from the panel of summoned talesmen, the panel is said to be "busted," and either the case is continued to the next term of court or additional jurors are recruited as quickly as possible. The panel was quickly busted, and the sheriff was sent out to summon twenty more talesmen. This panel was also busted, and the sheriff got sent out again for twenty more talesmen. In this fashion, the lawyers busted five twenty-member panels of talesmen in addition to the original panel of twenty-four. At the end of the day, they had six jurymen chosen, selected, and sworn. They were halfway to the necessary total of twelve. The judge ordered the sheriff to bring in twenty more talesmen for the beginning of court on Wednesday. The sworn jurors were sequestered for the night, and the defendant went back to jail.[11]

On Wednesday morning, the sheriff presented twenty new talesmen, and the lawyers were able to select and swear two jurors out of that panel. The sheriff went out again and brought in twenty more talesmen, and they selected and swore three more jurors. Now they were just one juror shy of the required total, and Judge Thomas could see the light at the end of the tunnel. He changed his strategy. In summoning the one hundred twenty talesmen of the supplementary panels, the sheriff had gone out and recruited jurors whose names were duly drawn from the pool of those qualified to serve.

With the finish line so near, Judge Thomas became weary of the long waits for the sheriff to return with additional panels of twenty. He now ordered the sheriff to pull four potential jurors "from the bystanders." This meant that the sheriff was to look into the audience and pull four men at random to serve as talesmen.[12] He would have no trouble finding four bystanders, because the courtroom was full of spectators. In a world without television, court proceedings were grand entertainment, and trials were well attended even when the stakes were small. Given the high-profile nature of the case against Truett, it was standing room only in the courtroom. One might wonder about the impartiality of jurors so selected.

The rest of the day was consumed with one four-man panel of bystanders after another being busted without getting that elusive twelfth juror. At the end of the day, the eleven jurors were sequestered, and the sheriff was ordered to have four more bystanders ready for examination the next morning. They went through seven more four-man panels of bystanders before they were able to swear the twelfth juror. The *Illinois State Journal* estimated that before the jury was seated, the lawyers had exercised approximately twenty peremptory challenges and three hundred to four hundred challenges for cause.[13]

In many respects, it can be said that the trial of a case is over when the judge says to "swear the jury." If a lawyer has the wrong jury, it makes no difference how good his case is or how brilliant a lawyer he may be—he is going to lose. With the right jury, the lawyer has already won the case unless he blunders. The defense team had reason to believe that they had gotten the right jury. Of the twelve jurymen, it has been documented that Alexander Trent had served with Lincoln in the Black Hawk War, Levi Cantrell had served on a land committee with Lincoln, Nicholas Moore and George W. Fagan were former clients, and Philip Clark later became a client. It is not unlikely that Lincoln knew even more members of the jury.[14]

By the time the twelfth juror was sworn, Douglas had to be exhausted. He was a one-man band competing against an orchestra of four of the most formidable criminal defense lawyers in the state, not to mention the as-yet-unproven Lincoln. Douglas soldiered on, however, with the presentation of the case.

As the trial progressed, it became clear that there were at least four crucial questions to be answered: (1) When did Truett arm himself? Did he leave the room for the express purpose of going to his overcoat to arm himself? (2) Did Truett pull the gun before or after Early picked up the chair? (3) Did Truett cock the pistol before returning to the room or on being confronted with the raised chair? (4) Was Early holding the chair in front of himself as a shield or overhead as a weapon?

If Truett left the room for the express purpose of arming himself for a confrontation with Early, if he cocked the pistol before returning to the room, if he pulled the pistol before Early picked up the chair, and if Early held the chair in a defensive posture rather than as a weapon, Truett was guilty of murder. If, however, Truett already had the gun in his pocket, if his only reason for leaving the room was for a private conversation with Ewing, and if he pulled and cocked the pistol only in response to Early threatening him with the chair, Truett was guilty of manslaughter at most and might even be innocent on a self-defense theory.

The first question could not be answered because of the absence of General Ewing. Truett left the room with Ewing for a private conference. What did they talk about? Could Ewing shed any light on whether Truett retrieved the gun from his overcoat after their conversation? These questions cried out for an answer. It is likely that Ewing's testimony would have been damaging to Truett. Ewing was a confidant and political ally of Truett. If he had anything helpful to say, he would almost certainly have been present to say it. Here is another place where the prosecution likely dropped the ball. Douglas should have found out what Ewing had to say and summoned him to testify at the trial. Ewing might have made a reluctant witness, but there are ways to corkscrew the truth out of uncooperative witnesses.[15]

The prosecution could give a qualified answer to question two. Neither Reed nor Roberts saw the gun until after Early hoisted the chair, but in his dying declaration, Early stated emphatically that Truett had pulled the gun before he picked up the chair. As to question three, Reed swore he never heard the distinctive sound of a cap-and-ball pistol being cocked. Truett must have cocked the pistol before he came back into the room. The evidence was unanimous on the fourth question. Reed and Roberts testified, and Early's dying declaration stated, that Early had held the chair straight out in front as if to shield himself from the firing of the pistol, not overhead to strike Truett.

On October 12, the last day of the presentation of evidence, the prosecution perpetrated another blunder. Douglas asked that the newly appointed state's attorney for Sangamon County, David M. Woodson, be sworn in and allowed to take charge of the case. Although relieved of command, Douglas remained on the case to assist. Woodson, thirty-one years old and a member of the bar for only five years, had not yet achieved the distinction he was to enjoy in later life. He served as a judge of the First Judicial Circuit from 1848 until 1867, when he returned to private practice. When he took over the prosecution of Truett, however, he was inexperienced, ill prepared, and assisted by the talented but seemingly unenergetic and undermotivated Douglas.

The prosecution had no answer for the two medical experts. Dr. E. H. Merryman testified that the nature of Early's wound left no doubt in his mind that

Early had lifted the chair over his head to strike Truett. If he had not so lifted the chair, it would have stopped the bullet. Dr. William S. Wallace corroborated Merryman's testimony, and the defense rested. This testimony contradicted not only the testimony of Reed and Roberts and the dying declaration of Early, but also common sense, yet the prosecution inexplicably had no answer for it.

Experts frequently believe that their expertise extends far beyond their chosen field, and it seems that Merryman and his cohort were speaking far beyond their qualifications when they said that the nature of the wound proved that Early had been attacking Truett. If Early had indeed been attacking Truett, he approached him in a most ungainly manner, sidling toward him like a crab, intending to strike an awkward sidewise blow with the chair. Remember, the bullet traversed Early's torso from left to right. Had Early been attacking Truett in normal fashion, he would have been facing Truett so as to bring the chair down in front of him and onto Truett. With his body in this position, the bullet would have traversed the torso from front to back.

Using a dose of common sense, the prosecution could have constructed a far more likely scenario: Truett was circling Early from right to left, trying to get a clear shot around the chair, and Early was mirroring Truett's movement, trying to keep the chair in the line of fire. When Early bumped into the settee, he could no longer mirror Truett's circling, and Truett maneuvered to Early's side, where he got a clean shot past the chair. The best evidence for the defense was the fact that Truett moved backward as he circled and Early sought to stay close to him. This fact could be interpreted as Early attacking Truett, but if Truett pulled the gun before Early picked up the chair, Early had as much right to use force to defend himself as did Truett. If Truett kept the gun leveled at Early and backed out of arm's reach, he could shoot Early from a distance, and Early could do nothing to defend himself.

Final arguments began shortly after the conclusion of the evidence, but they continued long into the afternoon. Judge Thomas decided to recess the trial and resume arguments the following day at 8 A.M. Arguments resumed Saturday morning, October 13, and continued until 7 P.M. Both Douglas and Woodson spoke for the prosecution, and both Logan and Lincoln argued for the defense. Logan had Lincoln give the closing summation. Stephen T. Logan was the captain of a "dream team" of criminal defense attorneys and undoubtedly the craftsman of the defense theory. How was it that he allowed the least experienced member of the defense team to deliver so important an address as the closing argument to the jury? Logan probably thought the young man knew everyone in Central Illinois and felt Lincoln was the ideal choice to close for the defense. Even at that stage of his career, Lincoln had a reputation for being a powerful speaker. As one observer put it, despite Lincoln's "rawness, awkwardness, and uncultivated manner, [he] was expected to make a strong speech in the case, and that expectation was not disappointed."[16] Logan later described Lincoln's speech as "short but strong and sensible."[17]

The *Peoria Register* summarized the prosecution argument:

> This being the evidence, it was contended by the attorneys for the prosecution that a clear case of murder was made out—that the killing itself implied malice by law—that express malice was proven from the fact of his getting the pistol that night after seeing Early—the expression of his countenance before speaking to Early—the determined manner in which he spoke to Early—the abuse—the repeated insults—the provoking epithets—these too spoken by a cowardly man to one his superior in size, strength, and courage—all went to prove that he was prepared to execute vengeance, and had the advantage of Early in having a cocked pistol well loaded—which pistol he drew, and it was seen by Early before he rose from his seat. That Early evidently had a right to take a chair or anything else to protect himself from a man standing before him with a pistol, and calling him a damned scoundrel, a damned rascal, a damned hypocrite and a damned coward. The prosecution contended that Truett was the assailant from the beginning—that he sought the controversy—urged on the quarrel for the purpose of seeking an opportunity to take Early's life—and that when Early lifted the chair before him Truett passed round so that he might safely shoot after a sham appearance of retreat and that Early pressed towards Truett to prevent him from shooting rather than stand still and be shot down by the deliberate aim of his antagonist.[18]

The *Register*'s summary of the defense argument was somewhat shorter:

> For the defense it was contended that Early had a deadly weapon, to wit, a chair, within striking distance of Truett—that Early could have immediately crushed Truett with the chair—that he intended to do so, or that Truett supposed he intended to do so—that Truett was authorized to make the demand about the authorship of the Peoria resolution—that his pride of character was much wounded by the resolution—that the frailties and passions of human nature should be somewhat indulged— that he had suffered in prison seven months, &c. &c.[19]

After Judge Thomas had instructed the jurors on the law to apply to the evidence, Sheriff Elkin escorted them upstairs to the offices of Stuart and Lincoln to deliberate on their verdict. After three hours of deliberation, the jurors arrived at their verdict. Did they open the trapdoor to announce that they had a verdict? However they communicated, Sheriff Elkin escorted them back into the courtroom, and they published their verdict: "We the jury find the defendant not guilty as charged in the indictment."[20]

Truett may have been found not guilty by the jury, but his reputation in Illinois was stained ever after, and Whig newspapers referred to him as an "acquitted murderer." Truett eventually left Illinois, taking his temper with him. He prospered as a merchant in San Francisco, where he put the lie to his prosecutors' accusation of cowardice by challenging a man to a duel. Truett survived the duel unscathed, but his antagonist took a bullet in the leg. Truett later moved to Montana, where he built a water supply system. He died in Helena in 1869.[21]

Lincoln had taken only a small part in Truett's defense among such a host of formidable lawyers, but that small part contributed mightily to the successful verdict. He emerged from the case with a burnished reputation and prospects of a bright future as a trial advocate. His next murder case did not end quite so happily.

2.

PEOPLE versus WILLIAM FRAIM, April 23, 1839

AS EARLY AS 1720, SETTLERS IN THE MIDWEST WERE TAKING THEIR GOODS to market down the waterways of the Mississippi River and its tributaries. They would build boats with the lumber they harvested from the midwestern forests, fill the boats with nonperishable goods, and float them down the river to New Orleans. Some of the tributaries were barely navigable, meaning that the boats had to have a shallow draft to avoid getting stuck on sandbars and the like. Propulsion was not a problem, as they simply let the boats drift along on the river current. The boats tended to be flat and rectangular, and hence they were called flatboats.

No more than four men were needed to sail such a boat down the river, but the trip was not without peril. River pirates infested the banks and would sometimes attack the flatboats when they were moored near the shore for the night. But the real danger came on the return trip. Flatboats could float with the current, but it was impossible to navigate them against the current. A flatboat was good for one trip down the river, and when it arrived in New Orleans, it would be sold for lumber or firewood, leaving the sailors with nothing to sail back up the river. If a flatboat man was fortunate enough to have a horse, he could ride, but most walked back home. This was when they were in the greatest danger of attack from pirates, as they walked home with their pockets full of money. Flatboat men meeting with pirates on the road home could expect to go home with empty pockets, if they were able to go home at all. Lincoln's first job after leaving home was to sail flatboats downriver to New Orleans. Once, as he and his boat mates had moored their craft for the night, his boat was attacked by half a dozen pirates. Legend has it that Lincoln single-handedly cleared the deck of pirates while his boat mates shouted encouragement.[1]

Another breed of river sailor was the keelboat man. Keelboats were designed to take dry goods up the river from New Orleans to the midwestern settlers. They were shallow-draft vessels but were more boatlike in appearance than flatboats. The sides of the boats had runways down which men trod, pushing

Flatboat akin to the one Lincoln used to sail the Mississippi River. FROM BROOKS, *ABRAHAM LINCOLN AND THE DOWNFALL OF AMERICAN SLAVERY*, 40, IN AUTHOR'S LIBRARY.

the boats along with poles pressed to the river bottom. The keelboat man would stand at the prow end of the runway, push the end of his pole to the bottom of the river, place the top of the pole to his shoulder, and walk to the stern end of the runway. He would then lift his pole, do an about-face, and walk back to the prow. With two lines of men on either side of the boat pushing against the river current, a keelboat could make fourteen miles a day. Keelboat men, supposedly "half-horse, half-alligator," were a hardy lot, and the hardiest of the keelboat men was Mike Fink. At just one inch shorter than Lincoln and weighing 180 pounds, Fink was an arrogant, aggressive braggart who used to boast, "I can outrun, out jump, throw down, knock down, drag out, and lick any man in the country. I'm a salt-river roarer! I love the women and I'm chock full of fight!" Rivermen who made such claims were required to back them up, and Fink earned a reputation as both a brawler and a marksman.[2]

Almost one hundred years after the first midwestern settler flatboated his goods down the Mississippi, steam-powered riverboats began to ply the waters of the Mississippi and its tributaries. The first riverboat sailed up the Illinois River in 1828, making landfall at Pekin. By 1833, three riverboats ran a regular route between St. Louis and Peoria. In 1850, riverboats made at least 788 voyages down the Illinois to St. Louis. The riverboat offered flatboaters a faster, but possibly not safer, way to return home after selling their goods in New Orleans. On the riverboat, the men always faced the danger of fire or explosion, and some rather unsavory characters habitually traveled on riverboats. The cabins on these boats were chronically overbooked, and the majority of passengers simply booked passage and slept on the deck as best they could. A cabin passenger paid $8 to sail from St. Louis to Peoria. Deck passengers paid $2.50.[3]

The sailors who manned the riverboats were every bit as rough-hewn as the flatboaters and keelboaters. The riverboat sailor remembered as William Fraim was a twenty-one-year-old Irishman when he fought his way into the history books by killing a ferryman named William Neathammer. Riverboat navigation on the Illinois River had to be suspended in the wintertime because the river froze completely over. In February 1838, Fraim's riverboat, the *Hero*, was iced in at Frederick in Schuyler County. Since the river could be impassable for as many as four months, the deckhands could do little other than lounge around and frequent the saloons. On February 17, Fraim went ashore and found a saloon in which to slake his thirst. He had a mighty thirst, and by the time Neathammer entered the saloon, Fraim was drunk. Neathammer was not being very careful about where he blew his cigar smoke. Fraim objected to Neathammer's secondhand smoke and told him, "Don't blow smoke in my face."

"I thought this was a free country," replied Neathammer, "and I'll smoke where I please."[4] Fraim swatted at the cigar to knock it out of Neathammer's mouth. Neathammer raised an arm to defend himself against the blow, and Fraim pulled a butcher knife, plunging it to the hilt in Neathammer's chest. Neathammer "instantly died."[5] That spur-of-the-moment fit of anger began Fraim's journey to the gallows and into a footnote in Abraham Lincoln's biography.

Fraim was immediately arrested, a coroner's jury convened, and it found the death of William Neathammer to be the result of Fraim's unlawful act. Fraim was remanded to custody without bond to await the next term of court and put into the log jailhouse in Rushville, Illinois. All of Schuyler County was up in arms. Neathammer was a well-liked local and Fraim an unknown outsider. When outsiders go to small counties and kill local citizens, their prospects of winning an acquittal are usually bleak. On June 6, State's Attorney Henry L. Bryant presented Fraim's case to the Schuyler County grand jury, and it indicted him for murder with malice aforethought. A man charged with a capital crime had a right to have a lawyer represent him, and T. Lyle Dickey of Rushville was appointed to represent him.

Dickey and Lincoln were friends, and Dickey recruited Lincoln to help him defend Fraim. Neither man was paid a penny for his services—the privilege of admission to the Illinois bar carried with it the duty to accept unpaid appointments to defend indigents charged with capital crimes. There is no record of Lincoln ever having appeared for Fraim more than one time, that being when the case went to trial. Dickey probably handled all the pretrial litigation up to the eve of trial, and then Lincoln stepped in to assist.

At this point in his career, T. Lyle Dickey was as young and inexperienced as Lincoln, but he would distinguish himself as both a lawyer and a soldier. Although he had a college degree, he got his license to practice law by reading law and was admitted to practice in 1835 at the age of twenty-four. The first years of his legal career were spent as a prairie lawyer, until he relocated to Chicago in 1854. Whenever Lincoln had business in Chicago, he used Dickey's law office as a base of operations. Dickey was a wily and successful criminal trial lawyer, with a remarkable ability to talk judges and prosecutors into seeing things his way. In one murder case he defended, the law of manslaughter had recently been changed, and the statute setting the penalty for manslaughter had been repealed and replaced by another. Dickey convinced the judge and prosecutor that since the penalty provision in effect at the time of the murder had been repealed, if his client were convicted of manslaughter, he could not be sentenced but had to be set free. This was, of course, wrong; otherwise, every Illinoisan who had previously been convicted of manslaughter would have to be turned out of prison. The jury found the defendant guilty of manslaughter, and the judge set Dickey's client free.[6]

When the Civil War broke out, Dickey became a colonel in the U.S. Army, distinguishing himself in combat at Forts Henry and Donelson, as well as at Shiloh. He became chief of cavalry on the staff of General Ulysses S. Grant and later assumed command of the four brigades of cavalry in Grant's army. After the war, he became a circuit judge, a U.S. senator, and a judge on the Supreme Court of Illinois. Of Dickey and his service on the bench, it was said that he was "possessed of wonderful memory, and with a remarkable power of analysis, his judgments were always received with profound consideration, and his opinions on important cases have generally been sustained."[7]

Dickey handled the pretrial litigation of the Fraim case vigorously, leaving no stone unturned in his efforts to free his client. He first obtained a continuance, citing the unavailability of witnesses, and then prevailed on the court to change the venue of the case. The wisdom of this last maneuver is evidenced by the fact that public opinion was so hot against Fraim that he had to be jailed in another county to prevent his being lynched. The judge moved the trial to Hancock County, where Fraim would become the first man tried for murder in the newly built courthouse.[8] When the case got to Hancock County, Dickey did something that seems strange on its face. On April 23,

1839, the day of Fraim's trial, Dickey filed a written plea of not guilty signed by his client, which read as follows: "Fielding Fraim who is indicted herein, by the name of William Fraim, being in custody defends and says that he is not guilty of Murder in manner and form as charged in said indictment and of this he puts himself upon the country."[9]

A general plea of not guilty did not have to be reduced to writing. Under the common law, however, a number of special pleas had to be made in writing. For example, today the defense of former jeopardy is asserted by a motion to dismiss, but under the common law it was asserted by a written plea of *autrefois convict* or *autrefois acquit*, and the validity of this plea would be decided by the judge before a jury was selected.[10] If it was valid, the indictment would be dismissed and the defendant freed without trial. Another type of written plea was called a plea in abatement, filed when the indictment charged the defendant by the wrong name.[11] This sort of plea was usually in the nature of a housekeeping motion, because all the prosecutor had to do was to go back into the grand jury room and get the grand jurors to indict the defendant under his proper name.

Why would Dickey do such a thing when the error was so easily fixed? Such a plea could be considered a complex maneuver to get Fraim freed from jail. In the normal situation, sustaining a plea in abatement causes no problem—the prosecutor just gets another indictment. In Fraim's situation, sustaining a plea in abatement could be catastrophic. If the indictment were dismissed, the Hancock County grand jury had no authority to indict for a crime that happened in Schuyler County. The Schuyler County grand jury was not in session. The state's attorney would have to wait until the next term of court in Schuyler County before he could get another indictment. Fraim, who would have been freed when the indictment was dismissed, would be long gone by that time.

Lincoln had successfully used a similar stratagem in an assault to murder case he had handled two years before, *People v. Cordell*. In that case, Lincoln's client had attacked Josiah Abrams with the handle of a scythe, breaking his arm and bruising his head.[12] Unfortunately, the indictment misspelled Cordell's name. Before his client entered a plea, Lincoln moved to quash (dismiss) the indictment, and the court granted the motion.[13] When the state's attorney declined to seek another indictment against Cordell, Abrams filed a civil suit against Cordell seeking damages for his broken arm. Lincoln did not fare quite as well in this suit. Abrams got a judgment against Cordell for $100.[14]

The ploy might have worked in Fraim's case except for one minor problem: written pleas had to be filed before the entry of an oral plea of not guilty. If an oral plea of not guilty had already been entered, the defendant had to obtain permission from the judge to withdraw his oral plea.[15] Dickey and Lincoln applied for leave to withdraw the oral plea of not guilty, but the judge refused. This meant that for purposes of being prosecuted for murder, the defendant's name was William Fraim no matter what his parents named him. The young lawyers took exception to the judge's ruling and had him certify the exception. This was an extremely important thing to do. In antebellum Illinois, in order to be able to appeal a conviction to a higher court, the defendant had to "take exception" to the contested ruling, and the judge had to certify the exception as an appealable issue.

Justice was swift for the riverboat sailor. In a trial lasting less than a day, the jury returned a verdict reading, "We the jurors, find the defendant guilty of *Murder* as charged in the indictment."[16] The verdict was neither dated nor signed, but it was still valid because it was returned in open court with the jury present.[17] Judge James H. Ralston had no choice but to sentence Fraim to be hanged. Before the judge could pronounce the sentence, Lincoln filed a motion for arrest of judgment. In the motion, he made several complaints about the legal sufficiency of the indictment to charge a crime:

1. The record in this cause does not sufficiently show that an indictment was found by a grand jury of the county against the Defendant Fraim.
2. The record in this cause does not show that a grand jury was empanelled at the term of the court at which the indictment purports to have been found.
3. There is no sufficient record in this cause to authorize the court to try the Deft [defendant] and pronounce judgment upon him.
4. The record from the Schuyler circuit court is defectively and imperfectly certified.
5. The said record is otherwise informal erroneous and insufficient.
6. The indictment is bad in this, that it does not show with sufficient certainty in the conclusion, whether the Deft was the murderer or the murdered man.
7. The indictment is bad, in the conclusion in not showing that the murder was committed in the manner and by the means before stated in the indictment.[18]

This motion is a good example of the lawyerly art of "flyspecking" or "nitpicking." The indictment admittedly was not a model of clarity, but common-law pleadings seldom were. When compared with other examples of indictments from that era, it is no more confusing than any other. Lincoln's motion for arrest of judgment was spurious.

The motion, which had been handwritten and signed by Lincoln, has an interesting history. After Lincoln's assassination, documents in his hand became sought-after souvenirs. Pleadings written by Lincoln began disappearing from courthouses all over Illinois, and the motion for arrest of judgment vanished from the court file. It surfaced in Spokane, Washington, in 1909, the year Joel E. Ferris, who grew up in Hancock County, moved to the state. Not long after his arrival in Washington, he found himself in the office of a Spokane businessman, who produced the document and said he was given it as a gift. This revelation touched off an intense lobbying effort, which eventually resulted in the return of the document.[19]

Judge Ralston took the motion under advisement until the next day, when he denied it. He then proceeded to sentence Fraim:

> And it being demanded of the prisoner by the Court what he had or knew to urge in this behalf why judgment should not now be pronounced against him, and the said defendant having nothing to urge except what had been before urged in this behalf: It is therefore considered by the court that the said William Fraim be hanged by the neck till he be dead. It is further ordered by the court that the sheriff of the said County of Hancock do cause execution of this sentence to be done and performed upon the body of him the said William Fraim on Saturday the eighteenth day of May next between the hours of twelve o'clock Meridian and two o'clock post meridian of said day on a gallows to be erected within one mile of the town of Carthage in said County. It is further ordered that the said William Fraim pay all the costs of this suit. And the said William Fraim is committed to the custody of the sheriff of said county, to be by him kept in close confinement until this sentence is executed. It is further ordered that the clerk of this court make and certify a copy of this order and deliver the same to the sheriff of said county which shall be sufficient authority in the hands of said sheriff to carry into effect the foregoing judgment.[20]

No appeal was taken to the Supreme Court. It may be that Dickey and Lincoln believed the odds of getting the case reversed were slim and decided not to appeal, or it may be that Fraim did not wish to take an appeal. Whatever the reason, the failure to take the appeal ensured that Fraim had a mere three weeks to live.

Although Schuyler County had a log cabin jail, Hancock County had no jail at all. Fraim was imprisoned in the room where the jury decided his fate. The jury room was on the second floor of the courthouse, and it looked out on the old courthouse, a log cabin that had been made into a school. The windows of the jury room had no bars, and the doors had no locks. A ball and chain attached to Fraim's ankle held him securely, and he was watched by a round-the-clock guard who never left him unattended. Seemingly resigned to his fate, Fraim was cheerful and befriended his guards. He made other friends as well.

The children attending the school were fascinated by Fraim. During recess and at dinnertime (antebellum midwesterners called the midday meal "dinner"), they played on the grounds before his window, and he talked to them, joking and throwing pieces of candy out the window to them. When the children ventured too close to his window to pick up the candy, he poured water on them from his cup. While Fraim talked and joked with the children, the authorities built a gallows in a ravine southeast of town. The ravine made a kind of natural amphitheater, convenient for the crowds of spectators at the execution, which was expected to be well attended. School would be let out, crowds would come from miles around, and families would bring picnic lunches.[21]

Fraim made a special impression on a wide-eyed seven-year-old girl. In the early 1900s, as a mature widow and grandmother, Eudocia Baldwin wrote a reminiscence of her acquaintance with Fraim, whom she remembered as a cheerful young redhead called Charlie who was full of jokes and pranks. On the morning of the execution, long before sunrise, she heard the rumble of wagons rolling into town as people came from as far as one hundred miles away to see the execution. She stayed home that day because of the canceled classes. She became agitated as the hours dragged on toward noontime and the appointed hour of Charlie's execution. The family sang hymns to soothe her jangled nerves, and as they sang a hymn about the righteous being gathered home to heaven, she wondered about Charlie's fate. "It was quite sure my baby brother and Sister Alice were in that 'home,'" she wrote, "but I did not know whether poor Charlie's kindness to us children would make him good enough to be taken to be with them."[22] As the time drew near, her father and brothers got into the wagon to go to the execution. She tried to join them, but they refused to take her.

Later, her mother took her into the near-deserted town to visit a friend. She got separated from her mother, and as she walked alone down the street, a man drove up in a wagon. "Sis," he called out, "would you like to ride out and see the hanging?" She hesitated but a moment. "Why yes, would you take me?" He replied, "Of course. Jump in," and before she knew it she was beside him in the wagon going to see the execution. Of the hanging, she wrote:

The place of execution was less than a mile away, southeast of town, and we soon reached the edge of the crowd. From there, by slow degrees, he edged his light buggy through the press of people and the jam of vehicles, to the very heart of it all, to the piteous spectacle that had drawn together the vast throng. Fortunately for my peace of mind, we were only in time to see a perfectly still figure, whose face was covered by a black cap, and whose body was attired in a blue jacket and white trousers. For, at one time in his short life, poor Charlie had been a sailor.[23]

Mrs. Baldwin's brother later described the hanging to her. As he stood on the gallows erected in the natural amphitheater, Fraim made a brief final speech. He told the women in the crowd that there would be less crime if they would stay home and tend to their households. Then, as the black hood was about to be placed over his head, he lifted his hand to delay the executioner. He took one long look at the crowd and lifted his eyes toward heaven. Raising his arms, he spoke his last words: "Oh, eternity, eternity, I dread thee!"[24]

Thus Fielding Fraim, aka William Fraim, made history for all the wrong reasons. He was the first person tried for murder in the Hancock County Courthouse. He was the first and only murderer hanged in Hancock County,[25] and he was the only client of Lincoln's to go to the gallows for murder.

3.

PEOPLE versus SPENCER TURNER, May 23, 1840

WHEN LINCOLN BEGAN PRACTICING LAW, ILLINOIS WAS DIVIDED INTO A NUM-
ber of multicounty circuits, each presided over by a circuit judge. Each county
in the circuit held two terms of court per year, and the judge traveled a circuit
going from county to county to meet each term of court. Terms lasted from
one to two weeks, depending on how much business each county had. Lawyers rode the circuit with the judge, trying to pick up business from would-be
litigants. Illinois was then a sparsely populated state with poorly maintained
roads over vast stretches of prairie. The only practical way to get from place to
place was on horseback. When he first started riding the circuit, Lincoln either
borrowed or rented a horse because he was too poor to own one. Eventually
he put together enough money to buy a horse, and later, when the roads got
better, he bought a buggy. Toward the end of his practice, railroads made
travel between counties much easier and faster.

Lincoln lived in Springfield, which served as both state capital and the Sangamon County seat. Unlike the other counties of the state, Sangamon had three
terms of circuit court per year. Initially it was the central county of the ten-
county First Judicial Circuit. When the circuits were reorganized in 1839, Sangamon County became a member of the nine-county Eighth Judicial Circuit.
Over the course of Lincoln's career, the Eighth Circuit was reconfigured a number of times. At its largest, it covered fifteen counties. By the time Lincoln was
elected to Congress and went to Washington, the Eighth Circuit included only
four counties, but when he returned, it covered fourteen (see the appendix).[1]

After Lincoln ended his career as a congressman, he and the judge "were
the only members of the entire bar who regularly made the rounds of all
the fourteen county seats—the judge because his duties demanded it, and
Lincoln because he loved the nomadic and arduous life."[2] This meant that
he could be gone from home as much as six months out of the year. It was in
DeWitt County that Lincoln tried his next murder case, once again having
the distinction of trying the first murder case in a newly formed county.[3]

28

In the early morning hours of April 18, 1840, in the town of Clinton, pass-
ersby found Matthew K. Martin lying senseless on the ground, bleeding from
a two-inch gash near his right temple. They carried him to the nearest house,
which belonged to Miles Gray. A doctor came and determined that Martin
suffered from drunkenness, exposure, and a blow to the head from a blunt
object. Although the doctor did what he could, Martin died at 5 A.M. on April
18. At that time in Illinois, whenever it was suspected that someone had died
as a result of foul play, the county coroner held an inquest to determine who,
if anyone, had killed the deceased.

Because the coroner was unavailable, Justice of the Peace J. C. McPherson
acted as coroner, and the body remained unmoved until McPherson completed his inquest. McPherson had the constable summon twelve talesmen
to serve as a coroner's jury, and when they assembled, he held the hearing
over the dead body. Eight witnesses testified before the jury, which rendered
a verdict finding that Martin "came to his death by a severe blow upon his
head with a club struck by Spencer Turner . . . , together with his own impru-
dence in keeping himself in a state of intoxication and exposure in rain and
inclemency of weather on the night previous to his death."[4]

McPherson took off his acting coroner's hat, put his justice of the peace hat
back on, and issued a warrant for the arrest of Spencer Turner. In deciding
what charge to make against Turner, McPherson had a problem. Two doctors
had attended Martin and examined him after his death, and they testified
equivocally before the coroner's jury. Martin had died as a result of the gash
that Turner made on his head or exposure because he was too drunk to come
in out of the rain or a combination of the two factors. Did that constitute
sufficient proof that Turner's beating had killed Martin? McPherson was not
sure, so he hedged his bets. He issued the warrant for assault and battery
with a deadly weapon, which was not a felony but was considered a "high
misdemeanor."[5] McPherson may have had his doubts about whether Turner
should be charged with murder, but he had no doubt that Turner's offense
was serious. He set the bond at $10,000, an extremely high bond for a mere
misdemeanor. Constable G. S. Bennett immediately arrested Turner, and
Turner immediately posted bond. There was nothing left to do but to await
the arrival of the circuit judge and state's attorney at the beginning of the
next term of court, scheduled to commence in May.

Each new term of court in the small towns of Illinois was anticipated with
excitement, and entertainment-starved settlers would flock to each session.
They were especially excited about the Turner case because he was the first
person accused of homicide in the newly formed county. Whether he would

stand trial for murder had yet to be decided. The man who would have the greatest say in the question was David B. Campbell, who served as state's attorney until his death in 1856. Campbell had a reputation as "a fair lawyer but a good prosecutor [who] would never prosecute one charged with crime unless thoroughly convinced of his guilt."[6] The first order of business when opening a term of court was to select and swear a grand jury. After the judge swore in the grand jurors, they would retire to a private room, where they took the testimony of witnesses and decided whether to bring formal charges against the accused. Campbell, as state's attorney, had a great deal of influence over the bringing of charges, because he presented the evidence to the grand jurors, advised them on the law, and drew up the formal charges when they found a true bill of indictment.

Although the term of court should have started on a Monday, the grand jury did not return an indictment against Turner until Friday. The grand jury may have been so late to indict Turner for any number of reasons—possibly the term was delayed because the roads were so impassable that the judge and lawyers were late getting to town, or possibly there were some issues with obtaining the attendance of important witnesses. Campbell may have been tardy with his indictment of Turner, but he wasted no time in putting the young man on trial. He called the case up for trial the very next day, and by the end of that Saturday, the jury returned its verdict.

Doctor James Brown and Doctor Thomas Laughlin, both of whom had testified before the coroner's jury, testified before the grand jury as well. Apparently their equivocation about the cause of Martin's death did not concern Campbell as it had McPherson. Without knowing more about the precise nature of the doctors' testimony, it is hard to fault Campbell for bringing a homicide charge against Turner, but he can be faulted for not engaging in some alternative pleading. He charged Turner with a single count of murder, and the trial jurors would have to find Turner not guilty if they were not satisfied that the beating caused the death. Turner would still be guilty of assault and battery with a deadly weapon, but on a murder indictment, the only lesser crime they could find him guilty of was manslaughter. Campbell could have and quite probably should have included a second count charging the assault and battery.

When the circuit-riding lawyers arrived in a town for the opening of a term of court, they were mobbed by would-be litigants seeking their services. We have a record of Lincoln handling only two cases at the May term of court, but he most likely handled the cases of any litigants who approached him. One such litigant was Baron Lowry, who was being sued because he had failed to pay off a $110 promissory note he had signed the year before. Lincoln probably charged Lowry no more than a $5 fee, but he most likely asked for cash in advance. The second litigant to approach Lincoln was Spencer Turner.

Court records show that Turner retained Lincoln as his lawyer the very morning of the day he stood trial for murder. The conventional wisdom among criminal defense attorneys is to have the fee either fully paid in advance or secured by a lien. Criminal defendants are notorious for not paying their lawyers. If they are acquitted, they believe their lawyers only demonstrated the obvious and deserve no fee. If they are convicted, they think their lawyers did a poor job and deserve no fee. After Lincoln's death, a story began circulating that held that instead of receiving a promissory note, Lincoln took a horse in payment for his services, and the horse almost immediately either died or went blind.[7] The court record belies this claim. Lincoln had Turner execute an unsecured promissory note as a fee for his services. The note read, "Clinton, May 23rd 1840: Ninety days after date I promise to pay A. Lincoln two hundred dollars for value received." Lincoln took the precaution of having Turner's brother William cosign the note.[8] As things turned out, he was wise to do so.

It may well be that Turner already had representation when he hired Lincoln. In antebellum Illinois, if someone was charged with murder and had money, he hired not only the best lawyer he could find but also as many lawyers as he could afford. Turner also had the services of two other lawyers, Stephen A. Douglas and Kirby Benedict. It may have been at Benedict's insistence that Lincoln was brought into the case at such a late date. There was no love lost between Douglas and Lincoln, but Benedict was a good friend of Lincoln's and often roomed with him on the circuit. Douglas drove a somewhat harder bargain than Lincoln: he got his $200 fee paid half in cash and half with an unsecured note. The notes to both Lincoln and Douglas went unpaid for over a year. There is no record of what arrangements were made with Benedict for his fee, but he must have commanded an equal sum. His contemporaries thought him to be "a lawyer of considerable talent and genius," saying that "for oratorical power . . . he was equal to any of the best speakers . . . in the west."[9]

Benedict had "a fog-horn of a voice, which he used most recklessly when excited." On one occasion, when Benedict had been particularly bad about "roaring to a jury at an evening session," his fellow lawyers had the sheriff "arrest" him on a bench warrant "for making loud and unusual noises in the night time." After court adjourned, they held a mock trial at a tavern, where he was convicted and sentenced to either pay a heavy fine or use his "fog-horn" voice to argue for a new trial. He supposedly argued so lustily that they threatened to hold him in contempt for overdoing it.[10] Mock trials of this sort became a custom among the lawyers on the Eighth Circuit, and Lincoln was

Stephen A. Douglas, a perennial Lincoln foe. Douglas was allied with Lincoln, however, in the Turner case. PHOTOGRAPH COURTESY OF THE LIBRARY OF CONGRESS.

usually heavily involved in them. By the time Lincoln became president, Benedict had left Illinois and been appointed chief justice of the Territory of New Mexico. The newly elected president's constituents urged him to remove Benedict, a Democratic appointee, and appoint a loyal Republican. Lincoln flatly refused. When asked to justify his decision, Lincoln replied that he had "enjoyed too many happy hours in [Benedict's] company, and that he was too grand and glorious a fellow for [Lincoln] to lay violent hands upon."[11]

While Campbell was busy getting his indictment for murder, Lincoln was busy defending the lawsuit against Baron Lowry. William Pratt complained that Lowry had signed a promissory note but when it came due refused to pay. When a complaint is made in a civil case, some sort of answer must be made contesting the claim; otherwise, the complainant wins by default. Lincoln immediately filed a written plea in the case alleging that "the defendant comes and defends the wrong and injury . . . and says he does not owe to the said plaintiff the said sum of money in his said petition mentioned, in manner and form as the same is therein stated; and of this he puts himself upon the country."[12] The practice of putting oneself "upon the country" when entering a plea goes back to medieval English practice, when cases could be decided by means other than by a jury. When entering a plea, the defendant had to state how he wished to be tried, whether by combat, ordeal, or some other means. When the defendant stated that he put himself upon the country, he was saying that he wished to be tried by a jury. Lincoln did not get his jury trial, but he did try the case that Friday, and the lawyer on the other side was his good friend and sometime roommate Kirby Benedict. The judge, sitting without a jury, found that Lincoln's client did indeed owe the money and entered judgment accordingly.

The actual trial of Turner was not a notable event, except that it was the only time in their legal careers that Stephen A. Douglas and Abraham Lincoln were on the same side of a lawsuit. Lincoln made the final appeal to the jury, but we have no record of what he said.[13] It is almost certain that the defense of the case rested on the issue of causation, emphasizing that the victim's drunkenness contributed heavily to his death. Lincoln biographer John J. Duff, himself a lawyer, advanced the theory that Lincoln argued self-defense in tandem with the causation defense.[14] Trial lawyers do not like to put all their eggs in one basket when defending a case, and they frequently argue multiple defenses. It is important in such instances that the defenses be compatible; lawyers often lose credibility with the jury when arguing conflicting defenses. For example, a lawyer would look foolish arguing simultaneous defenses of alibi and self-defense. Causation and self-defense, however, are compatible defenses that can easily be argued together. Justice McPherson had his doubts about the cause of death when he had Turner arrested for assault and battery with a deadly weapon, and at the end of the trial the jury shared those doubts. Their verdict read, "We the jury find the Devendnt not gilty. Clinton May 23—1840 [signed] Henry Wilbray, Foreman."[15]

What the Turner brothers did next supports the conventional wisdom about getting paid in advance. They did not pay Lincoln's promissory note when it came due. They did not pay the note to Douglas either, but Douglas had already gotten his compensation by discounting his note to S. M. Tinsley & Company in Springfield. Eventually both Lincoln and the Tinsley Company were forced to sue in order to collect on their notes.

On September 8, 1841, Lincoln filed suit against the Turner brothers alleging "trespass on the case." The Turners were duly summoned to appear in court, and the suit came before the court on October 7. The court awarded Lincoln a default judgment because the defendants did not honor their summons by coming to court. It appears that they had as much respect for court process as they did for promissory notes. They did not pay the judgment. Lincoln was patient. He gave them plenty of time to pay, but after the passage of two more years, he took further action. On April 4, 1843, Lincoln petitioned the court to issue a writ of *scire facias*, which meant that he was asking the court to order that the defendants come to court show cause why they should not be required to pay the judgment.

The Turners finally took notice of the proceedings against them and hired Clifton H. Moore to defend them. Moore was only twenty-four years old when he was admitted to the bar in July 1841, and he moved to DeWitt County shortly afterward. Because Moore was never able to fully support himself in the practice of law, he supplemented his income by speculating on land.[16] As a young lawyer with little business, Moore took his clients as he found them, and when the Turners came to him, he took their case. He probably did not take a promissory note as payment for his services. The case was continued from term to term until it finally came to trial in 1846.

Moore filed a plea of *actus non*, alleging that the signing of the promissory note created no lawful obligation because his clients were under age twenty-one at the time they signed.[17] Because they were technically still children, no contract signed by them had any legal force. On this issue, they put themselves "on the country." Lincoln answered the plea by filing a "replication" denying that the defendants were under twenty-one when they signed the note.[18]

The case went to trial on April 26, 1846, after both sides agreed to a bench trial. Evidently Lincoln was able to introduce satisfactory proof that the Turners had been over twenty-one. The judge found for the plaintiff and entered judgment for $213.50. Lincoln waited another year for the Turners to pay his fee, but they still refused. Finally, on March 17, 1847, Lincoln obtained a writ of execution commanding the sheriff to seize $213.50 worth of the Turners' "goods, chattels, lands, and tenements" to satisfy the debt. The sheriff served the writ on April 29 by confiscating the Turners' interest in a parcel of land in DeWitt County. Lincoln may have charged modest fees, but he was relentless in collecting his debts.

4.

PEOPLE versus ARCHIBALD AND WILLIAM TRAILOR, June 18, 1841

THE TRAILOR CASE IS UNIQUE BECAUSE IT IS THE ONLY MURDER CASE FOR which written accounts of the trial from Abraham Lincoln exist. Lincoln tried many interesting murder cases in his career, but the facts of the case under consideration were so bizarre that he felt compelled to reduce them to writing. He wrote the first account in a letter to his good friend Joshua Speed shortly after the conclusion of the trial.[1] He wrote in a conversational, humorous style that was much more relaxed than his second account of the trial. This second account, bearing the title "Remarkable Case of Arrest for Murder,"[2] was written several years after the event in a somewhat more formal style. It is noteworthy that the two accounts, written five years apart, are so lacking in discrepancies. The following reconstruction of the events of the case relies heavily on Lincoln's reminiscences and is supplemented by John Carroll Power's account in *History of the Early Settlers of Sangamon County, Illinois* and Paul Angle's *Here I Have Lived: A History of Lincoln's Springfield, 1821–1865.* Both Power's and Angle's accounts agree closely with Lincoln's, but Power's account departs far from fact in describing the climax of the trial.

The citizens of Sangamon County called it "probably the most remarkable trial that ever took place in Springfield, and beyond a doubt one of the most dramatic trials that ever took place in the whole country,"[3] but it began quite simply. William Trailor had two younger brothers: Archibald, better known as Arch, and Henry. The three came to Illinois in 1829, and each settled in a different community. William married and bought a farm near the village of Greenbush in Warren County, about one hundred miles northwest of Springfield. After giving him several children, his wife died and left him a widower to run his farm and take care of his family alone. A sober, industrious man, he became well liked by his neighbors despite his penchant for telling boastful tall tales and his tardiness in paying his bills.

William took in a boarder named Archibald Fisher, who had been a school-teacher before a gun exploded in his face, seriously injuring him and apparently causing some sort of brain trauma. Ever after, he suffered from ill health and sometimes had what his doctor called "aberrations of the mind." When lucid, which was most of the time, he supported himself by doing odd jobs, moving from house to house living with anyone who would take him in. Fisher, being a thrifty man, managed to save quite a sum of money. He had moved in with William Trailor and was living with him just before the chain of events that led to the "remarkable case."

At the end of May 1841, Fisher wanted to register some land at the land office in Springfield, and William decided to accompany him. They set out for the newly christened capital of Illinois in a Dearborn wagon, a one- or two-seater with a roof and sometimes sides that is drawn by a single horse. Their route took them by Henry Trailor's farm in Clary's Grove, and William decided stop in and visit him. They visited with Henry for a day or so, and then continued on their way to Springfield. Henry decided to go to Springfield also, and he accompanied the two on horseback, as the wagon did not have enough room for three men. At some time during the trip, the Trailors became aware that Fisher had with him a large quantity of gold coins.

The three men arrived in Springfield about noon on May 31 and took lodging in a boardinghouse run by William H. Myers but owned by Arch Trailor. Arch differed from his brothers in that he had never married and did not farm. He worked as a carpenter and had gained a reputation in Springfield as a down-to-earth, hardworking man. Like his brother William, he had money troubles.

After eating the noon meal, which they called "dinner," the three Trailor brothers left the boardinghouse with Fisher to take a tour of the town. The Trailors returned about suppertime, but Fisher was not with them. When asked what had happened to Fisher, they said that they had been walking on a footpath through a wooded area northwest of town, when Fisher stepped into the woods and walked off. After supper, the three brothers left to look for Fisher. First one brother, then another, and finally the third came back to the boardinghouse reporting that they could not find Fisher anywhere.

The next morning, they searched again for Fisher, and this time some of the other residents of the boardinghouse helped, but the search proved fruitless. When they returned for dinner, William and Henry said they were going to give up the search and go home. The residents of the boardinghouse urged them to stay and search further, pointing out that if William left, Fisher would not have a ride home. Henry and William left after dinner, but they did not take a direct route to Clary's Grove. Instead, they were seen going off in another direction toward a brickyard.

A day or two later, Henry returned to Springfield to renew the search for Fisher. Arch and several residents of the boardinghouse helped Henry in the search, which again proved fruitless. Henry put an ad in the *Sangamo Journal* that read:

A MAN BY THE NAME OF Fisher arrived in this city on Monday last from Warren County with the undersigned, and has not been seen or heard of since about 4 o'clock of that day. He is at times deranged, caused by an injury on the head. He is about 35 or 40 years of age, 5 feet 10 inches high, sandy whiskers, black hair—had on a blue broadcloth coat, brown jean pantaloons, and a white fur hat about half worn. He is a carpenter by trade. Any person knowing anything of the above man, will much oblige his friends by leaving word at this office or at the subscriber's residence, in Clary's Grove, Menard County. HENRY TRAILER.[4]

William did not return to help in the search. Instead, he made his way back to Warren County, where he began spending gold coins. When asked where the money came from, he said Fisher had died in Springfield and willed $1,500 worth of gold coins to him. The details of William's story did not seem to make sense, and the Greenbush postmaster, a man by the name of Tice, sent a letter of inquiry to the postmaster in Springfield. When James W. Keyes, the Springfield postmaster, received the letter, he sounded the alarm and roused the townsmen to action.

In the general excitement, two men stepped forward to give some direction to the search. William H. May, the former congressman who had been involved in the Truett case, now serving as mayor of Springfield, assumed the role of leader of the search. He had as his co-captain Josiah Lamborn, who as the attorney general of Illinois also had the duty of serving as the Sangamon County prosecutor. One of Lamborn's fellow Illinois lawyers, Usher F. Linder, described Lamborn in his memoirs:

He was considered by all the lawyers who knew him as a man of the tersest logic. He could see the point in a case as clear as any lawyer I ever knew, and could elucidate it as ably, never using a word too much or one too few. He was exceedingly happy in his conceptions, and always traveled the shortest route to reach his conclusions. He was a terror to his legal opponents, especially those diffusive, wordy lawyers who had more words than arguments.[5]

Judge James H. Matheny said of Lamborn that in the "discharge of his duties as the prosecutor of criminals his soul kindled with a strange and vengeful fire. Nothing moved him from his purpose. With the instincts of a bloodhound he tracked the skulking wretch to his lair and with pitiless heart crushed the hopeless victim."[6]

May and Lamborn organized search parties, and the searchers marched abreast over the prairie in all directions. Teams went into cellars, cells, pits, attics, and barns looking for Fisher. They went to the graveyard and dug up all the fresh graves to make sure that there had been no unauthorized additions to any of them. They excavated any spot of recently dug earth and disinterred many dead horses and dogs. Arch had such a sterling reputation that nobody suspected him of wrongdoing, but his brothers were not so fortunate. Amid talk of lynching Arch's brothers, two deputy sheriffs were dispatched, one to arrest Henry and the other William.

Deputy Sheriff Josiah Wickersham rode to Clary's Grove and easily located Henry. He placed Henry under arrest, brought him back to Springfield, and turned him over to May and Lamborn. For the next three days, they questioned him, using every stratagem they could think of to get him to confess. Henry steadfastly denied wrongdoing. Lamborn, although a relentless prosecutor, did not enjoy a savory reputation. After the case concluded, several people accused him of coercing a statement from the none-too-bright Henry. One claimed that Lamborn told Henry the circumstantial evidence was strong against him, and if he did not want to be hanged with his brothers, he had to confess and agree to testify against them. Finally, Henry began to crack. At first he said that he "guessed" the body could be found in Spring Creek between the Beardstown Road bridge and the mill owned by Adam and Horace Hickox.[7] With a little more coaxing, he made a full statement. Lincoln later summarized Henry's statement in the following language:

> Henry stated that his brothers, William and Archibald had murdered Fisher; that they had killed him, without his (Henry's) knowledge at the time, and made a temporary concealment of his body; that immediately preceding his and William's departure from Springfield for home, on Tuesday, the day after Fisher's disappearance, William and Archibald communicated the fact to him, and engaged his assistance in making a permanent concealment of the body; that at the time he and William left professedly for home, they did not take the road directly, but meandering their way through the streets, entered the woods at the North West of the city, two or three hundred yards to the right of where the

road where they should have travelled entered them; that penetrating the woods some few hundred yards, they halted and Archibald came a somewhat different route, on foot, and joined them; that William and Archibald then stationed him (Henry) on an old and disused road that ran nearby, as a sentinel, to give warning of the approach of any intruder; that William and Archibald then removed the buggy to the edge of a dense brush thicket, about forty yards distant from his (Henry's) position, where, leaving the buggy, they entered the thicket, and in a few minutes returned with the body and placed it in the buggy; that from his station, he could and did distinctly see that the object placed in the buggy was a dead man, of the general appearance and size of Fisher; that William and Archibald then moved off with the buggy in the direction of Hickox's mill pond, and after an absence of half an hour returned, saying they had put him in a safe place; that Archibald then left for town, and he and William found their way to the road, and made for their homes.[8]

At news of Henry's confession, the townsfolk became incensed and renewed their talk of lynching. Arch, previously above suspicion, now became a prime candidate for mob justice. Lamborn and May had him arrested, as much for his own safety as anything else.

A quick search of the wooded area described by Henry did not locate Fisher, but the searchers did turn up a number of things that tended to back up Henry's story. In the wooded area Henry described, which was near a brickyard, they discovered scuff marks on the ground, indicating a struggle. They found a wooden stick with two hairs attached to it. Lincoln's friend Dr. E. H. Merryman examined the hairs and pronounced them human, not head hair but body or beard hair. Merryman thought they were more likely from a beard because they appeared to have been cut. Leading away from the scuff marks were drag marks, such as would have been made if a human body had been dragged across the ground. They followed the drag marks to a set of wagon tracks, which went off in the direction of Spring Creek. The wagon did not leave a continuous trail, but when the searchers arrived at Hickox's millpond on Spring Creek, they found the wagon tracks again. The tracks led into the water as though someone had backed the wagon to the shore of the millpond to dump a body into the creek.

Hundreds of townsfolk gathered at the millpond to search for Fisher's body. They opened the sluices to drain off the water, raked around the edge of the water, dragged the millpond, and found nothing. Deciding that simply opening the sluices had not brought down the level of the pond far enough, they determined to tear down the dam and drain all the water off. One of the Hickox brothers protested the destruction of his means of livelihood, but the crowd threatened to lynch him if he did not cooperate. The dam came down. They found nothing. In the midst of all this excitement, Deputy Sheriff Maxey returned with William in custody. William was put in jail on June 17, 1841. The next day, two things happened: Henry's ad ran a second time in the *Sangamo Journal*, and a preliminary hearing was held in the case.

According to the criminal procedure of the day, whenever someone was arrested and unable to obtain his release from jail, he could request a preliminary hearing to determine whether there was sufficient evidence to warrant keeping him in jail. For ordinary cases, the hearing was held without a jury before a justice of the peace. In capital murder cases, two justices of the peace presided over the hearing. The defendant had a right to be present at the hearing and to be represented by counsel. His counsel could cross-examine the prosecution witnesses and call witnesses on his behalf. William hired three lawyers to represent him: Stephen T. Logan, Edward D. Baker, and Abraham Lincoln. Josiah Lamborn prosecuted, and William L. May sat as one of the justices of the peace.

Stephen T. Logan,
Lincoln's senior
partner from 1841 to
1844. FROM LAMON,
LIFE OF LINCOLN, 333.

One might have cause to suspect May's impartiality. He headed up the search effort. He helped browbeat a confession out of Henry. He and Lamborn were the architects of the case against William and Arch. How likely would he be to rule the evidence insufficient to hold the two Trailors in jail pending indictment by the grand jury? Apparently the defense team had sufficient confidence in him to go to trial before him, but they certainly were taking a gamble. The Christian Church, where they held the hearing, was packed with spectators.

Captain Wharton Ransdell, a tavern keeper, testified first. He saw William and Henry when they left town to go home. The two men did not take the direct route back to Menard County but went off in another direction. The last Ransdell saw of them, they were headed toward the brickyard near the trees where the scuff marks were found. Henry took the stand next and testified to the following facts:

1. He and William drove off from Springfield in the direction that Ransdell said.
2. He stood lookout while William and Arch drove the Dearborn to the wooded area.
3. William and Arch brought a body out of the thicket and placed it in the Dearborn.
4. They drove off toward Hickox's dam while he continued to stand as a lookout.
5. In a half hour, William came back alone and said they had put Fisher's body in a safe place.
6. William said that he had hit Fisher in the head with a club, knocking him to the ground, and that Arch had finished Fisher off by choking him to death.

The defense went after Henry hammer and tongs, but he weathered the storm of cross-examination without faltering.

Lamborn then called a lady whom the sources say was respectable but fail to identify. The lady testified that she saw Arch, whom she knew, with two men whom she did not know, going into the wooded area near the brickyard. She pointed out William as one of the unknown men and gave a description of the other. That description fit Fisher. She further testified that one to two hours later, she saw William and Arch come out of the wooded area without the third man. Other witnesses testified that since Fisher's disappearance, Arch had been passing an unusually large number of gold coins. Lamborn then put on evidence of the results of the crime scene investigation and rested.

The defense called one witness, a doctor from Warren County by the name of Gilmore. Dr. Gilmore testified that he had known Fisher for many years, and that Fisher had twice lived with him. Fisher built a barn for Gilmore the first time he lived with him. The second time Fisher lived with him, Gilmore was treating him for a chronic disease. Fisher's health had been ruined when his gun exploded in a shooting accident. Since the explosion, Fisher suffered from chronic poor health and occasionally had "aberrations of the mind." The morning of William's arrest, Gilmore had been away from home. While away from home, Gilmore learned that William had been arrested for the murder of Fisher.

Gilmore finished his business and returned home around 11 A.M. When he got home, he was astonished to find Fisher there. The man was "in very feeble health and could give no rational account as to where he had been."[9] Gilmore immediately set out to catch the deputy and have him set William free. Gilmore caught up with the deputy late that night in the town of Lewiston. He explained to the deputy that Fisher still lived and William could be freed, but the deputy told him he had served an arrest warrant on William, and duty required him to deliver William to the proper authorities in Springfield. Gilmore rode on in to Springfield to tell his story to the proper authorities. When Gilmore arrived in Springfield, his story fell on deaf ears. Lamborn decided that Gilmore was an accomplice of the Trailors and was trying to trick him into releasing them. One person did believe him, though—Arch's partner, Myers. Myers immediately took off for Warren County to bring Fisher back to Springfield. Lamborn's cross-examination almost certainly centered on getting Gilmore to explain why he did not bring Fisher with him to Springfield. Gilmore had a ready answer: Fisher was so sick that he feared to move him.

A number of Springfield men knew and respected Dr. Gilmore, and the defense called them to vouch for Gilmore's truthfulness. Postmaster Tice had set off for Springfield when he heard that Fisher was alive, and he arrived in time to testify at the hearing. As he had only heard Fisher was alive and had not seen the man with his own eyes, he could only testify that Dr. Gilmore was a well-respected man in Warren County. Through all this testimony, Henry stoutly maintained that "no power on earth could ever show Fisher alive."[10]

William May found himself in a difficult situation. Finding the evidence insufficient would be an admission that he had acted like a damn fool in rushing to judgment against the Trailors. May, however, was just one of two presiding officers. The other justice, William Lavely, had no such difficulty. Bitter pill though it was, May had to swallow it and find the evidence insufficient. They ordered the prisoners released.

The day after his client was freed, Lincoln sat down and wrote a long letter to his good friend Joshua Speed, telling him about the case. In it he almost gloated over the reaction of the crowd to the release of Arch and William:

It was amusing to scan and contemplate the countenances, and hear the remarks of those who had been actively engaged in the search for the dead body. Some looked quizzical, some melancholy, and some furiously angry. Porter, who had been very active, swore he always knew the man was not dead, and that he had not stirred an inch to hunt for him; Langford, who had taken the lead in cutting down Hickoxes mill dam, and wanted to hang Hickox for objecting, looked most awfully woebegone.[11]

The crowd had been angry for two weeks over the supposed injustice to Fisher; now they were angry about the supposed incompetence of Lamborn. They even talked of lynching the attorney general. As one member of the crowd said, it was "too damned bad, to have so much trouble, and no hanging after all."[12]

A few days later, Myers returned with Fisher, very much alive but not well. A group of remorseful townsfolk got together and drafted a proclamation that they published in the *Illinois State Journal.* The last paragraph read:

We deeply regret that our fellow citizen, Archibald Trayler, should have been suspected of so foul a crime; and that the respect we have long held for his integrity and upright deportment has been in no wise diminished by the accusation made against him before the circumstances were known; and that we are convinced that all such suspicions and accusations are utterly unjustified and untrue and are not justified by the circumstances developed on the examination are strongly repelled by his past peaceful conduct and amiable character.[13]

Arch Trailor became a sullen, morose man who shunned the society of his fellow townsmen, never speaking about the circumstances of the case. Two years after the trial, he died for no apparent reason. He had lived approximately one year longer than William, who likewise never talked about the case. Henry outlived his brothers, but not by much. He was reported to be a "broken, deranged man" to the day of his death.[14]

Again Lincoln had taken an unsecured promissory note as his fee, and again his client failed to pay it. Lincoln wound up suing and getting a judgment against William's estate, but he never collected a cent. He never forgot the case either. In 1846, he published his article, "Remarkable Case of Arrest

for Murder," in a Quincy newspaper.[15] In it he said that he would not speculate on the mystery of what really happened between Fisher and the Trailors,
but he did speculate on what would have happened to them if Fisher had not
shown up alive: "It seems he had wandered away in mental derangement, and,
had he died in this condition, and his body been found in the vicinity, it is
difficult to conceive what could have saved the Trailors from the consequence
of having murdered him. Or, if he had died, and his body never found, the
case against them, would have been quite as bad."[16]

It seems clear that had Fisher not shown up alive but was in fact dead, it
would have been because Arch and William had succeeded in killing him. The
best interpretation of the evidence points to the following scenario: the two
brothers robbed Fisher, attempted to kill him, believed they had killed him,
and threw his body into the millpond. Henry may have been coerced, but
he told the truth (table 4.1). If Henry told the truth, then Arch and William
robbed Fisher, tried to kill him, and tossed him into the millpond (table 4.2).
The killing failed, being tossed into the water brought Fisher back to consciousness, and he wandered back to Warren County. Other explanations have been
advanced, but none fit the evidence as well as the failed murder attempt theory.

The week following the hearing, the *Sangamo Journal* published the earliest
theory about what had happened: Fisher became deranged and wandered off.
Then, when the finger of suspicion pointed at Henry, he made up the story
implicating his brothers to shield himself from prosecution. This theory falls
to pieces when we consider how thoroughly Henry's story was corroborated
by other witnesses.

Dr. Alexander Shields, who was Arch's physician when Arch died, advanced the next theory:

> William Trailor had a great fancy for Captain Ransdell's niece, and she
> had a fancy for him, and the captain was intensely opposed to it. Trailor
> was determined to steal the girl, and she was willing to be stolen, and
> in order to be prepared for the theft, the three men went down into
> the timber to find if there were any byroads that would lead into the
> Beardstown road; then Fisher is sent home on foot, and arrangements
> made with the girl to meet him in the timber. When he departed from
> home he took that direction, and, the girl being unable to escape the
> vigilance of the captain and his spies, did not appear; after waiting a
> reasonable time, he went to the Beardstown road on his way home.[17]

This explanation explains nothing and accounts for none of the evidence,
nor does it make any sense. The next theory to surface comes from the pen

TABLE 4.1. Did Henry Tell the Truth?

Henry's Statement		Other Evidence		Conclusion
William told me he and Arch killed Fisher	+	William told everyone in Warren County that Fisher was dead	=	Henry told the truth
I wasn't involved in the killing	+	The respectable lady saw Arch and William with Fisher, but not Henry	=	Henry told the truth
The killing occurred in the woods by the brickyard	+	Searchers found signs of a struggle in the woods by the brickyard	=	Henry told the truth
When William and I left for home, we went to the brickyard	+	Ransdell saw William and Henry riding toward the brickyard	=	Henry told the truth
Arch and William drove the Dearborn to the woods	+	Searchers found wagon tracks going to the edge of the woods	=	Henry told the truth
They went into the woods and came out with a body	+	Searchers found drag marks from the scuff marks in the woods to the wagon tracks	=	Henry told the truth
They drove off toward Hickox's mill	+	The wagon tracks went in the direction of Hickox's millpond	=	Henry told the truth
William came back alone and said the body was in a safe place	+	Wagon tracks led to the edge of the millpond	=	Henry told the truth

of John Carroll Power, who wrote his speculations in 1876, some thirty-five years after the incident:[18]

1. Fisher had simply become deranged and wandered off.
2. Henry was coerced into giving a false confession.
3. The hair found on the club was first thought to be human, but later determined to be from a cow.

TABLE 4.2. What Conclusions Can We Draw?

Henry's Statement		Other Evidence		Conclusion
William told me he and Arch killed Fisher	+	William told everyone in Warren County that Fisher was dead	=	William believed Fisher was dead
I wasn't involved in the killing	+	The respectable lady saw Arch and William with Fisher, but not Henry	=	Only Arch and William were involved in the attack on Fisher
The killing occurred in the woods by the brickyard	+	Searchers found signs of a struggle in the woods by the brickyard	=	Arch and William attempted the murder in the woods by the brickyard
When William and I left for home, we went to the brickyard	+	Ransdell saw William and Henry riding toward the brickyard	=	William and Henry were going to dispose of Fisher's body
Arch and William drove the Dearborn to the woods	+	Searchers found wagon tracks going to the edge of the woods	=	Arch and William went into the woods to dispose of Fisher's body
Arch and William went into the woods and came out with a body	+	Searchers found drag marks from the scuff marks in the woods to the wagon tracks	=	Arch and William took Fisher's unconscious body out of the woods and put it on the Dearborn
They drove off toward Hickox's mill	+	The wagon tracks went in the direction of Hickox's millpond	=	Arch and William took Fisher to Hickox's millpond
William came back alone and said the body was in a safe place	+	Wagon tracks led to the edge of the millpond	=	Arch and William put Fisher into the millpond

4. The wagon tracks going into the millpond were made by William the day before he and Henry left for home. He had given up the search and headed home the day before, but his brother Arch caught him as he was fording the millpond and persuaded him to come back.
5. The scuff marks in the woods were made by a group of girls who had been playing there the day Fisher went missing.

Power's first point, that Fisher had become deranged and wandered off, is correct as far as it goes, but Fisher's derangement most likely resulted from being clubbed in the head, choked almost to death, and dumped in the millpond.

The validity of Power's second point, that Henry was coerced into confession, depends on whether coercion always produces a false confession. It does not. If a coerced confession can be corroborated in detail, it is unlikely to be false. If Henry gave a false confession, then Arch and William were the victims of an unlikely series of coincidences that corroborated the confession in detail.

His third point is that the hair on the club was from a cow rather than a human. If that is true, it is a remarkable coincidence that someone went into the woods and clubbed a cow in the exact spot where William was supposed to have clubbed Fisher and that the cow's hair was sufficiently similar to human hair to fool Dr. Merryman. Further, if it were cow hair, it simply removes the club as a piece of corroborating evidence for Henry's confession but does nothing to disconfirm the confession.

The fourth point, that the Dearborn made the tracks going into the millpond when William made an abortive attempt to go home on the day of Fisher's disappearance, makes no sense at all. If William were going home, he was heading in the wrong direction. If William were trying to ford the river, he was exercising extremely poor judgment in trying to ford at the millpond—the widest and deepest part of the river.

As to the fifth point, that the scuff marks on the ground were made by girls playing, it is certainly an unfortunate coincidence that they were playing right at the beginning of drag marks that led to the wheel marks of the Dearborn.

A final reason to discount Power's hypothesis is the fact that he got the facts of the case dreadfully wrong. Power was dismissive of Lincoln's article on the "remarkable case." Of Lincoln's account, he wrote that it was "principally true, but contains some glaring errors, which, by the aid of men who took part in the proceedings, I have been able to avoid."[19] Obviously he did not know that Lincoln wrote it. To borrow a phrase, the most glaring error in Power's account comes when he says that the defense called one witness: Archibald Fisher. Power claimed to have thoroughly investigated the original news accounts of the affair and to have interviewed eyewitnesses to the trial. How could he have gotten it so wrong? He got his story on the authority of an unnamed eyewitness whom he described as "a gentleman who was cognizant of the proceedings from beginning to end, and who is now a judge of one of the courts of Illinois." This anonymous judge gave a vivid description of Arch Trailor's reaction on seeing Fisher alive in court: "When the man he was accused of having murdered was led into his presence, he broke down and gave vent to his feelings in a flood of tears, followed by uncontrollable fits of sobbing and moaning."[20] All of this serves as a warning that an informant is not necessarily reliable simply because the person claims to be an eyewitness.

The final explanation of the mystery comes from the pen of Roger W. Barrett, who edited and published Lincoln's account of the case in a pamphlet. Barrett credited Henry's confession and the testimony of the corroborating witnesses and advanced an explanation that accounted for almost all the facts. His theory was as follows: Everything happened just as Henry said, but when Fisher went into the woods, he either suffered an epileptic fit and fell down into a catatonic trance or went temporarily crazy and attacked Arch and William, who defended themselves. Both scenarios ended with Arch and William standing over Fisher's apparently dead body. Arch and William, believing Fisher to be dead, relieved him of his money. Fearing they would be blamed, they threw Fisher's catatonic body into the millpond. Barrett observed, "The Trailors must have been puzzled when the pond was drained and no body found, and bewildered when Fisher showed up alive. . . . It is not to be wondered that Archibald and William would never reveal their part in this strange affair."[21] If Barrett's theory is correct, however, it is to be wondered why Arch and William did not just say what happened, omitting the fact that they rifled Fisher's pockets. None of the townsfolk knew how much money Fisher had. It is also difficult to make either story fit around Henry's statement that William clubbed Fisher and then Arch choked him to death.

If the objective is to exonerate Arch and William, then it is quite logical to invent factors for which we have no evidence, such as the tryst in the woods with Captain Ransdell's daughter or Fisher's insane attack on Arch and William. But Ockham's razor posits that if a simpler theory is available that explains the evidence without imagining factors for which there is no evidence, then the simpler theory is preferable.[22] Such a theory is available in this case. Simply following the evidence where it leads brings one to the conclusion that Arch and William robbed and attempted to kill Archibald Fisher.

5.

Various Criminal Cases, 1845–46

AFTER THE TRAILOR CASE, LINCOLN WENT FOR THREE YEARS WITHOUT TRY-
ing another homicide, then in a three-month period he tried three, but none
of them would be against Josiah Lamborn. In the wake of Lamborn's debacle
with the Trailor prosecution, the Democratic Party declined to nominate him
for another term as attorney general, and James A. McDougall succeeded
him. McDougall was said to be "one of the most brilliant men ever connected
with the Chicago bar,"[1] but he failed to display that brilliance in *People v.
Tinney*,[2] the next murder case Lincoln defended. Few records pertaining to
this case survive, but we do have the indictment drafted by McDougall. In
the custom of the time, the allegations in the indictment are redundant, and
the indictment is almost devoid of punctuation. With grammar corrected,
most of the redundancies omitted, and punctuation inserted, count one of
the indictment charged that on June 22, 1840, in one of the counties of the
Eighth Judicial Circuit (but not necessarily in Tazewell County), Edward B.
Tinney murdered John Kelsey by shooting him in the head with a single-shot
pistol, and that the bullet penetrated four inches into Kelsey's head, instantly
killing him. The second count of the indictment charged that four years later,
on June 22, 1844, Tinney unlawfully killed Kelsey again, this time in Tazewell
County, and this time without malice aforethought, by shooting a single-shot
pistol at him and grazing his head, causing him to fall out of a boat and into
Illinois River and instantly drown.[3] It does not take a law degree to recognize that the indictment had serious flaws. McDougall got his indictment
on September 7, 1844, and Tinney languished in jail for six months awaiting
the next term of court.

When Tinney's case came up for trial, the responsibility for his prosecution
had been transferred to David B. Campbell as state's attorney. Campbell had
inherited a mess from McDougall, and Lincoln took full advantage of the
mistakes McDougall made. He moved to dismiss the indictment for informality. Obviously Tinney could have killed Kelsey only once, and the single

49

bullet discharged from Tinney's gun could not have both grazed Kelsey's head and penetrated it to the depth of four inches. Lincoln wanted both counts of the indictment dismissed, but the judge had other ideas. Although the first count of the indictment was fatally defective because it did not charge that the crime occurred in Tazewell County, the second count was sufficient to charge a crime. The judge dismissed count one, which charged murder, and allowed the case to go to trial on the second count, which charged manslaughter.

The second count may have been legally sufficient to charge a crime, but was it charged correctly? What if the bullet had actually penetrated Kelsey's skull? Campbell was going to trial on an indictment charging that the bullet only grazed Kelsey's head. If Campbell proved penetration, Lincoln could move for a directed verdict of not guilty because of a variance between the pleadings and the proof. An additional problem was the allegation that Kelsey died instantly. Count two charged that Kelsey died from drowning, and neither drowning nor a graze from a bullet kills instantly. Campbell could not prove that Kelsey died instantly. That gave Lincoln another variance between pleading and proof. Even if the judge allowed the case to go to the jury, Lincoln could make the argument that Tinney did not kill Kelsey, Kelsey died because he fell out of a boat in the middle of the Illinois River and did not know how to swim. The jury found Tinney not guilty.

Lincoln tried his next murder case, *People v. Weaver*, in Champaign County. The Champaign County Jail figures prominently in the story of the trial of William Weaver. The county had no jail until 1839, when it set aside $850 to build a two-story log jail. The jail measured eighteen feet long by eighteen feet wide and had only one entrance on the second floor, which could be reached by an outside stairwell. Prisoners who were considered unruly or escape risks were housed on the first floor. To put a prisoner in the first-floor holding area, the jailer opened a trapdoor in the floor and put down a ladder. After the prisoner climbed down the ladder, the jailer took it up and closed the trapdoor. The first floor had two barred windows one foot high by one foot wide, through which light and air could come into the holding area. The jail had no heat, and the inmates would freeze in the winter and bake in the summer. It was surrounded by a stockade fence, and the townsfolk mistakenly believed it to be escape-proof.[4]

The old jail housed not only William Weaver, the first man tried for murder in Champaign County, but also Tom Johnston, a foster nephew of Abraham Lincoln. In 1856, when Lincoln was campaigning for John C. Frémont in his failed bid to win the presidency, Lincoln's nephew spent several months in the first-floor holding area of the jail. Johnston, while passing through Urbana, stole a watch from a watchmaker's shop owned by Mr. and Mrs. Green. He was quickly apprehended and placed in jail, protesting that he wanted to have Lincoln as his lawyer. The consensus of opinion was that he was so obviously guilty that he needed no lawyer, so nobody tried to notify Lincoln.

Not long afterward, Lincoln came to Champaign County to give a political speech for Frémont. He spied his old friend Henry Clay Whitney in the crowd, and during the handshaking that followed his speech, Lincoln told Whitney, "I want to see you all to yourself." They separated from the crowd, and Whitney asked what Lincoln wanted. Lincoln responded:

> There is a boy in your jail I want to see, and I don't want anyone to know it except us. I wish you would arrange with the jailer to go there, on the sly, after the meeting, and let us in. This boy is not my nephew, but when my father married the second time; his wife had a boy of about my age, and we were raised together, slept together, and liked each other as well as actual brothers could do. This boy is a son of him—my foster-brother. He is already under a charge of stealing a gun at Charleston. I shall do what I can for him in these two cases, but that's the last. After that, if he wants to be a thief, I shan't help him anymore.[5]

There was a great sadness in Lincoln's voice, and Whitney, who was a prominent lawyer and the son of the local justice of the peace, agreed to arrange the meeting.

As stealthily as possible, the two lawyers went to the jail and were admitted through the gate. They talked to young Johnston through the small grated window on the first floor. In describing the visit, Whitney wrote, "As we approached the one foot square hole through which we could converse with the prisoner he heard us and set up a hypocritical wailing, and thrust out toward us a very dirty Bible, which Lincoln took and turned over the leaves mechanically."

"Where was you going, Tom?" asked Lincoln. According to Whitney, the boy replied with incoherent wailing. Lincoln cut him short and said, "Now you just do what they tell you—behave yourself—don't talk to anyone, and when court comes, I will be here and see what I can do. Now stop crying and behave yourself."[6]

At the fall term of court, Amzi McWilliams, the state's attorney for Champaign County, went to Whitney and told him that he had consulted with Judge Davis. "If the Greens come into court and say they do not wish to prosecute," he said, "I will *nol pros* [dismiss] the case." Lincoln had again come to town campaigning and was scheduled to give a speech at a church that evening. The Greens lived quite near the church.

That evening, while another speaker was holding forth, Lincoln and Whitney slipped out of the church and went to the Greens' home. They found the Greens sitting at the table in their kitchen, and Whitney explained the purpose of their visit. The Greens agreed, and the next morning they went to the courthouse to tell McWilliams that they wanted the charges dropped. McWilliams entered a nolle prosequi (dismissal by the prosecutor). That was the last day of the term in Champaign County, and as the lawyers were leaving town headed toward the next county in the circuit, the entourage passed young Tom Johnston standing on the side of the road looking forlorn. Lincoln was seen to stop his buggy, dismount, and go over to the boy. He engaged the young man in earnest conversation for a brief time, gave him some money, and remounted his buggy.[7] Lincoln later managed to get the charges dropped in Charleston as well.

William Weaver's sojourn in the Champaign County Jail began on October 10, 1844, when Weaver, who had a reputation as a "drunken, reckless wretch, shot David Hiltibran in the right side with a rifle, without any apparent motive, except the fiendish recklessness that often attends men who have become besotted."[8] Weaver was immediately arrested and put in the jail's first-floor holding cell, and there he sat until the next term of court. In May of the next year, he stood trial on a charge of murder. Because Weaver, like Fielding Fraim, had no money, the judge appointed Lincoln and Asahel Gridley to represent him. James A. McDougall, who had been involved in the Tinney case, prosecuted, and he had more success against Lincoln this time. In a whirlwind prosecution, the grand jury indicted Weaver on May 7, the petit jury convicted him on May 9, and the judge sentenced him to death on May 10.[9] The judge scheduled the execution for June 27, and the county officials began to build a scaffold.

As Weaver languished in the first-floor dungeon, someone slipped him an auger, which he used to bore holes in the logs of the jail wall. Slowly but surely, he made a breach in the wall large enough to slip through. Just days before his scheduled execution, Weaver made his break for freedom. Attempts to find and arrest him proved futile, and he escaped to Wisconsin, where he changed his name and his habits and lived out his life as a law-abiding citizen.[10] Weaver's escape from Champaign County's supposedly escape-proof jail inspired other inmates, and breakouts became so common that the Urbana Union complained that the jail "might answer for the imprisonment of infants, or of men who are badly crippled, but will not do for the detention of rascals."[11] Finally, in 1857, the county built a more secure brick jail in the public square.

While Weaver patiently augered his way out of jail and out of an appointment with the hangman, Lincoln moved on to the next county on the circuit, and before the scheduled date of Weaver's execution, he had tried another homicide case. This case, *People v. Dorman*, provides a contrast between the efforts of lawyers who have received a fee and lawyers who have not. In the Weaver case, the defendant was indicted on a Wednesday, arraigned and tried on a Friday, and sentenced to death on a Saturday. It is unlikely that a lawyer was appointed to represent him until after the grand jury returned its indictment. On short notice and without much time for preparation, Lincoln and Gridley met their client and tried his case, and after Weaver was sentenced to death, neither lawyer took an appeal. The Dorman case took a very different course.

On February 22, 1845, James O. Dorman tried to break into Ellen Cox's home. Cox, who was pregnant, resisted Dorman's attempt to beat down the door. Dorman never got into the house, but Cox became ill. Doctors blamed the illness on her exertions in trying to keep Dorman out of her house. Cox's condition worsened, and finally she died on March 2. Since Dorman never got into the house with Cox and never touched her, the chain of causation from Dorman's banging on the door to Cox's death was tenuous. Apparently the coroner's jury was not satisfied that Dorman had caused Cox's death. Had they found Dorman criminally responsible for the death of Cox, one of the justices of the peace of Sangamon County would have issued a warrant for his arrest, and he would have been immediately arrested. The action of the coroner's jury should have caused Attorney General James A. McDougall to pause and reflect on the wisdom of pursuing charges against a man whom one jury had already failed to find guilty.

Heedless of the warning, McDougall indicted Dorman for manslaughter in Sangamon County Circuit Court on March 17. The indictment, which was a model of clarity for that day and age, charged that James Dorman went to the home of Ellen Cox and "did then and there unlawfully attempt to force an entrance"; that Ellen Cox, "sick and weak of body from her being then and there in a state of pregnancy ... was compelled to make great physical efforts to prevent" the breaking and entering; that she became "greatly alarmed and frightened"; and that her fright, coupled with her weakened condition, caused her to become ill, languish for several days, and die.[12]

When a grand jury indicts a defendant who is not in custody, the clerk of the court issues a capias (which is similar to a warrant) for the arrest of the defendant. This was done, and a deputy sheriff immediately arrested Dorman and put him in jail.[13] Dorman hired Lincoln for a fee of $50. Lincoln immediately moved for a change of venue, and the judge changed the venue to Menard County. This put the trial off until the beginning of the next term of court in Menard County. Because Champaign County had its term of court between Sangamon and Menard, Lincoln wound up trying the Dorman case sixteen days before Weaver's scheduled execution. The jury predictably found Dorman not guilty.

On August 28, 1845, in Menard County, Peter Parker hit Eliphalet Purse on the forehead with "a certain board of the value of six cents," inflicting a "mortal wound of the breadth of three inches and the depth of one inch." Purse died the next day.[14] David B. Campbell indicted Parker for manslaughter, and Lincoln defended with the assistance of a young attorney named Thomas L. Harris. Harris was soon to make his mark in the world, but not as a lawyer. When the Mexican-American War broke out the following spring, Harris raised a company of volunteers that was incorporated into the Fourth Regiment, Illinois Volunteer Infantry, under Colonel E. D. Baker. The regiment elected Harris major, and he became second in command under Baker. He fought at the Battles of Vera Cruz and Cerro Gordo. At Cerro Gordo, Colonel Baker became brigade commander when General Shields was wounded, and Harris assumed command of the regiment. Harris acquitted himself so well that after the war, the Illinois legislature presented him a sword for gallantry in battle. While Harris was distinguishing himself on the battlefield, Lincoln was committing political suicide by opposing the war as a freshman congressman. Lincoln did not run for reelection. He stepped aside so his old partner Stephen T. Logan could run on the Whig ticket. Harris ran on the Democratic ticket and defeated Logan.[15]

The case went to trial on June 9, 1846, before the Honorable Samuel H. Treat, but there were other cases on the docket that day. Before Parker could be tried for manslaughter, Jonathan Page had to be tried on a charge of horse theft. David B. Campbell prosecuted Page with Lincoln and Harris defending, and the jury found Page not guilty.[16] When it came time to try Parker, Campbell had better luck, and the jury found him guilty as charged. Because Parker was under the age of eighteen, the judge sentenced him to only sixty days in jail. After Parker had served a month, Harris drafted a petition asking that Governor Thomas Ford "grant a liberation" to Parker. Harris collected the signatures of the clerk of court, the sheriff, eight jurors, and seventy additional petitioners. The governor granted the pardon.[17]

Lincoln was not finished when he concluded the trials of Page and Parker. He had one more matter to be heard before the court. Squire Powell had sued Iven Worth in justice of the peace court for $27. When the jury decided the case in Worth's favor,[18] Powell hired Lincoln to take an appeal to circuit court. Apparently, when an appeal was taken from the justice of the peace court to circuit court, the case was completely retried. The court minutes for June 9 report that in the case of *Powell v. Worth*, "This day came the parties in proper person and by their attorneys, and this cause by agreement is tried by the court, and the court having heard the evidence, the Plaintiff dismisses his suit at his costs."[19]

Judge Treat stayed busy that day. In addition to trying the two felony cases and hearing Lincoln's appeal, he tried one other civil case without a jury and presided over the publication of an indictment by the grand jury.[20] David Logan, acting as attorney general pro tem, indicted James and George Denton for the ax murder of Cassius Brown. Sometimes when the prosecutor was unavailable or unable to handle a case, a prosecutor pro tem would be appointed. Because Campbell, the regular prosecutor, had his hands full that day trying felony cases, Logan was appointed to step into the breach and work with the grand jury.

Appointment as prosecutor pro tem was not the only way a private attorney could become the prosecutor on a case. If the victim or the victim's family thought the elected prosecutor was not equal to the task of prosecuting a case, they could hire a more experienced attorney to associate with him in the trial. Prosecutors themselves often called on members of the private bar to assist them. Sometimes, as in the Denton case, more than one private lawyer became involved in the prosecution. And sometimes, as in the next case, one of those private prosecutors was Abraham Lincoln.

6.

PEOPLE versus JAMES AND GEORGE DENTON, June 12, 1846

OF ALL THE MURDER INDICTMENTS FROM LINCOLN'S CASES THAT HAVE SUR-vived to the present, the indictment drafted by David Logan has to be the most concise, clear, and understandable. Count one of Logan's indictment charged that both James and George Denton used an ax to chop and strike Cassius Brown in the head, neck, and left side of the body. Count two charged that both men were guilty of the murder, but that only George Denton had an ax.[1] Because only George Denton was in custody, Logan asked that a capias be issued for James's arrest.[2] He was arrested almost immediately and was in

Earliest known photograph of Lincoln, taken shortly after he tried the Denton case. PHOTO-GRAPH COURTESY OF THE LIBRARY OF CONGRESS.

court represented by counsel on June 11. There were two new prosecutors on the case as well: Josiah Lamborn and Abraham Lincoln.

The Denton case is notable for two things: the distorted picture of the trial that has come down to us in the Lincoln lore and the remarkable aspects of the case, which have gone virtually unnoticed. This chapter first recounts the stories passed down about the trial, then attempts a reconstruction of what happened when Cassius Brown met his death, and finally traces the course of the prosecution, from its ill-conceived inception to the odd maneuverings of the lawyers to its almost inevitable conclusion.

According to Carl Sandburg, the Dentons got into a dispute with their brother-in-law Cassius Brown, the three men squared off against each other with axes, and Brown lost the battle. During the voir dire examination of the jury, Lincoln was heard to remark, "I would like to throw the whole panel out, for I know every single one of them; but I can't object to a man among them."[3] Lincoln became convinced that such a jury would never convict, and for all practical purposes he simply gave up the fight. During the weeklong trial, he left the questioning of all witnesses to another prosecutor, and when the time came to argue the case to the jury, he declined to make an argument. Unsurprisingly, the jury acquitted. Sandburg ends his account of the trial with the remark "Lincoln never made much of a record when called in as a prosecutor."[4]

Sandburg's account of Lincoln quitting the case in midstream echoes some other stories about Lincoln, especially one about a case in which Lincoln found out midtrial that his client had lied to him. Ward Hill Lamon reported Lincoln's reaction: "In a closely-contested civil suit, Lincoln had proved an account for his client, who was, though he did not know it at the time, a very slippery fellow. The opposing attorney then proved a receipt clearly covering the entire cause of action. By the time he was through, Lincoln was missing. The court sent for him to the hotel. 'Tell the judge,' said he, 'that I can't come: my hands are dirty; and I came over to clean them!'"[5]

Another example of Lincoln's supposed inability to argue the wrong side of a case comes from a story that has been told and retold concerning his first appearance before the Supreme Court of Illinois. The standard version of the story says that after taking his appeal to the supreme court, Lincoln realized that he had no case. Being unable to argue when the law was so clearly against his client, Lincoln appeared before the court and made the following brief speech:

This is the first case I have ever had in this court, and I have therefore examined it with great care. As the Court will perceive, by looking at the abstract of the record, the only question in the case is one of authority. I have not been able to find any authority sustaining my side of the case, but I have found several cases directly in point on the other side. I will now give these cases, and then submit the case.[6]

Lincoln then handed the authorities up to the court and sat down, refusing to argue for a position that he knew was wrong. This story of Lincoln's candor in his first appearance before the Illinois Supreme Court came from William Henry Herndon, who claimed to have gotten it from Justice Samuel H. Treat. Lincoln biographer John T. Richards thoroughly investigated the story and determined that it contained several inaccuracies: Justice Treat was not on the bench when Lincoln first appeared before the supreme court; Lincoln represented the appellee, not the appellant, when he made his first appearance before the supreme court; and Lincoln won his case the first time he appeared before Justice Treat.[7]

John J. Duff provided a very different picture of Lincoln's involvement in the Denton trial. According to Duff, Lincoln was called in to assist "that rather unsavory character, Josiah Lamborn," and when the case came up for trial on June 11, 1846, George got a severance from James, who stood trial alone. The trial lasted two days and eventually ended in a hung jury. Lincoln then began to lobby Lamborn to drop the charges because there were no eyewitnesses to the crime. When Lincoln finally prevailed on Lamborn to drop the charges, it was a "considerable achievement," given "Lamborn's obsessive zest for prosecuting." Duff disagreed with Sandburg's opinion of Lincoln as a prosecutor. He said that Lamborn was a highly talented trial lawyer with ample self-esteem, and allowing Lincoln to associate with him in the trial was a "flattering recognition of [Lincoln's] capabilities."[8] Moreover, the fact that Lincoln could amicably work with Lamborn was a testament to Lincoln's ability to get along with people, because as a prosecutor, "Lamborn was ruthless, fighting always with the invective which made him the most feared prosecutor in the state."[9] Reinhard H. Luthin simply repeated Duff's account but omitted the character sketch of Lamborn.[10] Duff also mentioned a puzzling fact: Stephen T. Logan, Lincoln's old senior partner, served as co-counsel for the defense along with Thomas L. Harris, a prominent member of the Springfield bar.[11] How was it possible for Stephen T. Logan's son and junior partner, David Logan, to obtain the indictment against the Dentons, and then for the elder Logan to defend one of the men whom his son had indicted? The Logan firm's apparent conflict of interest is the first of the remarkable aspects of the case that have gone unnoticed.

The Sandburg version of the trial portrays Lincoln as being unable to effectively prosecute a case he did not believe in and generally not being a very good prosecutor at all. Duff's version has Lincoln, the able prosecutor, working alongside Lamborn to prosecute the case. In Duff's account, after the jury hung, Lincoln had the good judgment to decide the case was not worthy of prosecution and the ability to persuade the rabid prosecutor Lamborn to agree. A careful reading of what remains of the court record shows that neither version is correct.

As best can be reconstructed from the court record, Cassius Brown had a reputation for a violent temper and a habit of carrying a handgun. He and his brothers-in-law, the Dentons, got into a heated disagreement that went from words to blows to homicide. Only three people witnessed the brawl, and of those three only the two Dentons were available for comment when it was over. Brown did not die immediately but languished until the next day before succumbing to his wounds. He did live long enough to make a dying declaration accusing the Dentons of murdering him, but one might question how much faith should be put in the dying declaration of a man suffering from head wounds caused by repeated blows from an ax.

We can infer that the coroner convened a jury, and it returned a verdict finding that Brown had been killed by the Dentons. The Dentons may have actually testified at the coroner's inquest. They were not yet the defendants in a criminal prosecution and thus were not barred from giving testimony. If they did testify, they certainly swore that George struck the fatal blows in self-defense. Warrants were issued for the Dentons' arrest, and they were duly arrested and placed in jail.

Two justices of the peace, sitting as committing magistrates, held a preliminary hearing to determine whether probable cause existed to warrant the continued detention of the brothers pending a grand jury indictment. Probable cause is a much lower burden than proof beyond a reasonable doubt. The courts of antebellum Illinois defined probable cause as "a reasonable ground of suspicion, supported by circumstances sufficiently strong in themselves to warrant a cautious man in the belief that the person accused is guilty of the offence with which he is charged."[12] A reasonable doubt, on the other hand, was defined as "such a doubt as would induce a reasonable man to say, 'I am not satisfied that the defendant is guilty.'"[13] The committing magistrates found no probable cause to believe that James Denton had committed murder and released him.[14] They found probable cause against George Denton, but the fact that it was a close decision is reflected in George's release on bail pending trial.[15] When a judge releases a defendant facing a capital murder case on bail, that means the judge believes the case against the defendant is weak. Prosecutors should sit up and take notice whenever a committing magistrate finds no probable cause to believe that a person has committed a crime. If a committing magistrate says, "I don't believe the defendant is guilty," then it is highly unlikely that a jury will say, "We are satisfied beyond a reasonable doubt that the defendant is guilty."

Because a procession of prosecutors handled various aspects of the case, it is not clear who represented the people at the preliminary hearing. Thomas L. Harris probably represented the Dentons at the preliminary hearing, and Stephen T. Logan probably did not. It would be strange if two members of the same firm were simultaneously on both sides of a death penalty case. The far more likely scenario is that the elder Logan did not become involved in the litigation until after his son had gotten the indictment and withdrawn from the case. It is reasonable to assume that Harris represented both Dentons at the preliminary hearing and then only George Denton when the indictment was returned. When his brother was indicted, the elder Logan stepped in and took over the representation of James.

Now we come to the next remarkable aspect of the case: the Dentons were the only witnesses to the killing. With both of them arrested and charged, they could not give evidence in their own defense, nor could they be compelled to give evidence against each other. What did the prosecution plan on using as evidence that they killed Brown? Aside from the questionable dying declaration, the only evidence that appears to have been available to the prosecution was admissions made by the brothers to other witnesses. These admissions, however, would not be confessions. They would be evidence that George killed Brown, but they would bring with them the baggage of being evidence that George acted in self-defense. Both brothers clearly agreed that James not only did nothing to contribute to Brown's death but also tried to stop the fight. Consequently, there was almost no evidence whatsoever to convict James and precious little to convict George.

That is the way Nathan Dresser, one of the justices of the peace who held the preliminary hearing, saw the evidence when he ruled that James be released from jail. He might have made the same ruling for his brother, had the prosecutor not done some well-choreographed maneuvering to obtain more evidence against George. The prosecutor solved the problem of the lack of evidence against George by asking the justices to decide James's case before they decided George's. When the justices made a finding of no probable cause for holding James and released him from custody, he was no longer a defendant and no longer had a privilege against self-incrimination. The prosecutor could then compel James to testify against his brother. As soon as James was released, the prosecutor placed him on the stand to testify against George. We can be sure that James testified reluctantly and tried to slant his testimony in such a way as to help his brother as much as possible. Despite James's reluctance to give evidence against his brother, he testified to sufficient facts that, taken with the dying declaration and circumstantial evidence garnered from other witnesses, established probable cause to believe George was responsible for unlawful homicide.[16] The reasonable thing for the prosecutor to do in such a situation was to have been content with simply prosecuting George and using James as a prosecution witness.

At this point, however, another remarkable thing happened: David Logan indicted both James and George. How could a grand jury indict when the committing magistrates found no probable cause? A preliminary hearing is an adversarial proceeding at which the defendant's attorney may cross-examine the prosecution witnesses and call defense witnesses. A grand jury proceeding is not adversarial. The defendant has no right to counsel, no right to cross-examine the prosecution witnesses, and no right to call defense witnesses to testify before the grand jury. In such a situation, probable cause is much easier to prove. Logan faced a situation where he had a highly suspect dying declaration that gave some evidence that James was guilty; he might arguably have had probable cause, but he had good grounds to question whether he had proof beyond a reasonable doubt. When the chances of conviction are slim to none, prosecutors do well to say, "No, we cannot prosecute this case." Logan seemed to be saying, "It's a long shot, but let's give it a try anyway."

When Josiah Lamborn stepped into the role of prosecutor, he inherited a very marginal case from David Logan. He had two options: either he could recognize the deficiencies in the case and drop the charges against James so he could be used as a witness against George, or he could adopt Logan's attitude and pursue the charges against both. Considering his zeal for prosecution, it is unsurprising that he pursued charges against both. We should not judge the younger Logan too harshly for filing a marginal case, nor Lamborn for going forward with it. The only exculpatory evidence came out of the mouths of the brothers, and it was reasonable to assume that at the very least they embellished their testimony to make themselves look more innocent than they actually were. The heartfelt belief that the defendant lies when he says he is innocent has prompted many a prosecutor to file a case with little prospect of achieving a conviction. So long as probable cause exists, so long as the prosecutor sincerely believes the defendant guilty, and so long as the prosecutor conducts the prosecution according to the highest standards of ethical conduct, he commits no ethical breach by pursuing charges.

At the arraignment on June 11, George moved to sever his case from James's and have a separate trial from his brother. As grounds for his motion, George alleged the following:

> The Defendant George W. Denton, being duly sworn states on oath that he is informed and verily believes that it is necessary in order to obtain a fair trial of this Indictment, that there should be separate trials granted the Defendants; that he deems it essentially necessary that he should have the benefit of the testimony of his co-defendant James Denton on his trial.
>
> That the unfortunate affray which resulted in the death of Brown the deceased took place when no other person was present except Brown the deceased and these two Defendants. He further states that the said James Denton took no part whatever in the fray except to endeavor to prevent it, that he neither assisted, aided, abetted, advised, or encouraged it; that whatever violence was used by the affiant toward said Brown was used in his necessary self-defense against the assault then made on him by said Brown with a gun; and that he used no more violence than seemed reasonably necessary to defend himself against such an assault as was made by said Brown, which was of such a character as to put this affiant in great danger of his life.
>
> That on the trial before the examining court the Defendant James was discharged on the ground that there was no evidence to criminate him. That he believes he will be able to prove his justification on the ground of self-defense fully by said James; and that without the testimony of said James the case need be tried and decided on the evidence of circumstances, on what are alleged to be death bed declarations of the deceased made, as the affiant believes, when the sanity of the deceased was, to say the least, extremely doubtful and uncertain, and on admissions alleged to have been made by defendants which were, at the examining court, in part at least greatly perverted.[17]

Harris supported the motion for severance with an affidavit from Nathan Dresser, the justice of the peace, which said:

> Nathan Dresser, having been first duly sworn, states that he was one of the justices who examined the Defendants in this case when they were arrested on the charge of the Murder alleged in this Indictment; that

on said examination the defendant James Denton was discharged on the ground that there was no evidence sufficient to criminate him in the estimation of the examining court. That James Denton was then examined as a witness and his testimony, elucidated the facts and circumstances proved by other witnesses, was confirmed by the facts and circumstances found to exist; and from the testimony as it appeared before the examining court, he apprehends that the facts of the case cannot be certainly arrived at or fully understood without his [James Denton's] testimony.[18]

Judge Treat was impressed by the argument and ordered the defendants be tried separately. The logic of the motion to sever dictated that the weaker case, the one against James, be tried first so that his charges could be disposed of before he testified on behalf of his brother, George. Treat ordered that George's case be continued to the next term, leaving the prosecution with no choice other than to try the weaker case first. When prosecuting a series of connected cases, the prosecutor wants to try the best case first. The results of the first trial can have a domino effect on all following trials. An acquittal in the first trial means that the prosecutor will almost certainly have to try every single one of the rest of the cases, but a conviction in the first trial can often place the prosecutor in a much stronger position when confronting the remaining cases. The maneuvering of the defense counsel had prevented the prosecution from putting its best foot forward, and it was just going to have to live with the judge's ruling.

Then something else remarkable happened. The prosecution sorely needed more evidence than it had against James, and the only source of such evidence was George. The prosecutors engaged in some more maneuvering, and the upshot was that George became available to testify against James. There is no record as to who devised the scheme, and we are left to speculate whether it came from the minds of the two most towering intellects involved in the case—Lincoln and Logan—or whether other lawyers were architects of the stipulation. The prosecution needed George's testimony to have any hope of getting a conviction, and the defense believed that James needed his brother's testimony to have his best chance at an acquittal. Why not agree that George could testify at his brother's trial and that his testimony would not be used against him in his own trial? This analysis led to an agreement that was memorialized in the minutes of James's trial: "Be it remembered that on the trial of the foregoing cause, George W. Denton was introduced and testified as a witness by the consent of the parties, and it was stipulated by the people that his testimony then given should never be used as evidence against him in the trial of this indictment as against him or of any other indictment preferred against him for the same charge."[19]

The case went to trial on June 12, and it is difficult to tell in hindsight whether the prosecution or the defense made the better bargain. The jury hung. Would the jurors have convicted if they had not heard George's testimony that James merely tried to stop the fight? Would they have acquitted if they had not heard the admissions George made that tended to indicate guilt? We will never know. What does seem obvious, however, is that the prosecution should have tried to engineer a situation where it tried George first and had James testify under the same sort of agreement made for George's testimony.

When the case came back up for trial in October 1847, Lincoln was not there, but it was not because he felt the case did not deserve to be prosecuted. It was because he had just been elected to Congress and was traveling to Washington to take up his office.[20] Evidence for the proposition that Lincoln did not desert Lamborn is that when the case came back up for trial, Lincoln's junior partner, William H. Herndon, assisted Lamborn. If Lincoln thought the case unworthy of prosecution, he would not have sent Herndon to take his place at the retrial. It seems that in the interim, Harris and Logan decided that the prosecution had made the better bargain with the agreement for George's testimony. There would be no such agreement at the retrial. It also seems that Harris decided George would have a better chance without his brother's testimony than with it, so he agreed to consolidate the two cases for trial. Lamborn faced a much more difficult task on the retrial: he had neither George's testimony nor Lincoln's help, and he faced both Harris and Logan on the other side. Herndon's help was not enough to overcome those difficulties. The jury acquitted both men on the retrial.

7.

Various Criminal Cases, 1850–53

WHEN HE RETURNED FROM WASHINGTON IN JULY 1849 AFTER HIS ONE TERM as a congressman, Lincoln began rebuilding his law practice,[1] but it was not until July of the next year that he tried another homicide case: *People v. Davis.*[2] When William D. Davis, a Mexican-American War veteran, got arrested for the murder of a Mr. Louthan, he hired three lawyers to represent him: O. B. Ficklin, A. G. Jones, and A. P. Dunbar. Prosecutor pro tem Thomas A. Marshall represented the people at the preliminary hearing, opposing all three of Davis's lawyers. Justices of the Peace Nathan Austin and William Collins found probable cause to believe that Davis had killed Louthan, but for a lesser charge of manslaughter. Having his charge reduced to manslaughter made Davis automatically eligible for release on bail, and the justices set bail at $1,000. A man who could afford three lawyers could afford to make $1,000 bail, and Davis soon had his freedom.

State's Attorney Alfred Kitchell took a different view of the case than the justices had: he indicted Davis for murder. Davis failed to appear for arraignment, and the court ordered that he be taken into custody. His lawyers got the venue changed from Coles County to Clark County, and when the case went to trial on July 1, 1850, Davis had a fourth lawyer—Abraham Lincoln. The jury found Davis guilty of manslaughter and set his punishment at three years.

After Davis had served two years, a group of Coles County citizens got together and petitioned the governor to pardon Davis on grounds that he had a wife and two small children and that he had "lost one of his hands in the U.S. Army on the Rio Grande in 1846."[3] Lincoln lent his support to the effort by writing a letter to the newly elected governor, Joel A. Matteson:

> Sir: In July 1850, a man by the name of William D. Davis, was tried and convicted of the crime Manslaughter and sentenced to the Penitentiary for the term of three years, by the circuit court of Clark County, whither his case had been taken by a change of venue from Coles county.

Coles County Courthouse, where the prosecution of William D. Davis began but did not conclude. In most of Lincoln's murder cases, the venue was changed to another county. PHOTOGRAPH COURTESY OF THE LIBRARY OF CONGRESS.

> I assisted in his defense, and thought his conviction was right, but that the term fixed was too long under the circumstances. I told him that if he should behave himself well for a considerable portion of the time, I would join in asking a pardon for the remainder. He has a young family, and has lost one of his arms. He has now served about five sixths of his time; and I understand, the Warden, who is now in Springfield, testifies that he has behaved well. Under these circumstances I hope he may be released from further confinement.[4]

This was one of the few times when Lincoln took up his pen to urge a pardon that his plea fell on deaf ears. Davis served out his full term, and it is said that Lincoln never quite forgave Matteson for ignoring his request.[5]

Lincoln tried his next homicide case in November 1852. It involved a great-nephew of the frontiersman Davy Crockett. John Crockett was a feeble-minded twenty-six-year-old who could perform simple menial tasks if someone stood over him. When left to his own devices, he would just lean on his plow and stare off into the distance. Crockett's community believed that he was "not quite an idiot." Young Crockett might not have been capable of performing complex tasks, but he was perfectly capable of taking another human's life. A. D. Thornton served as the lead counsel for the defense, and Lincoln assisted. Thornton was a distinguished, college-educated lawyer who eventually became a judge on the Illinois Supreme Court.[6] The defense was mental incompetence, and the evidence was plentiful.

Despite the excellence of his attorneys and the quality of the evidence of his incompetence, the jury convicted Crockett of manslaughter and set his punishment at two years. The citizens of Moultrie County were so shocked by the verdict that they immediately began a petition drive, collecting hundreds of signatures advocating for the release of young Crockett. Lincoln assisted the drive by writing the wording of one of the petitions, and the wording was copied and used for three more petitions. Thornton sent the petitions to Governor Augustus C. French with a cover letter outlining the evidence of Crockett's feeble-mindedness, and Lincoln endorsed Thornton's letter, saying, "I assisted in the defense of J. A. L. Crockett; and, of course, heard and noted the evidence; and I concur generally with the statement of Mr. Thornton, above. I think him, most clearly, a proper subject of the Executive Clemency."[7] Additionally, seven of the jurors who found Crockett guilty signed the petition for clemency. Even the judge, David Davis, wrote a letter to the governor recommending a pardon, and State's Attorney David Campbell endorsed Davis's letter concurring in the recommendation.[8] Governor French granted the pardon, and Crockett never spent a day in the penitentiary at Alton.

Lincoln was still taking unsecured promissory notes in payment of his legal fees, and he took one from Crockett's father, Elliott. Elliott died without ever paying the note, and Lincoln wound up suing the elder Crockett's estate for his legal fees. Lincoln got a judgment, but he never collected on it.[9]

In September 1852, Lincoln became involved in Tazewell Circuit Court in a protracted lawsuit involving seven cows. Daniel Crabb and Andrew J. Walls obtained a writ of replevin to recover cattle that they claimed had been unlawfully taken from them by Andrew Wallace. The way replevin worked was that the complainant filed paperwork asking for the writ and posted a bond for the return of the property. Upon the posting of the bond, the court would issue a writ of replevin immediately, and the sheriff would go out and confiscate the property. At this point, the ownership of the property was not decided, but the plaintiff could hold the property pending a trial to determine the lawful owner.

It often happened that plaintiffs would obtain a writ of replevin, get their property back, and then dismiss their suit without the court ever adjudicating who the lawful owner of the property was. Usually the defendant was too poor to hire a lawyer, and he would lose his property. Crabb and Walls got their writ of replevin. The sheriff took the cows from Wallace and gave them to Crabb and Walls, and then Crabb and Walls dismissed the suit. In this case, however, Wallace had enough money to hire a lawyer. In fact, he had enough money to hire three lawyers: Abraham Lincoln, Edward Jones, and Alexander H. Saltonstall.

Wallace probably came to have three lawyers in this way: Many lawyers did not travel the circuit. They eked out a living in the town where they lived and usually supplemented their income by pursuing a second occupation. These town-bound lawyers were good enough at drawing up papers, but they lacked the trial skills of the circuit-riding lawyers. When court came into session, and the circuit riders came to town, the town-bound lawyers would associate the more skilled circuit riders to help them try their cases. Lincoln was a popular choice of the town-bound lawyers. Edward Jones was also a lawyer who commanded a great deal of respect. He had not only read law in a law office but also attended the Virginia Law School. In addition to being a highly successful practitioner, he had a military bent, having served with distinction in both the Black Hawk War and the Mexican-American War.[10] Wallace's team of lawyers promptly got the case reinstated and scheduled it for trial in the first term of court the following year.

Lincoln arrived in Tazewell County for the opening of the term of court on May 2, 1853. He spent the first week handling a hodgepodge of civil cases, including *Crabb and Walls v. Wallace*. While Lincoln and his co-counsel spent the week engaged in pretrial maneuvering, State's Attorney David Campbell spent the week presenting cases to the grand jury and prosecuting the true bills they returned. By the end of the week, Campbell had completely finished his docket, but *Crabb and Walls v. Wallace* was not yet ready to be tried. Having no further business to transact, the grand jury was released, and David Campbell left town to go to DeWitt County, the next stop on the Eighth Circuit, to do some advance preparation for the arrival of Judge Davis and the circuit-riding lawyers after the second week of the Tazewell County term had ended.[11]

Over the weekend, a horrific crime occurred. Two surviving news articles give us all the known particulars. The *Illinois State Register* simply said, "Last week at Pekin a man committed a rape upon a little girl, seven years of age,"[12] but the *Peoria Democratic Press* reported:

> It appears that a fellow by the name of Thomas Delany, on Saturday last, committed a horrible outrage upon the person of a little girl, seven

years of age, daughter of a widow lady residing in Wesley. The fact being discovered, the citizens became justly incensed, seized the scoundrel, who denied the charge, took him to the river, tied a rope about his neck, with a large weight to the end of it, and threatened to throw him in the stream, if he did not confess his guilt. This he did upon condition that they would give him a fair trial.[13]

From the pleadings in the court file, we can flesh out some detail: The widow and her seven-year-old daughter, named Jane Ann Rupert, made their home in the small community of Wesley just outside Pekin, the county seat of Tazewell County. The girl's uncle, Paul N. Rupert, lived next door. Not far from the Ruperts resided an Irish immigrant by the name of Thomas Delny, who worked as a miner. Delny drank to excess, which may have played a part in the incident.

It appears that on Saturday, May 7, Paul Rupert discovered evidence that Delny had sexually molested his niece. Rupert then sent for a doctor to examine Jane Ann and went looking for Delny at the head of a mob. They found him, and Rupert accused him of raping Jane Ann. Delny steadfastly denied doing any such thing. The mob grabbed Delny and took him to the river. They tied one end of a rope around his neck and the other end around a heavy weight and made ready to throw him into the river. Delny, pleading with them for his life, offered to confess if they would allow him a fair trial. The mob agreed, and Delny confessed. They turned him over to the sheriff.

The very next day, Sunday, May 8, Justice of the Peace Thomas Pinkham convened a preliminary hearing. A single justice of the peace could conduct preliminary hearings in most matters, but the crimes of rape and murder required two justices. Pinkham recruited a neighboring justice of the peace, James Harriott, and they took testimony on the allegation. Harriott later figured prominently in another of Lincoln's cases, sitting as the judge in *People v. Armstrong*, known as the Almanac Trial.[14] At the end of the preliminary hearing, Pinkham and Harriott found probable cause to believe that Delny had committed the crime and set his bail at $2,000. Since Delny was unable to make bail, he was committed to the common jail to await indictment by a grand jury when the next session of court was convened in November.[15]

Although the duly elected prosecutor, David Campbell, was no longer present in the county, Judge David Davis decided to go ahead and try Delny in the current term of court and get him safely off to prison at Alton. On Monday morning following the preliminary hearing, Judge Davis sent the sheriff out to summon the necessary number of talesmen to make up a special grand jury.

While the sheriff was out summoning jurors, Lincoln was busy trying a case. Luke Crittenden had lost a boat, and M. A. Sweeny had found it. Citing the well-established legal principle of "finders keepers," Sweeny refused to return the boat to Crittenden. Crittenden hired William B. Parker, who associated Lincoln to help him try the case. Sweeny hired Samuel W. Fuller, who associated Edward Jones. Lincoln would thus try *Crittenden v. Sweeny* against Edward Jones, and then turn around and try *Crabb and Walls v. Wallace* with Jones. Fuller, Lincoln's other adversary that day, later joined a law firm in Chicago and served as an ally in the last major case Lincoln tried, the Sand Bar Case.[16]

Lincoln had no sooner gotten a $300 verdict for his client than Judge Davis "ordered, that Abraham Lincoln, Esq., act as Prosecutor for the People during the remainder of this present term."[17] Lincoln took charge of the newly assembled special grand jury and began to present the case of *People v. Delny* to them. Before the day was over, they had returned a two-count indictment charging Delny with rape. Lincoln drafted the indictment, which was a model of brevity, clarity, and careful pleading. The first count alleged that Delny "then and there violently, and against her will, feloniously did ravish and carnally know" Jane Ann Rupert. The second count merely charged that Delny, being over the age of fourteen, "did unlawfully and carnally know" Jane Ann Rupert, "a female child under the age of ten years."[18]

The next day, May 10, Lincoln tried *Crabb and Walls v. Wallace*. The jury returned its verdict finding that the cattle lawfully belonged to Wallace. Lincoln had little time to rest. He called up the case of *People v. Delny*. One point about which the court records leave us wondering is whether Delny had a lawyer. Nothing in the records clearly indicate that he did, but record keeping in the courts of antebellum Illinois left much to be desired. Delny could very well have had a lawyer without anyone making note of it in the court records. There is evidence, however, that Delny stood trial without the benefit of counsel.

The first notation in the court minutes reads, "This day came as well the People by their attorney as the defendant in proper person."[19] The term "in proper person" often, but not always, meant that the defendant was unrepresented. After Lincoln called Delny before the court, Delny was given a copy of the indictment and was offered a list of the witnesses called before the grand jury. It is unclear whether he actually received the list of witnesses. Judge Davis's bench docket states that Delny waived receiving a copy of the witness list,[20] but the court minutes reflect that he received a copy.[21] These documents would have been helpful if Delny could read, but we do not know whether he was literate. The judge then asked Delny how he pleaded, and Delny entered a plea of not guilty and "put himself upon the country."

Now, if Delny were represented by an attorney, the next thing that should have happened was a motion for change of venue. Having narrowly escaped a lynch mob, Delny certainly had reason to "fear that he would not get a fair trial in Tazewell County on account that the minds of the inhabitants were prejudiced against him." The court then proceeded to jury selection, but Delny had witnesses he needed to subpoena. He gave the names of his witnesses to the clerk, and a subpoena was duly issued for Constant Filbert, Dutch Billy the Cooper, Simmonds, Henry Bloom, Jn. McCook, and M. Hayl. It was an *instanter* subpoena, which meant that the people receiving the subpoena were supposed to drop everything they were doing and immediately go to the courthouse. This was important, because the day was far gone, the trial was in progress, and it could be over before the witnesses got to the courthouse. Apparently none of Delny's witnesses testified on his behalf. There is no evidence that the subpoena was ever served. An examination of the subpoena reveals that a deputy sheriff had gotten it and checked off the names of the persons to be served, but there is no return of service endorsed on the back of the subpoena.[22] A deputy sheriff would hardly neglect to endorse a return of service on a subpoena. The return of service was his evidence that he was entitled to a fee for having served the subpoena. All the prosecution witnesses, however, were present and accounted for. Their subpoena had been issued the day before, and they had all been duly served. The deputy's return of service states that he was entitled to $2.60 as payment for serving that subpoena.[23]

The absence of Delny's witnesses and the absence of any evidence of a complaint about his missing witnesses are strong indicators that Delny stood trial without benefit of counsel. Any competent defense attorney would have complained loudly about going to trial on such short notice without being able to procure the attendance of the defense witnesses. Trials against unrepresented defendants usually take one of two courses: either the defendant simply sits at the counsel table looking lost and helpless, and if he mounts any defense at all, it is ineffective, or the defendant acts out inappropriately, repeatedly violating the rules of procedure, obstructing the orderly trial process, and alienating the jury.[24] A defendant who takes either of these courses does not improve his chances of gaining an acquittal. Delny most likely adopted the first course of action.

The jury convicted Delny and set his penalty at eighteen years in prison. Judge Davis sentenced him to eighteen years at hard labor with one year in solitary confinement. Lincoln received $5 for his services as prosecutor pro tem. Judge Davis's docket entries sum up the trial succinctly: "A special Grand Jury summoned, Monday 2nd week and bill found. List of jurors and witnesses waived. Copy of Indictment furnished. Arraigned. Plead Not Guilty. Jury Sworn. Verdict guilty—confinement penitentiary 18 years. Arraigned for sentence. Judgmt of Court—To be confined in Penitentiary for 18 years—one year in solitary confinement—residue at hard labor. Sheriff to have 15 days to convey him to Alton."[25]

The prosecution of Thomas Delny was neither Lincoln's finest hour as a trial lawyer nor Davis's finest hour as a judge, but given Delny's near lynching, they seem to have found themselves in an awkward position and took what they considered the least undesirable path. But Thomas Delny got railroaded. There was nothing fair about his trial. He was facing a possible sentence of life in prison; he deserved to have a lawyer, and it would have cost nothing to supply him with one. As a price for the privilege of admission to the bar, lawyers were expected to take indigent appointments without compensation.[26] Delny should have been given a change of venue. He should have been given an opportunity to procure the attendance of his witnesses. Even if he was guilty, this does not change the fact that his trial was grossly unfair because of the denial of these three things. In American jurisprudence, it is not sufficient that the guilty be convicted. The guilty must be properly convicted. If the proper safeguards are not afforded to the guilty, what is to prevent them from being denied to the innocent?

Although the trial of Thomas Delny was grossly unfair, it seems to have been the least undesirable alternative open to Judge Davis. A little less than ten years before Delny's trial, in Carthage, Illinois, an enraged mob stormed the jail and killed Joseph and Hyrum Smith. The Smiths' jailers were not willing to risk their lives or to take the lives of fellow citizens to save the Smiths. Delny's jailer was in a similar situation. The mob had already come within a hairbreadth of killing Delny; anything less than rapid retribution was likely to culminate in a lynching. Davis must have analyzed the situation like this: If they waited until the next term of court, the mob would tire of waiting for justice, storm the jail, and lynch Delny. Moving Delny to another county to await trial would simply result in the sheriff being waylaid as he transported the prisoner, and the prisoner being lynched. Delny had to be tried immediately. But if a lawyer were appointed for Delny, he might move for a change of venue, the trial would be delayed, and the mob would either storm the jail and lynch Delny or waylay the sheriff as he transported Delny to the new county. Therefore, Delny could not have a lawyer. Ironically, if Davis had either waited until the next term to try Delny or appointed a lawyer, he could say he had done the "right" thing even though Delny was dead. And whom did Davis trust to handle the prosecution of this most delicate case? Abraham Lincoln.

Delny could look forward to spending the next eighteen years of his life at the penitentiary in Alton, Illinois. It did not promise to be a pleasant eighteen years. Prison reform was decades in the future, and living conditions in the prison were squalid at best. The term "hard labor" was not just a euphemism. The convicts worked, and they worked hard, but Delny had a bit of good luck with the form of hard labor to which he was assigned. Many convicts were leased out to private industry to work as quasi-slave labor, and Sebastian Wise rented Delny to work in his flour mill, adjacent to the prison. Wise found Delny to be a good worker. Delny worked in the flour mill for almost six years, until something happened that ultimately led to his early release from prison. The people of Alton did not like having a prison in their community. They felt that it depressed property values and that convict labor robbed them of job opportunities. In 1859, after much lobbying by the citizens of Alton, the state decided to move the prison to Joliet,[27] and Sebastian Wise confronted the prospect of losing a good worker.

Wise was determined to keep Delny as a worker, and he was a man of action. At his earliest opportunity, he approached his old friend Governor William H. Bissell. Could Bissell do him a huge favor and pardon Thomas Delny? Such an excellent worker as Delny certainly deserved leniency. Bissell did not completely brush Wise off, but he did not unequivocally promise to pardon the man. On February 11, 1859, Wise wrote and reminded Bissell that he wanted Delny pardoned.[28]

It seems that if a convict did not have a large number of friends to petition for his release, he could do just as well by getting rented to a politically powerful businessman and impressing the businessman with his work ethic. Bissell granted the pardon. At the end of the May 1853 term of Tazewell Circuit Court, however, Delny's pardon was far in the future, and Lincoln had little time to contemplate the finer points of whether justice had been done in the case. He had another murder case to try at his next stop on the circuit.

8.

PEOPLE versus MOSES LOE, May 19, 1853

ON MONDAY MORNING, AUGUST 30, 1852, JAMES GRAY HAD BUSINESS IN Springfield. A new term of court was beginning, and the town would be crowded with itinerant lawyers and would-be litigants, all trying to have their suits heard before the Honorable David Davis, circuit judge. Gray intended to be one of those litigants, but he anticipated that he might run into some trouble on the way. He asked his friend Benjamin Morris to ride with him, and Morris agreed. They saddled their horses and began to make their way along the ill-maintained road to the city. When they got to the Nippers residence in the Lick Creek area, they found the trouble that Gray had feared.[1]

Moses Loe lounged under a tree on the side of the road, whittling with a bowie knife, a poor tool for whittling but an excellent weapon for killing. Loe had been there since sunrise, when Williamson Nippers and his sister Jane got up, Williamson to feed the livestock, Jane to cook breakfast. Ira Parker saw him there later that morning, just leaning against that tree, scraping the end of a stick with his bowie knife.

Gray spoke to Jane as he and Morris rode past. The two rode on toward Springfield, and as they approached Loe, Gray asked him if he had eaten

Bowie knife resembling the one likely used by Moses Loe. FROM SCHAUBS, "MOUN-TAIN MEN AND LIFE IN THE ROCKY MOUNTAIN WEST."

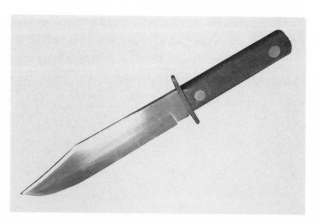

breakfast. Loe said something that Morris could not quite understand. The only word he clearly heard was "threatening." Then Gray noticed something about the way Loe was holding the knife and told him to put it down. Loe refused, saying, "You accused me of fighting boys less than me. Now you can fight a boy less than you."

In reply, Gray spurred his horse and cantered back up the road away from Loe. Loe ran after him, picking up a stout stick, then slowed to a walk but continued toward Gray. Gray dismounted and also picked up a stick. As Morris watched, the two men engaged and Gray fell to the ground. Loe stabbed at Gray's neck and then stomped the prostrate man. Gray called for help, and Morris dismounted. As Morris ran toward the two men, he saw Gray regain his feet, blood streaming from his mouth.

It was shortly after breakfast when Williamson Nippers noticed Gray and Morris riding down the lane toward Loe, but he thought nothing of it at the time. When the yelling started, both he and Jane went to the front door. They saw the three men in a sort of confrontation. Jane called Williamson back when he charged out of his house to see what was going on, but he continued down the road toward the confrontation. As Williamson ran toward them, Gray turned his horse and fled back down the road toward the Nippers home, with Loe on foot in hot pursuit. Gray got some eighty yards past the Nippers home when Williamson saw him dismount and pick up a club. Gray's attempts at self-defense proved ineffective.

After the fight, Loe left the scene and the Nippers siblings did what they could to assist Gray, who was bleeding from neck and mouth. Morris rode for a doctor, but the doctor could do little. While they tried to save Gray, the constable searched for Loe. He could not find Loe until the next day, but as soon as he found the man, he took him to jail. At the jail, Edward D. Meacham questioned Loe.

"Moses, I'm sorry about what happened," he began.

"I'm sorry, too," replied Loe.

"Did you give him a mortal wound?" asked Meacham.

"I suppose I did," he replied.

"Do you have the knife?"

"Yes."

"Give it to me, please." Loe handed the knife over to Meacham. "Moses, can you tell me how you did it?"

"I hit him with the club first and knocked him down. Then I stuck him with the knife. I held it like this," he said, indicating his grip and demonstrating his stabbing motion. Loe left out the detail that he had then stomped his victim.[2]

The day after Loe's arrest, the *Illinois State Journal* ran a brief article on the case.[3] In a separate article, the *Journal* reported that court was in session, and the grand jury was expected to immediately take up the case.[4] On the same day that the *Journal* ran its articles on the killing, State's Attorney David Campbell had the grand jury indict Loe for murder. The indictment charged that

> Moses Loe in and upon one James Gray in the peace of the people then and there being unlawfully feloniously willfully and of his malice aforethought did make an assault and that the said Moses Loe with a certain knife of the value of six cents which he the said Moses Loe in his left right hand then and there had and held the said James Gray in and upon the right side of the neck of him the said James Gray then and there unlawfully feloniously willfully and of his malice aforethought did strike and thrust giving to the said James Gray then and there with the knife aforesaid in and upon the said right side of the neck of him the said James Gray one mortal wound of the breadth of one inch and of the depth of one inch of which said mortal wound the said James Gray from the said thirtieth day of August in the year aforesaid until the thirty first day of same month of August in the year aforesaid at the county and state aforesaid did languish and languishing did live on which said thirty first day of August in the year aforesaid and before the finding of the indictment the said James Gray in the County and State aforesaid of the said mortal wound died, and so the Grand Jurors aforesaid upon their oaths aforesaid do say that the said Moses Loe the said James Gray in manner and form aforesaid feloniously willfully unlawfully and of his malice aforethought did kill and murder Contrary to the form of the Statute in such cases made and provided and against the peace and dignity of the said people of the State of Illinois.[5]

By the standards of the times, Campbell's indictment was a model of clarity and conciseness. Things were moving swiftly, and it looked as though Loe might receive as speedy a trial as Thomas Delny had. Any hope for a speedy resolution of the case vanished, however, when Abraham Lincoln took up the defense and moved for a change of venue. The affidavit for change of venue, written in Lincoln's own hand, read as follows:

> Moses Loe, the defendant to a certain indictment for murder pending in the circuit court of the county aforesaid, being first duly sworn states on oath that he fears he will not receive a fair and impartial trial on

said indictment in the circuit court of the county aforesaid, where the trial is pending, on account that the minds of the inhabitants of said county wherein said trial is pending are prejudiced against him, he therefore prays the court to award him a change of venue to the next nearest county where the cause aforesaid does not exist.[6]

Loe signed the affidavit with an *X*, swore to it, and the motion was granted. The wording of the motion for change of venue is awfully brief and alleges no facts supporting the defendant's fear that he would not get a fair trial. When a litigant filed a motion seeking specific relief, he was expected to give a concise statement of why he was entitled to the relief beyond the mere fact that he wanted it. As many motions as Lincoln filed for changes of venue, and as many times as his motions were granted, it seems that in antebellum Illinois all a litigant had to do was to file an affidavit saying he was afraid he could not get a fair trial and ask for a change of venue. The motion would almost automatically be granted. This may have been because everyone knew everyone else in the sparsely populated counties of the time, and it was very difficult to get good juries out of such small pools of potential jurors. Whatever the reason, Lincoln seems to have had a knack for getting the venues changed in his murder cases.

This delay of the trial could simply prove to be a minor bump in the road. They could move the trial to DeWitt County, next in the circuit rotation, and continue the march toward a speedy resolution of the issue. The indictment was filed in Sangamon County Circuit Court on September 1, Lincoln got the venue changed on September 4, and the paperwork was filed in the new county on September 22,[7] a delay of merely three weeks. On October 9, however, Lincoln advanced another reason to delay the trial:

I, Moses Loe, the defendant to a certain indictment, for the supposed murder of one James Gray pending in the circuit court of the county aforesaid by change of venue from the county of Sangamon, being first duly sworn states on oath that he cannot safely go to trial at the present term of this court because of the absence of Thomas Blankenship and Elizabeth Grass, who, he is advised and believes, are material witnesses for him on such trial that affiant expects it will be proved by the prosecution that he, affiant, on the morning of the killing of said Gray, came to and remained alone upon the grounds where the killing afterwards occurred, a considerable length of time before the arrival of said Gray, and he expects, in explanation of that part of his conduct, to prove by said Blankenship that said Gray told said Blankenship on the evening before the killing that he, Gray, had an appointment with this affiant to meet and fight with each other at the time and place where and when the killing afterwards occurred. Affiant states that there was in fact such appointment made the day before the killing by said Gray and affiant, but that no other person was present at the making of it; that having been in close confinement ever since the killing, he has had no opportunity of finding out persons to whom said Gray may have spoken of said appointment; that he has learned that he, said Gray, had so spoken to said Blankenship, but did not so learn until it was too late to procure his attendance at the present term of the court, that affiant expects there will be some other evidence tending to prove the fact of such appointment, but none of so satisfactory a character as that of said Blankenship; that said Blankenship resides in Sangamon county and affiant expects to procure his attendance at the next term of the court—Affiant further states that since his arrival here on the sixth inst he learned, for the first time, that one Mary Grass, whose name is not endorsed on the indictment, is to be used as a witness against him; and that it is expected she will testify that several weeks previous to the killing, and about the time affiant bought the knife with which said Gray was wounded on the day of the killing, she heard this affiant say he intended to kill said Gray with said knife—Affiant expects and believes said Mary Grass can not and will not testify that he, affiant, ever spoke in her presence of said knife more than one time; and that affiant expects to prove by said Elizabeth Grass that she was present with said Mary, when affiant once spoke of said knife, and that she understood and remembers what he then said, and that he did not speak of or allude to said Gray that what affiant [illegible] say on that occasion was that if one Thompson Lacy should assail him, affiant, as he had believed, he had threatened to do, he, affiant would defend himself with that knife—that said Elizabeth Grass resides in Morgan county, and affiant believes he can procure her attendance at the next term. & that this application is not made for delay, but that justice may be done—.[8]

Notice that in the affidavit for change of venue, Lincoln has Loe say, "I'm afraid I won't get a fair trial because the people are prejudiced against me," but not why he thinks the people are prejudiced against him. In the motion for continuance, he has Loe say, "I want a continuance because I can't get Thomas Blankenship and Elizabeth Grass served with subpoenas to have them testify on my behalf," but he goes on to say what they are going to testify to and why that testimony is important. Apparently judges were much stingier in granting motions for continuance than they were in granting motions for change of venue.

As to his need for the testimony of Elizabeth Grass, he clearly stated grounds for a continuance. The prosecution intended to call Mary Grass, who would testify that shortly after Loe bought the bowie knife, he told her he was going to use it to kill Gray. This is clear evidence of premeditation and malice aforethought. If Elizabeth Grass could impeach that evidence, it would be crucial to the defense. Lincoln included in the affidavit the facts to which he expected Elizabeth Grass to testify: she had been present at the conversation between Mary Grass and Moses Loe, and Moses said he intended to use the knife on Thompson Lacy, not James Gray. The only way that David Campbell could defeat the motion for continuance on these grounds would be to stipulate that he would not use Mary Grass as a witness. If Mary did not testify, then there would not be any need for Elizabeth to testify. Campbell was not willing to do this, so the case was continued.

The second ground Lincoln mentioned in the motion was problematic. Thomas Blankenship stood ready to testify that the day before the killing, Gray told him that he had an appointment to fight Moses Loe at Lick Creek near the Nippers house. This is hearsay, and at the time of Loe's case, there was no exception to the hearsay rule that would allow it into evidence. Current Illinois law would allow such a statement, but that law is over one hundred years too late to have helped Loe. Under current Illinois law, a homicide victim's statement of intent is admissible to establish his intent to do something and that he acted in conformity with that stated intent.[9] In the 1850s, however, Illinois recognized no such exception. Lincoln's law library contained a copy of Greenleaf's *Treatise on Evidence*, but Greenleaf's chapter on hearsay recognized no exception that would allow this statement by Gray into evidence.[10] It was no matter at this point, however. Elizabeth Grass's absence was sufficient grounds to continue the case.

When the case eventually did come on for trial in May of the next year, David Campbell had a problem: Mary Grass was not there. Deputy Sheriff Charles Small had duly served her with a subpoena, but she was nowhere to be found.[11] Campbell had two alternatives, neither of which was palatable: he could ask for a continuance to try to procure her attendance in six months, or he could go to trial without her. Waiting six months was not a happy solution because, from a prosecution viewpoint, cases are not like wine—they do not get better with age. The nonattendance of Mary Grass was a function of the aging process of the case. She had been available six months before, when the case was continued, but she got lost in the delay. What other evidence might be lost with another six-month delay? The other alternative was to go to trial without her, but he would have a much weaker case if he did. Mary's testimony was his best evidence that Loe had premeditated the murder.

Campbell settled on a half measure. He would put the case off as long as he could during the current term of court, hoping that Mary could be located and brought into court before time ran out. She had not been found by the end of the day on May 16. May 17 ended with no sign of Mary. Finally, on May 18, Campbell made his decision—he would go to trial without her. He made a reasonable decision. Although it would have been nice to have such direct proof of premeditation, he really did not need any proof of premeditation at all to get a murder conviction. Under then-existing Illinois law, murder was "the unlawful killing of a human being, in the peace of the people, with malice aforethought, either express or implied."[12] Express malice existed when the defendant had a "deliberate intention unlawfully to take away the life of a fellow creature which [was] manifested by external circumstances, capable of proof."[13] In other words, malice was express when the murder was premeditated. Implied malice existed "when no considerable provocation appear[ed], or when all the circumstances of the killing, show[ed] an abandoned and malignant heart."[14] Campbell had very good evidence of malice aforethought even without Mary's testimony, and the conventional wisdom predicted an easy murder conviction.

The trial commenced on May 19, 1853, and David Campbell called Benjamin Morris as his first witness. An artifact survives from the trial of Moses Loe that we do not have for the vast majority of Lincoln's cases—the notes of the witnesses' testimony taken in Lincoln's own hand. On December 5 and 6, 1894, the Lincoln Memorial Collection of Chicago was liquidated at auction in Philadelphia, and these notes on the trial of Loe were auctioned off along with a number of books from Lincoln's law library. Lincoln's notes sold for $55.[15]

Morris testified to the facts set forth above, and when Campbell turned Morris over to Lincoln for cross-examination, it looked very bad indeed for Loe. Lincoln did, however, weaken Morris's testimony by bringing out these additional facts: Gray told Morris that Loe wanted to meet him at Lick Creek to fight. Gray asked Morris to come with him in case Loe was at Lick Creek. Loe made no move to go toward Gray until after Gray took off on his horse, and then Loe followed him.

Edward D. Meacham testified next, and in addition to giving the details of Loe's statement, he testified to his examination of the knife. There was only a small amount of blood on the tip of the knife, giving Meacham hope that the wound was not fatal. Unfortunately, the carotid artery lies very close to the surface of the throat, and it takes no great depth of penetration to sever it.

It also developed in the testimony of Jane Nippers that as Gray sat on his horse confronting Loe under the tree, Gray laughed at Loe, and that Gray continued to laugh as he rode away from Loe. Jane did not know anything about the actual fight because she went back inside her house when Gray got off his horse.

When Campbell rested, Lincoln called Thomas Blankenship and asked him what Gray had said about Loe. Either Campbell did not object or Lincoln made an argument that persuaded the judge to allow this despite its lack of support from legal authority. Blankenship testified that on the Sunday before the killing, Gray had asked him, "Do you want to see some fun?" Blankenship asked what he meant, and Gray replied, "Moses Loe and I are going to fight at the mouth of the lane in Lick Creek tomorrow morning." Blankenship was the most important defense witness called. He testified to substantive facts that mitigated the killing.

The two remaining witnesses called by Lincoln were more in the nature of smoke and mirrors. James Carter testified that Loe lived about three-quarters of a mile away from the scene of the crime—a fact that gave Loe an innocent reason for being in the vicinity. It also tended to show that Loe chose a place near home to attack Gray. Apparently he did not want to get tired from too long a walk. Dr. Goodbread testified that he thought the blood from Gray's mouth did not come from the cut in his throat. So Gray was bleeding from the mouth from being hit in the head with a club by Loe rather than from being stabbed in the neck with a knife. This is hardly exculpatory evidence.

The jury had these facts to sort through: On the one hand, Loe had armed himself with a huge knife to meet Gray. Loe chased Gray when Gray cantered away on his horse. Loe picked up a club, knocked Gray down with the club, and while Gray lay on the ground, stabbed Gray in the throat. Then Loe stomped the dying man. This certainly looks like malice aforethought. But on the other hand, Gray had an appointment with Loe to fight, and he kept it. Gray laughed at Loe. He thought it was funny that Loe, on foot, was trying to catch him on his horse. Gray did not have to stop or pick up the stick. He ignored several opportunities to avoid getting himself killed. The stab wound to Gray's throat was only an inch deep; it just happened to be in an unfortunate spot. These facts did not make Loe legally innocent, but they certainly could be argued in mitigation to reduce the crime to manslaughter, which was a killing in the heat of passion upon provocation.[16] Lincoln was probably aiming for a manslaughter conviction, and the jury did not disappoint him in that regard. He had cause to be disappointed by the sentence they recommended, however. Their verdict read, "We the Jury find the Prisoner Moses Loe guilty of Manslaughter in the highest degree and therefore affix the penalty accordingly which is Eight years confinement in the Penitentiary of Illinois."[17]

In other words, they came very close to finding Loe guilty of murder, and because of that, they voted to impose the heaviest sentence allowed by law. In those days, the jury was not given a preprinted form to sign, but wrote out the verdict in longhand on a scrap of paper. A verdict was normally signed by the foreman, but Loe's verdict bore the signatures of all twelve of the jurors. The judge sentenced Loe to eight years at hard labor in the state penitentiary at Alton, with three months to be served in solitary confinement.[18]

As can be seen from the way this case played out, a criminal prosecution is not a zero-sum game with clear winners and clear losers. In many cases, the prosecution would count a manslaughter conviction a win, but in the Loe case, the evidence of malice was so strong that Campbell most certainly felt that he had lost. Lincoln, on the other hand, had won a Pyrrhic victory at best. He had kept his client's neck out of the hangman's noose, but Loe had received the maximum sentence allowable by law.

Strangely enough, while Lincoln was defending Loe against David Campbell's charge of murder, he was simultaneously defending Campbell against a charge of dereliction of duty. Abraham Smith, a justice of the peace in Vermilion County, believed that Campbell was too lax in his prosecution of illegal liquor sales. Smith began publicly berating Campbell, saying he had refused to present liquor sale cases to the grand jury, had appeared drunk for grand jury proceedings, and sometimes had even been too drunk to come to grand jury proceedings. Smith said that he had offered to draw up indictments for Campbell to present to the grand jury, and that Campbell had replied, "If you draw them up, you might as well prosecute them." Campbell reached his limit with such accusations and hired Lincoln and Ward Hill Lamon to file a slander suit against Smith, asking for damages in the amount of $2,000. The case commenced in May 1852 and was tried on June 1, 1853, just under two weeks after the Loe trial. Lincoln wrote the jury instructions, and the jury returned a verdict awarding Campbell $450 and requiring Smith to pay the costs of prosecution.[19]

In August 1857, after Loe had served more than half of his sentence, seven of the jurors in the case signed a petition to have Loe pardoned. Lincoln endorsed the petition in the following language:

I defended Moses Loe in the case mentioned, and, with the exception of the assistance of a younger man at the trial, who volunteered merely to try his hand, the whole defence rested on me. I know Loe to have been a very young man at the time of the offence, and that more than half his time, (originally eight years) has elapsed since his conviction. As to his previous character, or his conduct in the State prison I know nothing; but willing to trust the numerous and very respectable gentlemen who speak to these points, I cheerfully join the request that he be pardoned for the remainder of his term.[20]

The petition contained some seventy additional signatures, and Governor Bissell granted the pardon.[21] As shall be seen in chapter 10, Lincoln had an active postconviction practice in petitioning for pardons for convicted criminals.

9.

PEOPLE versus DAVID LONGNECKER, June 3, 1856

JACOB PIATT AND W. D. KERR OWNED A DRY GOODS STORE IN MONTICELLO, the seat of Piatt County. Apparently they kept late hours, because at 9 P.M. on April 19, 1854, they had several potential customers, G. W. Reid, Josiah Reed, and J. A. Hill, all in various locations about the store. Another man, a ne'er-do-well by the name of Jacob Ater, had been sitting in the store for about half an hour when David Longnecker came in. Longnecker was a local lawyer who was not considered one of the leading attorneys in Illinois. When he came in, he found Piatt behind the counter examining some oilcloth tablecloths.

"Major Longnecker, what do you think these table cloths would be worth?" Piatt asked. Longnecker examined the tablecloths.

"I'd say about $1.50," he replied. Longnecker then turned to leave the store.

At this point, Ater interjected himself into the discussion of the value of the tablecloths: "That's a damned lie." Longnecker stopped, turned around, and walked back into the store.

"You're a damned loafer. You do nothing but lay round town and drink whisky." Apparently Longnecker wanted to redirect the conversation from the worth of the tablecloths to the worth of Jacob Ater.

"You are a damned liar," Ater retorted, seeming more than willing to trade insults with Longnecker.

"Pay me what you owe me is all I ask of you," said Longnecker, again changing the subject.

"I owe you nothing," replied Ater.

"You're a damned liar. I have a judgment against you for $40," Longnecker countered.

"If you have," Ater said, "you got it by fraud."

"You are a damned dirty dog," Longnecker said.

Ater stood up, stepped back a step or two, and raised his chair off the floor. "Don't call me a damned dirty dog."

Longnecker replied, "You damned dirty dog; don't strike me with that chair." At this time, the action became confused. G. W. Reid saw Ater raise the chair as if to strike Longnecker. He then saw Longnecker hit Ater in the chest and say, "Don't raise a chair to me you damned dirty dog." J. A. Hill saw Ater strike at Longnecker with the chair. Jacob Piatt maintained that he was looking in the other direction and saw nothing. Josiah Reed, who happened to be coming out of the back storeroom when the fight broke out, saw Ater draw back the chair as if to strike; heard Longnecker say, "Don't you strike me with a chair you damn dog you"; and saw Longnecker lunge at Ater. Reed saw no weapon in Longnecker's hand. W. D. Kerr, who had been in the storeroom with Reed, came out in time to see Longnecker lunge at Ater, but he did not see Ater do anything toward Longnecker.[1]

As Longnecker left the store, Ater turned to Kerr and said, "He stuck me. Go get Dr. Ward." The men could see blood streaming from Ater's neck. They got him into a chair and tried to comfort him as Kerr went for the doctor. Dr. Ward arrived almost immediately, examined Ater, and gave his prognosis: "He's going to die." They got Ater off the chair and laid him on the floor. Within seven minutes of the stabbing, Ater had died.

The story actually began two years earlier, on May 15, 1852, when James H. Hollingsworth went to Ater's home to ask Deborah Ater to come and help take care of his sick wife. Deborah agreed, but Jacob Ater did not. He was going out of town and wanted her to accompany him. Deborah departed with Hollingsworth for his home, but Jacob came after them and overtook them. Ater angrily insisted that Deborah leave town with him. When they got to Hollingsworth's home, Ater went into the home with them and continued to insist that Deborah leave with him. Hollingsworth asked Ater to leave his house, telling Ater that his wife was sick and he did not want any disturbance. Deborah firmly refused to go anywhere with Ater, and he knocked her down with his fist. He then began kicking her, swearing that he would kill her. Hollingsworth intervened, the two men struggled, and Ater got the better of Hollingsworth.

The two men separated and went into the street. A neighbor named Mrs. Johnson saw the fracas and called to Deborah to come to her house for her safety. Deborah retreated to Mrs. Johnson's home, but Hollingsworth came to her and asked her to come to his home and stay with his wife, assuring her that she would be protected at his home. She agreed, and the two started back for Hollingsworth's home.

As they went back to the home, they encountered Ater, who had collected a number of cronies to act as backup. Ater said to his cronies, "There comes the damned son-of-a-bitch and I will kill him." He threw a quart bottle at Hollingsworth, narrowly missing the man's head, and then attacked with his fists. Before Ater could reach his intended victim, Hollingsworth pulled a pistol, pointed it at him, cocked the hammer back, and pulled the trigger. The percussion cap was a dud, and the gun did not fire. Neither Ater nor his cronies remained in the vicinity to find out if Hollingsworth had a spare cap.[2]

Deborah Ater swore out an affidavit against Jacob Ater,[3] and Ater was duly charged with assault and battery. Ater went to David Longnecker, who drafted a complaint affidavit against Hollingsworth for Ater to put his mark on.[4] Hollingsworth was arrested for assault with intent to commit murder. He hired Abraham Lincoln, and one of Lincoln's first acts was to move for a change of venue.[5]

David Campbell actually indicted Hollingsworth for assault to murder. Interestingly, Deborah Ater's name was endorsed on the back of the indictment as a witness testifying before the grand jury, but it was struck through.[6] What this probably means is that Campbell prepared the indictment in advance, expecting Deborah Ater to appear and testify. She did not. With only the testimony of Jacob Ater and a few of his cronies, Campbell got a distorted picture of what had actually happened. It is probable that Deborah's case against Ater never materialized. Her absence from the Hollingsworth grand jury was most likely prompted by threats from Ater.[7] If Ater's threats could prevent her from testifying at Hollingsworth's grand jury, they could prevent her from testifying against him.

Hollingsworth could not testify in his own behalf, and if the only available witnesses were Ater and Ater's cronies, Campbell could convict Hollingsworth. Lincoln needed the testimony of Deborah Ater if he were going to save Hollingsworth from prison, but he was unlikely to get her into court to testify. Lincoln broke the horns of his dilemma by taking the deposition of Deborah Ater.[8] He confronted a few problems with using her deposition, though. Illinois law at the time allowed depositions only in civil cases,[9] and advance notice of the taking of the deposition had to be given to the other side.[10] Under the law, Lincoln would never be able to read the deposition into evidence. Lincoln most likely was thinking, "Campbell is a fair man. If he understands this woman is too terrified to testify, he'll do the fair thing and let me read her deposition into evidence." If that is what Lincoln was thinking, he was in for a surprise. Campbell did not let Lincoln read the deposition into evidence—he dropped the charges. Campbell understood the true role of a prosecutor—to seek justice, not to get convictions.

Longnecker represented Ater on at least one other charge, for disorderly conduct, which resulted in a fine.[11] By the time Ater had run up $40 worth of attorney's fees, Longnecker washed his hands of defending the man and sued him. The judgment he got against Ater was not worth the paper it was written on. The two men became enemies, and their feud ended on April 19, 1854, at Piatt and Kerr's dry goods store.

The dry goods store became even more crowded after Longnecker left. Justice of the Peace Thomas C. Stewart, acting as coroner, arrived at the store and assessed the situation. He instructed the constable to bring twelve talesmen to the store to act as a coroner's jury. When the twelve men had been assembled and sworn, Stewart began taking the testimony of the witnesses to the fight. The coroner's jury found probable cause to believe that Ater "came to his death by a wound inflicted by David Longnecker (supposed to be by a knife) on the 19th day of April 1854 in the house occupied by Messrs. Piatt & Kerr as a store in Monticello Piatt County and State of Illinois."[12] The next morning, Abraham Rizer swore out a complaint against Longnecker for unlawful homicide, and Stewart issued a warrant.[13] The warrant did not specifically state whether it was for murder or manslaughter, which by default meant that the initial charge against Longnecker was the lesser charge of manslaughter. That same day, Sheriff Sam Morain arrested Longnecker, who posted $1,000 bond.

On May 16, State's Attorney Elam Rust indicted Longnecker for murder. Longnecker was rearrested and arraigned, and he entered a plea of not guilty. By consent of the parties, the judge continued the case and released Longnecker on $2,000 bail. At this arraignment, Joel Seth Post, a lawyer from neighboring Macon County, represented Longnecker. On that day, Lincoln was in Clinton defending the Illinois Central Railroad in seven lawsuits.[14]

When court next met in October, Lincoln was again elsewhere. He had returned to politics, galvanized by Stephen A. Douglas's Kansas-Nebraska Act, which had the effect of repealing the Missouri Compromise of 1850, the act prohibiting slavery in U.S. territories north of latitude thirty-six degrees and thirty minutes. In a sort of warm-up for their more famous debates in 1858, Lincoln and Douglas were barnstorming Illinois and debating the Kansas-Nebraska Act. On October 16, 1854, the two were in Peoria, where each of them spoke for three hours.[15] The next day, when Longnecker appeared in court, they were in Lacon, Illinois, to engage in another debate. The debate fell through when Douglas announced he was too hoarse to speak and Lincoln refused to take advantage of "Judge Douglas's indisposition."[16]

Just as Lincoln was not willing to give a speech in Lacon, Longnecker was still not willing to go to trial in Monticello. He filed an affidavit for continuance, alleging that he required the testimony of Joseph Read, Dan McMillan, and Thomas C. Stewart, who were not available for trial. As he was required to do in order to prove his grounds for a continuance, Longnecker outlined what he expected to prove by the three men:

> The affiant expects to prove by said Read that at the time the pretended homicide was committed by affiant on the body of Jacob Ater the said Ater had a deadly weapon drawn to strike down or commit a great bodily harm on the affiant and that the affiant only acted in self-defense in the [encounter] that resulted in the death of the said Ater.
>
> Affiant expects to prove by said McMillan that on the nite of the pretended homicide the affiant and the said McMillan spent the time together for several hours up to within a few moments of the said [encounter] and that affiant conduct was of a peaceable character and that the said Ater was not allude[d] to in any way.
>
> The affiant expects to prove by the said Stuart [*sic*] that the said Ater was a desperate character and had feelings of hatred & malignancy against the affiant and a few days before the said [encounter] the said Ater told the said Stuart that he would take the life of affiant and that the said Stuart warned the affiant that the said Ater would take affiant's life and that the said communication was made to affiant a few days previous to the [encounter].[17]

The judge granted the continuance. A few days later, Longnecker moved for and got a change of venue. The judge moved the case to Mason County, where Longnecker's case was called up for trial on May 28. He again got a continuance.[18]

Longnecker was having difficulty getting his witnesses to come to court. One had moved out of state, and it would be impossible to compel him to return and testify. This witness was Thomas C. Stewart, the justice of the peace who had found probable cause to believe Longnecker guilty of manslaughter. Post got Elam Rust to agree to taking the witness's deposition, and on August 18, Longnecker sent written interrogatories to Stewart. On August 31, Stewart appeared before an officer authorized to take oaths and gave written answers to the written interrogatories. The most pertinent questions and answers were these:

> [Q] 9: Did you at any time before the death of the said Jacob Ater have any conversation with him respecting the said David Longnecker[?]

[A]:   I had.

[Q] 10: Did you at any time hear the said Ater make any threat against
         the life or body of the said David Longnecker[?] If yes state fully
         and particularly when it was & how long before his death and
         what he said[.]

[A]:   I heard him make threats against the life & body of David Long-
         necker. I cannot state the time positively, but it was a short time
         before Ater's death. He (Ater) said that he would take satisfac-
         tion out of him (Longnecker) and that he would cut or kick his
         damned old guts out.

[Q] 11: Did you ever communicate to the said David Longnecker what
         you heard the said Ater say about him in his lifetime[?]

[A]:   I did.

[Q] 12: Did you ever hear the said Ater say that he intended to take the
         life of the said David Longnecker[?]

[A]:   I did not. I never heard him make any threats only the one above
         stated.

[Q] 13: When you communicated the threat to the said David Long-
         necker which had been made by the said Ater if any what was
         the reply if any[?]

[A]:   He replied but I do not recollect what the reply was.[19]

On October 30, 1855, David Longnecker stood trial for murder in Macon
County. Elam Rust prosecuted, and Joel Seth Post and Richard J. Oglesby
defended. Lincoln was handling a mortgage foreclosure in Vermilion County
that day.[20] Longnecker's jury hung, with six jurors voting guilty of manslaughter and six voting not guilty.[21]

Finally on June 3, 1856, the time for retrial of Longnecker came, and
Lincoln went into battle at the climax of the prosecution. The jury hung
again, this time with seven voting for acquittal and five for conviction of
manslaughter. When a jury hangs once, a prosecutor might attribute it to
a bad jury pool, but when two successive juries hang on the same case, the
prosecutor must question the wisdom of trying the case a third time. Lincoln
attempted to persuade Rust to drop the charges by circulating a petition
imploring him to enter a nolle prosequi. Lincoln wrote the petition in his
own hand and put the first signature on it. Thirteen other members of the
bar added their signatures to the document.[22] Rust relented and entered a
nolle prosequi, thus ending the prosecution of David Longnecker for the
murder of Jacob Ater.

Lincoln handled another murder case while the Longnecker case was slowly making its way through the criminal justice system. On August 7, 1854, in Vermilion County, Walter Bosley had shot Egbert Barnett in the back. Because the wound was not immediately fatal, Daniel Morgan made a sworn complaint to Justice of the Peace J. D. Purkins. The complaint and warrant were somewhat unusual in that neither one of them named the crime that Bosley was supposed to have committed. Together the affidavit and warrant read:

> Daniel Morgan comes and on his oath complains against one Walter Bosley and says that a criminal offense has been committed at the County of Vermilion in the State of Illinois on the seventh day of August 1854 and says that a criminal offense has been committed by shooting one Egbert Barnett and that the said Daniel Morgan has just reason to believe that Walter Bosley has committed the same and he the said Daniel Morgan prays that a warrant may issue against the said Walter Bosley. . . .
>
> Whereas Daniel Morgan has made complaint before me J. D. Purkins one of the Justices of the Peace within and for Said County against Walter Bosley in the words and figures set forth in the aforegoing complaint by the said Daniel Morgan Subscribed and sworn to on this 7th Day of August 1854 You are therefore hereby commanded in the name and by the authority of the Said People to arrest the Said Walter Bosley and bring him before me or some other Justice of the Said County to answer said complaint and be dealt with according to law.[23]

The uncertainty as to what crime Bosley had committed was removed on August 15, when Barnett died. On October 27, 1854, the Vermilion County grand jury indicted him for murder; he was arraigned, entered a plea of not guilty, and moved for a continuance. On that day, Lincoln was in Chicago, giving a speech on the Kansas-Nebraska Act.[24] Then something occurred of which we have no record, but it resulted in the indictment being dismissed. The next record we have of court action came when state's attorney pro tem Leonard Swett indicted Bosley for murder on November 11.[25] (Leonard Swett makes an appearance again in connection with the trial of Isaac Wyant, discussed in chapter 12).

Ward Hill Lamon represented Bosley in the pretrial phase of the prosecution. Lamon, a giant of a man, associated with Lincoln on many cases outside Springfield as Lincoln rode the circuit. Lamon sometimes presented himself as a partner of Lincoln, but they were not true partners. Although they worked together on many cases, they also occasionally tried cases against each other.

Ward Hill Lamon, the Eighth Circuit state's attorney. Lamon later became a U.S. marshal for the District of Columbia and served as Lincoln's bodyguard. PHOTOGRAPH COURTESY OF THE LIBRARY OF CONGRESS.

It is difficult to tell precisely when Lincoln became involved in the Bosley case. He may have been involved from the outset, with the understanding that Lamon would handle pretrial matters and Lincoln would be there for the trial, or Lincoln may have become associated at the last minute. He certainly did not make any appearances in court before the actual trial.

The day that Bosley got indicted, Lincoln had a rather unusual experience. A special term of circuit court was being held in DeWitt County, and the grand jury returned an indictment against Archer Herndon for unlawful sale of alcoholic beverages. Archer Herndon was William H. Herndon's father, and the indictment was in Lincoln's handwriting.[26] It is not every day that a lawyer draws up criminal charges against his law partner's father. Although Lincoln assisted in the prosecution, his primary reason for being in DeWitt County was to defend a suit against the Illinois Central Railroad. Abial P. Cushman had sued the railroad for $500 damages, claiming that it had failed to properly maintain its fences, allowing cattle to get onto Cushman's property. The jury awarded Cushman $89.50,[27] and Lincoln wrote the judgment against his client for Judge David Davis to sign.[28]

The Bosley case finally came to trial on May 25, 1854, with Lincoln, Ward Hill Lamon, Jonathan Kilborn, and George W. Lawrence for the defense, and Leonard Swett for the prosecution. We know nothing of the circumstances of the killing other than the fact that Bosley shot Egbert Barnett in the back. Given that circumstance, it appears that it would have been difficult to craft a viable defense to a charge of murder. The defense team did well to get the jury to reduce the charge to manslaughter. The jury set Bosley's penalty at eight years, which indicates how close Bosley came to the gallows. It would seem that trying a capital murder case would be enough labor for one day, but Lincoln and Lamon handled eight more cases that day, three of which went to jury trial that term.[29]

Lincoln and Lamon collaborated on many cases, but as in *People v. Patterson* (see chapter 16), they often found themselves on opposite sides. Possibly the strangest case they collaborated on was the defense of the notorious horse thief George High, discussed in the next chapter.

10.

Lincoln's Pardon Practice

MARCH 19, 1856, PROMISED TO BE A BUSY DAY FOR ABRAHAM LINCOLN AND his old partners. Lincoln had two cases set for trial in two different courtrooms. He opposed his former partner Stephen T. Logan in *Taylor v. Humphries*, an action in ejectment in the U.S. Circuit Court for the Southern District of Illinois, and he was co-counsel with his other former partner, John T. Stuart, defending John Hibbs on a charge of manslaughter in Sangamon County Circuit Court. Luckily for Lincoln, both courts were in Springfield.

Lincoln probably began his day trying the case in federal court, and as soon as he got a verdict, he hustled over to Sangamon County Circuit Court to try the manslaughter case. The county court would have a much heavier docket than the federal court, and the state's attorney would have been willing to work with Lincoln by calling up other cases before the manslaughter case. Lincoln had a good morning, getting a verdict in favor of his client,[1] but he and Stuart had a bad afternoon—their client, John Hibbs, was convicted of manslaughter and sentenced to two years in prison.[2]

A little over a year after Hibbs's conviction, on May 8, 1857, Judge David Davis wrote a letter to Governor William Henry Bissell describing the circumstances of the case. He said that Hibbs and another man had been seen together in a field, and the other man had later been found in the field clubbed to death. Hibbs was found, heavily intoxicated, in a house a short distance away. There was no history of bad blood between Hibbs and the victim, and no indication that they were having difficulties the day the man died. Hibbs could remember nothing, claiming an alcoholic blackout. Davis went on to say that Hibbs had a wife and small children, he had served more than half of his sentence of two years, and he was deserving of a pardon. Below Davis's signature, in Lincoln's handwriting, appears this notation: "We defended John Hibbs, mentioned in Judge Davis' letter above; and we concur with the Judge, that a pardon now, after his having served about fourteen months of his two years, would not be improper." The note was signed by Lincoln and

Stuart.[3] A petition signed by seventy citizens of Sangamon County accompanied the judge's letter.[4] The governor almost immediately ordered that Hibbs be pardoned.[5] Throughout his career, Lincoln continued to advocate for his clients even after they were convicted at trial. His forum of choice for that advocacy was not, however, the Supreme Court of Illinois. He seems to have preferred to take his pleas to a forum where he did not have to make legal arguments—the Governor's Mansion. The remainder of this chapter departs from the chronological survey of homicide cases and looks at selected cases from Lincoln's pardon practice.

On October 15, 1841, Michael Hill was supervising a work crew cutting timber on his land in Sangamon County, when a neighbor of his by the name of Lewis approached him and angrily demanded that Hill pay him for a whiplash (the lash end of a whip).[6] Hill contended that he had paid for the whiplash, and the two argued. Hill ordered Lewis off his property, but Lewis refused to leave. In an effort to make Lewis leave, Hill hit him over the head with a barrel stave, knocking him to the ground. This rendered Lewis willing, but unable, to leave Hill's property. Hill offered to seek medical assistance for Lewis, but

Judge David Davis. Lincoln later appointed him to the U.S. Supreme Court. PHOTOGRAPH COURTESY OF THE LIBRARY OF CONGRESS.

Lewis refused, and two of Hill's men helped him home. Two days later, Lewis finally called a doctor. The doctor said Lewis was dying of a fractured skull, but he could have saved the man if he had been called in at once. Hill stood trial for manslaughter on March 31, 1842, and the jury convicted him, setting his sentence at one year and ten days.[7]

Lincoln and his then partner, Stephen T. Logan, defended the case at trial. Logan immediately asked the judge for a stay of sentence while Lincoln went out and collected signatures on a petition for pardon. The judge granted the stay, and Lincoln collected 147 signatures, including those of the jurymen.[8] On April 11, Logan reported to the judge that Governor Thomas Carlin had pardoned Hill, and the judge ordered that Hill be released from jail.[9]

In 1856, Lincoln defended David Thompson on a charge of murder in Woodford County Circuit Court. Lincoln had been appointed to represent Thompson, who was unable to pay for a lawyer. The record is too sketchy to give a precise reconstruction of the facts of the case. All that can be said with certainty is that Thompson shot a man named Patrick Morgan in the neck with a shotgun. Morgan languished for two weeks before dying. State's Attorney Amzi McWilliams indicted Thompson for murder, and on April 27, the case was tried to a jury. Lincoln was assisted at the trial by Norman H. Purple, who edited a volume on the laws of Illinois,[10] and John Clark. The jury returned a verdict of guilty of manslaughter and set the penalty at eight years. Two years later, supporters of Thompson began a petition to have him pardoned, and they asked Lincoln to endorse it. He agreed and endorsed the petition in the following language: "I was appointed by the court to defend the above named David Thompson. I thought at the time his conviction was wrong, and I am now clearly of opinion he ought to be pardoned—I have recently been at Woodford; was the universal sentiment that seems to be in favor of his pardon—."[11] The governor pardoned Thompson.[12]

A few days before Lincoln went to trial in the Thompson case, Edward Barrett had gotten into a brawl with Hugh Lynch at the home of Martin Helbert in Champaign County. In the brawl, Barrett stabbed Lynch in the stomach, inflicting a fatal wound. Lynch cried out that he was stabbed, and Martin Ryan tackled Barrett and disarmed him. Lynch died the next day. Prosecutor pro tem Ward Hill Lamon indicted Barrett for murder, and Barrett hired Lincoln to defend him. Lincoln worked out a plea bargain, and on October 23, 1856, Barrett pleaded guilty to manslaughter and Judge David Davis gave him a five-year sentence.[13] In 1859, a group of citizens of Champaign County got together a petition to have Barrett pardoned, and Davis wrote a letter in support of the petition for pardon.[14] The petitioners also presented the governor with a letter from Illinois State Prison attesting to Barrett's good behavior as a prisoner.[15] They did not, however, present him with a recommendation from Lincoln.

The most unusual pardon petition Lincoln ever became involved with was a campaign to have a horse thief pardoned. Just across the state line from Vermilion County, in Warren County, Indiana, lived a family by the name of High. The Highs had settled the Redwood Point area of Warren County in the late 1820s, and their home became a sort of gathering point for undesirables.[16] By the early 1850s, they had a horse theft ring operating out of their home. Isaac High was the patriarch of the family, but George High was the leader of the gang. They ran a multistate operation centered in the Wabash Valley and were soon terrorizing the citizens of Vermilion and Warren Counties. The Redwood Gang, as they were known, used intimidation tactics such as nighttime shootings into the homes of those who opposed them, anonymous threats, and other acts of violence. George High became infamous for his many escapes from custody, acquittals on perjured testimony, and other exploits.[17]

In the absence of effective law enforcement, citizens took the law into their own hands, forming "horse companies" or "horse theft detective agencies" to combat the horse thieves. These vigilante groups used intimidation tactics similar to the ones employed by the Redwood Gang, but they pledged that they would "never resort to such means unless it becomes positively and absolutely necessary to fight the enemy with their own weapons and the circumstance clearly justifies the means to be used."[18] In September 1853, a horse company led by Thomas McKibben finally ambushed and captured George High. Instead of lynching him, they decided to take him to the Vermilion County Jail to be dealt with by legal process. According to legend, as they took him to jail, High engineered an escape on his black stallion, Truxon. He led the horse company on a merry chase across the entire width of Illinois. When he arrived at the Mississippi River, he spurred Truxon into the water, certain the horse could swim the river, and neither the horse nor the highwayman were ever seen or heard from again.[19] The true end of George High was not quite so romantic.

Upon being jailed, High retained Lincoln and Lamon to represent him on two charges of horse theft. High's gang began to threaten the witnesses against him, including Thomas McKibben, in an effort to intimidate them into refusing to testify. McKibben called a meeting of his horse company, and they agreed on a proclamation that they published in the *Danville Citizen*. The proclamation generally resolved to use all necessary means to combat horse theft in general and the High clan in particular. It also included the following resolutions:

1. If any harm came to anyone involved in the arrest of George High, the horse company members would "pursue the suspicious part of the High tribe and deal out tenfold vengeance upon their heads."

2. If High were acquitted as a result of false testimony, they would "deal out street justice to him and those of his confederates who may fall into [their] hands."

3. If any man bailed High out of jail, they would "view him as a confederate of the said George High."

4. If any lawyer took "any ungenerous or unfair course to acquit High," they would withhold their "influence and patronage" from that lawyer.

The proclamation was signed by Thomas McKibben as president of the Ross Town Horse Company.[20]

Representatives of the horse company visited Ward Hill Lamon's office regularly to check on whether arrangements had been made to bail High out of jail. Lamon wrote to Lincoln saying that he would not be surprised if, when High was released on bail, the horse company killed him.[21] Fear for High's life may have kept him in jail for the fourteen months it took to get his case to trial. His father, Isaac, certainly had the money to bail him out.

When High's case came up for trial on October 27, 1854, wild rumors circulated that the Redwood Gang planned to break him out of jail. McKibben's horse company took preventive measures. Its members rode into town one hundred strong, making such a show of force that some feared they might break High out and lynch him.[22] In the courtroom, Lincoln moved for a change of venue and the judge granted it, moving the case to Champaign County, still well within the area of depredation by the Redwood Gang.[23] One year later, the case finally came on for trial in Champaign County, and Lincoln again moved for a change of venue. This time the judge denied the motion.[24]

The horse company probably had a considerable contingent of regulators present to see that nobody gave perjured testimony on behalf of High and to make sure that Lincoln did not use an "ungenerous or unfair course" to gain an acquittal. It was in this atmosphere that George High stood trial on two charges of horse theft. Two indictments were pending against High, and because they had not been consolidated, there would have to be two trials. The state's attorney called up the first indictment for trial. The lawyers chose a jury and presented the evidence and argument of counsel. The jury convicted High and set his sentence at eighteen months, and the judge sentenced him to eighteen months of hard labor. Then the state's attorney called up the second indictment for trial. The lawyers chose a second jury out of the pool of talesmen that had been sitting and watching the first trial, then presented the evidence and argument of counsel. The second jury found High guilty and set his sentence at eighteen months, and the judge sentenced him to another eighteen months of hard labor.[25] One might suspect that the second jury had been somewhat influenced by what they saw the first jury do.

High had been in prison for about a year when William McCullough wrote a letter to Governor Joel A. Matteson asking that he pardon High on the grounds that High's wife was very ill and needed him to come home and take care of her and her children.[26] Matteson in turn wrote a letter to David Davis, who had presided over the trial of High, asking whether he might be a suitable candidate for a pardon.[27] In reply, Davis pointed out that McCullough was from McLean County, but the crimes had occurred in Vermilion County. He then gave Matteson a brief history of the prosecution and took up High's character: "High is a man of good appearance & fine talents—rather uncommon talents—If he had common honesty he would have shone in any walk of life—." He then described how High lived at Redwood Point, a notorious gathering place for criminals, and how the horse company had been formed to "break up the rendezvous & to catch High & other horse thieves." Davis described how difficult it had been to capture High and closed with the observation that he did not think High's wife and children were in such dire straits as had been represented.[28]

Five days later, Davis had completely changed his tune. Lincoln wrote a petition for pardon stating that the signers of the petition were men who "took an active interest in prosecuting his conviction." According to the petition, these men now "think that public justice has been satisfied in his case; and as he is yet quite a young man, we hope and believe that some lenity toward him would be favorable to his reformation for the future." One of the signers of the petition was Thomas McKibben—the same Thomas McKibben who had worked so hard to arrest High, whom High had threatened to kill, and who had threatened to kill High. Judge Davis endorsed the petition, saying that the signers of the petition were the most respected men in Vermilion County and the sentiments they expressed were a "fair index of the public opinion of the county." He said he shared that opinion and recommended the pardon. Lincoln also endorsed the petition: "I have been acquainted with the circumstances of George High's case from the time of his arrest and I cheerfully join in the request that he might be pardoned."[29]

It has been hinted that Lincoln did something wrong with this petition, pulling the wool over the governor's eyes and obtaining the release of a desperate criminal. On the surface, it looks as though there may be some substance to this suggestion. Seven of the signers were lawyers (one of whom, Lamon, defended High), one was reading law, and one was a county judge.[30] A case could be made for the proposition that Lincoln simply got some of his friends and colleagues to sign a fraudulent petition, got his good friend David Davis to endorse it, and then endorsed it himself in such a way as to conceal the fact that he was the defense attorney in the case.

Four items of evidence tell strongly against the theory of chicanery. The first is the signature of Thomas McKibben, the captain of the Ross Town Horse Company. McKibben, who would "rather chase a horse thief than eat," would never be party to such a transaction. It has been suggested that he signed the petition because he and Lincoln were friends and fellow Republicans, and he did it as a favor.[31] He would have to have been a very good friend of Lincoln's indeed to sign a petition to pardon a man who had threatened to kill him. McKibben must have had a much better reason to sign the petition.

Second, over the course of five days, David Davis underwent a 180-degree change of attitude toward High. One remark Davis made in his first letter to Matteson explains both his change of attitude and McKibben's signature on the petition: "It was represented to me in Vermilion County (from which County I have just returned) that the horse company would take some action in relation to High's pardon soon. . . . I have no proper evidence on the subject & shall wait further developments in Vermilion Co. before uniting in any application for his pardon—."[32]

The third piece of evidence is the fact that the horse companies had a highly publicized policy that horse thieves "must be punished or leave our country."[33]

Finally, upon his release from prison, George High left Indiana and Illinois never to return, but he did not plunge his horse Truxon into the Mississippi River in an idiotic attempt to swim to the other side. He moved to Missouri, where he returned to his old habits.[34]

These facts suggest that someone brokered a deal between McKibben and High that called for High to be pardoned and to leave Illinois. High's sentence was not a long one, and nothing prevented him from going back into the horse theft business on his release. Nothing prevented McKibben and his band of vigilantes from making good on their mortal threats if High resumed his business in Illinois. A solution that provided for High's sentence to be shortened in return for his leaving Illinois comports with Lincoln's philosophy of "persuad[ing] your neighbors to compromise whenever you can."[35]

The governor granted High's pardon on November 10, 1856.[36] On November 26, the *Illinois State Journal* ran the following article: "Another Sheriff Shot.—Thomas McKibben, Sheriff elect of Vermillion county, Illinois, was found one day last week in his cornfield, dead, six balls having entered his body. By whom the bloody deed was committed, is not known."[37] No record can be found of sheriff-elect McKibben's slayer ever being brought to justice. Whether the murder victim was the same Thomas McKibben who was president of the Ross Town Horse Company is open to question. On October 1, 1860, someone named Thomas McKibben was elected president of a congress of the Horse Thief Detecting Societies of Indiana and Illinois and signed a proclamation responding to threats leveled against certain of its members and pledging to "spare no human effort, and stop at no expense" to bring the threateners to justice.[38] The next year saw Thomas McKibben enlisting in Company B of the Twenty-Fifth Illinois Infantry as a first lieutenant, and by the end of the war he had attained the rank of major.[39] Apparently High did not exact revenge on Thomas McKibben before leaving Illinois for good, and the Thomas McKibben who was killed shortly after High received his pardon was a relative of the intrepid horse thief detective of the same name.

Lincoln was sometimes ready to add his weight to a request for the pardon of someone he did not represent. On March 22, 1858, he wrote the following letter to Governor Bissell:

> Samuel Jones and Jerry Jones, at court here last week, were found guilty of stealing five shoats, or small hogs—I have been appealed to, to say something in favor of their being pardoned—They are father and son—I know nothing to say, except that he is an old citizen (I mean the father) and his neighbors appear now more anxious that he and his son should be pardoned, than I have known in any other case—This is really all can say—I was not concerned in the trial; and consequently did not listen to the evidence—.[40]

David Davis wrote a letter to Governor Bissell on October 24, 1858, asking him to pardon a young man named Orren Smith, who had been sentenced to a year in prison for theft. He did not immediately mail the letter, however. First he got Ward Hill Lamon, the prosecutor, to endorse the letter concurring with the request, and on November 3, Lincoln endorsed the bottom of Davis's letter, stating that he did not try the case but was in the courtroom when it was tried, and he concurred in the request for pardon.[41]

On June 8, 1860, Lincoln endorsed a recommendation by Judge Charles Emerson that Emanuel Fowler, who had been convicted of assault, be pardoned. In the endorsement, he wrote, "Believing that Judge Emerson knows what is right in this case, I join in the recommendation he makes."[42]

Two months later, on August 7, Mary Cunningham asked Judge Buckner S. Morris to write a letter recommending that her brother, who had served six years of an eight-year sentence for manslaughter, be pardoned. Morris wrote the letter, saying that the young man, Patrick Cunningham, had killed a Chicago police officer in a drunken rage, was extremely remorseful, and had behaved well while in prison.[43] The very next day, Mary went to Springfield to personally deliver the letter to the governor. Before she went to the governor's office, she went to Lincoln and asked him to endorse the letter. He did so in the following words: "I think it almost always safe to pardon a convict, when, as in this case, the Judge before whom he was convicted, recommends it."[44]

It appears that Lincoln could sometimes be persuaded to add an endorsement to a pardon petition, but when called on to do so he would not vouch for the character of a convict whom he did not know or believe in. The best he would do was to vouch for the character of those who urged the pardon.

11.

PEOPLE versus JANE AND THEODORE ANDERSON, November 28, 1856

GEORGE ANDERSON HAD A BLACKSMITH SHOP IN SPRINGFIELD, A PARTNER named William Talbott, a wife, three children, and a modest home not far from his shop.[1] George supplemented his income by taking in boarders. In addition to his family, one longtime boarder and a hired girl lived with him. The boarder, a young man named John Morgan, slept in the dining room near the master bedroom. The hired girl, Rebecca Law, slept with the children. George's bedroom opened out onto an enclosed backyard, and in the rear of the yard stood a privy. Across the street from the backyard was John Armstrong's woodworking shop.

Things began to go wrong for Anderson when his nephew, Theodore Anderson, came from New Jersey and began boarding with him. While boarding with the Andersons, Theodore became too friendly with his uncle's wife, Jane. George, an easygoing sort, tried to overlook the bond developing between Theo and his wife. He may have adopted a less easygoing attitude had he known that in early February 1856, Jane went with Theo to a photographer's shop and had a picture taken to give Theo.

Things came to a head toward the end of March, when Theo complained of insomnia and said he could get to sleep if someone combed his hair for him. Jane volunteered, and the two retired to Theo's bedroom. The next morning, George told Theo to find other lodgings, saying that Jane was overworked trying to care for so many householders. Theo decided to go to Jerseyville, and George accompanied him to the train station. As the two walked to the station, Cyrus Youst overheard a snippet of their conversation. Theo was apologizing to George, saying he was sorry he had done it. George replied, "Oh, well, it was nothing that I didn't do when I was a boy."

When he arrived in Jerseyville, Theo met Dr. J. L. White, and the two became friendly. Theo stayed in Jerseyville approximately two weeks before returning to Springfield, but shortly after he left, Dr. White noticed that a bottle of strychnine had gone missing from the cabinet in his examining room.

Upon his return, Theo began boarding with another relative, Charles Anderson, who lived just a few blocks from George. It was about this time that three things happened: a man in black started skulking around George's house at night, Theo started skulking around the house during the day, and George started getting sick at night. John Morgan first noticed the man in black and immediately told George. George went outside to investigate and found nothing, but he was concerned enough to borrow a revolver from his friend A. W. Coleman. Theo, the daytime skulker, usually stationed himself at John Armstrong's woodworking shop, talking with the workmen and watching George's backyard from his vantage point at the shop. Theo, a brick mason, had placed orders for a straightedge and a plumb bob with the woodworkers, and he frequently came by to check on their progress with the order and to peer into George's backyard.

When George first became ill, Jane sent for Dr. Ed Lord, the family physician, who immediately came in the middle of the night and administered medication to try to relieve the symptoms. Dr. Lord was puzzled by the symptoms, which recurred night after night with increasing intensity. If he had not had such implicit faith in Jane's love for George, he would have sworn that she was poisoning him with strychnine. But Jane showed such loving concern, such worry, and such compassion that Dr. Lord dismissed any such suspicions.

Dr. Lord decided to stay with George at night to be present when the symptoms came on. The first night, he stayed until the usual hour of onset, but no attack came. He went home, but no sooner had he gotten home than Jane sent for him—George had suffered another attack. This pattern repeated itself for several nights, until George told Dr. Lord that he thought the treatment was what was killing him. Dr. Lord suggested turning the case over to his partner, Dr. Ed Fowler. Dr. Lord discussed the case with Dr. Fowler, including his nagging suspicions of strychnine poisoning, and Dr. Fowler agreed to take the case.

Under Dr. Fowler's care, the pattern continued. No matter how late the doctor stayed up with George, the symptoms would hit his patient as soon as he left. Finally, Dr. Fowler sat up with George all night long, leaving first thing in the morning. Jane was fixing the family's breakfast as the doctor left. George had not had an attack all night long, but no sooner did he eat breakfast than he had another one. Jane immediately sent John Morgan for Dr. Fowler. When the doctor returned, he gave George the antidote for strychnine, and George improved. Fowler then told husband and wife, "There is something very wrong about this situation, and mark my words, I will get to the bottom of it!" George had no further attacks.

George slowly began to mend. He got strong enough to go buy a suit of clothes to fit his emaciated frame, and he visited the blacksmith shop. He began visiting friends, including his cousin Charles Anderson. On Sunday, May 11, 1856, he and Jane ate dinner (the noon meal) at Charles's home. Theo was present, and the three seemed to get along cordially. They were invited to come back to Charles's for tea the following Thursday evening, May 15.

That Thursday morning around 8 A.M., Harvey Samuel and Council Sampson saw Jane at the front gate of her home talking to a "tolerably young man." Jane had a dress to sew, and she spent most of the day working on it. Around 10 A.M., Jane went to Rebecca Dunning's house for some help cutting out the pattern for the dress. She stayed at Rebecca's until noon, when she left for home, saying she would return that afternoon to continue work on the dress.

Theo ate dinner at Charles Anderson's that day and then left for the livery stable, where he stayed from about 1 to 1:30 P.M. He had not been gone from Charles's long before Jane arrived on an errand connected with her dress. Jane left Charles's around 2 P.M., and Abijah Anderson escorted her home. It was about this time that Thomas Felton saw Theo walking with a lady on Washington Street, and Charles Pride saw Jane walking toward her home with a man whom he later swore was Theo.

Jane went back to the Dunning home around 3 P.M., and Rebecca helped her work on the dress until 4 P.M., when it became obvious that they needed some material that they did not have. Jane left to get the material and went to C. M. Smith's store. After purchasing the material from Smith, she returned to Rebecca Dunning's home around 4:10 P.M. During this time period, John Armstrong saw Theo go into a vacant lot with a woman he identified as Jane. He saw them talk a few minutes and then leave. W. M. Farnsworth saw Theo about this time with a woman, but he could not identify her as Jane. Jane stayed at the Dunning home until 5 P.M., when she left and went home. She did not go to tea at Charles Anderson's that evening, but George did. Around 6 P.M., both Abijah Anderson and Gideon Northerner saw Jane talking to Theo in the front yard of her home.

John Morgan ate supper with Jane that evening. While they were eating supper, George came home, and Jane said, "You have got back."

George replied, "Yes, but you did not come out there as you agreed," an apparent reference to Jane's not taking tea with him at Charles Anderson's.

Jane replied, "No."

George said, "But you could go off someplace else."

Jane remarked that she could.

George said, "If you are above going any place with me you can go where you have been and stay."

Jane smiled and said she would. Morgan decided that now would be an opportune time to leave the home. He then went to town and remained until nearly 9 P.M. Morgan arrived home around 9 P.M. and went to bed.

Theo left Charles Anderson's that evening around 6 P.M. with Benjamin Green and Henry Vaughn. The three of them walked around town for a while, and they separated around 8:30 at Spath's corner. Theo spent the rest of the night wandering around town, going to Freman's corner, the post office, and the alley behind the American house. He then decided to go home. His pathway would have taken him directly by George Anderson's home. Theo got home and got to bed around 9:30 P.M. The house was locked at 10 P.M., and after that time it would have been difficult for anyone to enter or leave the house without being detected.

Around 10:15 P.M., William E. Plank was passing down the alleyway between the rear of the Andersons' home and Armstrong's woodworking shop when he saw a man dressed in black step out from a lot directly opposite the Andersons'. The man bore some resemblance to Theo, but he was dressed differently from the way that Theo normally dressed.

Sometime around 10:45 P.M., Jane wakened Morgan. George had gone outside and not come back. Jane was frightened. Would Morgan go out and look for him? Morgan, only eighteen, was none too anxious to go looking for George, but he agreed to do so. He walked to the back door and looked out. The moon was waxing gibbous, with eighty-four percent of its disk illuminated.[2] In the light of the moon hanging high overhead, Morgan saw George's inert form lying face up near the privy. Morgan told Jane he thought George was dead. Jane insisted he go outside and make sure. Morgan refused. Jane sent him for the doctor. Morgan ran to Dr. Fowler's and roused him out of bed. On the way back to George's, he stopped at Charles Anderson's and woke them. Charles, Abijah, and Theo got out of bed and went to George's house.

When Dr. Fowler arrived at about 11 P.M., he found Jane standing in the doorway between the dining room and the bedroom. She said George had gotten up during the night and gone out, died, and no one knew it. Dr. Fowler found George in the backyard five or six feet from the privy door, lying across the path; his legs were straight, and his hands were drawn up to his side. His limbs were relaxed and not rigid, and the body was still somewhat warm. Dr. Fowler immediately suspected foul play. The privy door stood open, and a chamber pot lay in the doorway. Dr. Fowler went back inside and told Jane that George was dead. Jane said that after she had gone to bed, George complained of pain in his legs. She had gotten up and rubbed them, and asked him if she should stay up, but he told her to lie down and take her rest, saying that he would call her if he felt any worse.

In short order, a mob of people crowded into the Anderson home. Some were family, some well-wishers, and some merely curious. Both Theo and Jane discounted the possibility of murder. They both thought George had simply gone to the privy and been struck by one of his seizures; he then must have fallen and hit his head, fatally injuring himself. The scenario touted by Theo and Jane did not in any way fit the circumstantial evidence.

Dr. Lord arrived and made a minute examination of the body and its surroundings. George had on his underclothes, boots, and an overcoat with a revolver in the pocket. Dr. Lord saw an ugly wound on the back of George's head that looked sufficient to have caused death, but he felt it strange that he could find no signs of a struggle. The doctor found a stick or piece of plank on the ground seven or eight feet from the body. It was about three feet long and very heavy at one end. It seemed singularly adapted to inflict a heavy blow, but he could find no blood on it. He did find some hairs on the end of the club, and the hairs looked as if they had come from George Anderson. The absence of blood around the body was puzzling; head wounds are notorious for bleeding profusely. Dr. Lord thought that one explanation for the lack of blood might be that the blow was inflicted after George's death. A hammer was also found, and it was the right size to have made the hole in the back of George's head, but it had no blood or hair on it. Another weapon might have caused such a wound to George's head. It was a weapon that was quite common on the western frontier but is virtually unknown today—a slung-shot, a small, heavy weight sewn into a leather pouch on the end of a looped leather strap. They could find no slungshot on the grounds of the Anderson homestead, but some people thought they knew where they could find one.

Dr. Lord told Jane he needed to perform a post mortem examination on George. At first she voiced no objection, and they carried him into the bedroom where the two doctors began the post mortem. Jane then began to object, saying she could not bear to hear the sound of sawing on her husband's head and objecting to the removal of his stomach. When they told her the stomach would not be removed, she settled down. Contrary to what Jane had been told, the doctors did in fact remove George's stomach. Later testing showed that it contained a lethal dose of strychnine.

As the finger of suspicion pointed more and more at Theo and Jane, it was decided to inventory Theo's belongings. A deputation went to Charles Anderson's to search his belongings. They conducted a thorough search of

Theo's footlocker but did not find a slungshot. They did, however, find a bottle of strychnine, the photograph of Jane, and a packet of unsigned love letters. Theo had no explanation for the photograph or the love letters, but he said that he had gotten the strychnine in New Jersey to treat a skin condition. Neither Dr. Fowler nor Dr. Lord had ever heard of strychnine being used to treat skin conditions.

The coroner convened a coroner's jury, and it rendered a verdict of "death by the hand of some person or persons unknown." Theo was almost immediately arrested,[3] and Jane's arrest soon followed. Jane retained John T. Stuart, Benjamin S. Edwards, and William Campbell to represent her. The prosecutor was Amzi McWilliams, a competent but irascible attorney whom few other lawyers liked. After an arrest, the first stage of the prosecution is a preliminary hearing at which the prosecution has the burden of establishing lawful grounds for holding the accused to answer for the charges. In antebellum Illinois, they called this stage of the prosecution the "examination," and it was held before two justices of the peace.

John T. Stuart, Lincoln's first law partner. PHOTO-GRAPH COURTESY OF THE LIBRARY OF CONGRESS.

The prosecution has a low burden of proof at the examination. All that needs to be proven is probable cause to believe that a murder had been committed and that the accused had committed it. Difficulty in establishing probable cause at a preliminary hearing should serve as a red flag to the prosecutor that the case most likely does not merit prosecution.

The case against Jane Anderson was beset by problems of proof. How was George killed? Was he poisoned or bludgeoned? If he was bludgeoned, what was the strychnine doing in his stomach? If he was poisoned, how did his body get from the house to the backyard, and how did the head wound occur? How could Jane have poisoned George when she had no strychnine? How could she have gotten his poisoned body out to the privy to stage an attack without leaving drag marks? What about the mysterious man in black who was seen lurking around the house the night of the murder? Could he have done it? In addition to all these unanswered questions, McWilliams confronted the spectacle of all George's relatives lining up to testify on behalf of the accused. His strongest witnesses were the doctors, but even they had to admit that Jane was such a loving wife it was hard to believe she could harm George.

McWilliams had the photograph, the strychnine, and the love letters in Theo's footlocker. He also had the innuendo of several possible sightings of Jane meeting with Theo away from the home and of Theo mooning over Jane from Armstrong's woodworking shop. At the hearing, however, things did not go well. The identifications of Jane as the woman with Theo were iffy at best, and the love letters found in Theo's trunk could not have come from Jane—she was illiterate. Mary Anderson, Jane's fourteen-year-old daughter, caused something of a sensation when she testified from the stand that she and Theo were "lovers." In 1856, that term did not carry the intimate connotation it does today, but it gave Theo a reason other than infatuation with Jane to be gazing at George's backyard. The case against Jane collapsed, and the court entered a finding of no probable cause. She was released from jail, and her case should have been over.

McWilliams, however, was not a man to be discouraged by a setback. He had Jane rearrested and tried again to establish probable cause at a second examination. Although the newspapers gave a full report of the testimony of every witness at the first examination, the second examination rated a mere two sentences: "We mentioned yesterday that Mrs. Anderson was again arraigned before the court for the alleged murder of her husband. After undergoing a second trial she was discharged—there being no additional evidence adduced against her."[4]

While Stuart, Campbell, and Edwards were defending Jane at the preliminary hearing, Lincoln was in Urbana defending Father Charles Chiniquy against a lawsuit for slander. Chiniquy, a flamboyant Catholic priest, had taken to the pulpit and denounced one Peter Spink as a perjurer. Spink sued Chiniquy in Kankakee County Circuit Court, seeking $10,000 damages. Venue was changed to Urbana in Champaign County, and Chiniquy retained Lincoln to defend him. The trial lasted three days, and on May 22 the jury hung. The case got continued to the October term, and Lincoln eventually engineered an out-of-court settlement.[5] Father Chiniquy wrote a lurid and somewhat counterfactual account of the trial in his memoir, *Fifty Years in the Church of Rome*.[6]

In an examination held immediately on the heels of Jane's second examination, McWilliams persuaded the justices to find probable cause against Theo. If he had been circumspect, he would have indicted only Theo for murdering George by striking him on the head with a blunt object, either a hammer or a board. McWilliams, however, was intent on prosecuting Jane as well. At the next term of the Sangamon County Circuit Court, he indicted both Jane and Theo for murdering George.[7] He had Jane immediately rearrested, and the case was set for trial in the November term of the court.

On July 12, 1856, Benjamin S. Edwards wrote a letter to Judge David Davis asking two favors. He wanted Davis to call a special term of the Sangamon Circuit Court to hear Jane Anderson's case as quickly as possible, and he wanted Jane tried separately from Theo: "Mrs. Anderson who is in jail under an indictment for murder is anxious to have her trial—Will you inform us whether you would appoint a special term—and when—and if so whether you would allow her a separate trial—Which in our judgment from a full examination of the case is essential to her safety."[8]

Although the burden of proof always rests with the prosecution in every criminal case, the defense often finds it helpful to try to prove that someone else committed the crime. The likeliest someone else to put forward as solely responsible for the crime is a codefendant. When codefendants stand trial together, if one begins to blame the other, the other often reciprocates, and the jury is presented with the spectacle of two defendants, each trying to prove the other committed the crime. Such a situation is sometimes called a "cutthroat defense," and both defendant and codefendant usually end up with their throats cut. It is much safer for a defendant to obtain a separate trial, where the codefendant can safely be blamed without fear of reciprocal accusations.

Edwards's plea fell on deaf ears. There would be neither a special term nor a separate trial for Jane Anderson. With this joint trial, there would also be no cutthroat defense. Theo had no money to speak of, and it appears that

Jane paid his attorney's fees as well as her own. Both Jane's and Theo's law-yers would be working to throw suspicion on the mysterious man in black who was seen in the alley behind George's house on the night of the murder.

As he had with the David Longnecker case, Lincoln came late to the de-fense of the Anderson case. He was apparently hired on the eve of the trial, not by the accused, but by the attorneys already retained to defend the case. In 1899, Thomas Lewis, one of Jane's attorneys, wrote a letter to the *Illinois State Register* reminiscing about the case. Jane had raised $300 and hired Lewis, Stephen T. Logan, and Benjamin S. Edwards, giving them each $100. As Lewis recalled, Lincoln joined the case in the following manner: "Conscious as we were of the innocence of the parties, we offered Abraham Lincoln $25 each, making the fees $75 each. Lincoln accepted. . . . A feeling had sprung up against the woman, and a $200 fee was raised to employ an assistant for the prosecution. It was first offered Lincoln, as he told us. He declined. He said he would sooner defend the woman for nothing than prosecute her for $200."[9]

Lewis's recollection may be somewhat faulty. He went on to recall that the trial consumed ten days and that no fewer than 150 witnesses testified. The trial began on November 19, 1856, and concluded on November 28. Al-though Lewis gave an accurate estimate of the length of the trial, he greatly overestimated the number of witnesses called—only 54 witnesses actually testified at the trial.

When court convened on November 19, Amzi McWilliams could not have been happy. Public dissatisfaction with his handling of the Anderson case had resulted in his failure to retain his office. His party refused to nominate him for reelection, and Ward Hill Lamon had become the Eighth Circuit state's attorney.[10] In addition to his professional woes, McWilliams faced the daunting prospect of contesting his case against six opposing lawyers: Stuart, Edwards, and Lewis for the defendant Jane Anderson; and Lincoln, Stephen T. Logan, and John E. Rosette for Theo. McWilliams faced the most formidable array of legal talent that could have been mustered from the Springfield bar. Four of the defense lawyers were talented, well-respected advocates in the prime of their careers. Only Rosette, a young lawyer who served as a gofer during the trial, could be characterized as a lightweight. With a marginal case and a stellar array of adversaries, McWilliams would need something akin to a miracle to obtain a conviction. Additionally, he faced a tedious jury selection process. The attorneys worked through a panel of 240 prospective jurors before they finally swore 12 to try the case.[11]

The testimony for the prosecution went much as it had at the preliminary hearing, with a few notable exceptions. McWilliams offered no testimony about the hammer, which could have made a wound similar to the one on George's head. This left the stick, which probably could not have made such a wound, as the only possible murder weapon. Judge Davis ruled the unsigned love letters inadmissible in evidence.[12] Apparently the facts that they were not signed, that Jane was illiterate, and that Jane's daughter professed her love for Theo were sufficient to render the letters irrelevant. Lincoln objected to all the testimony that McWilliams had introduced at Jane's examination about people seeing Theo meeting with a woman who might have been Jane. Judge Davis also held this evidence inadmissible.[13]

McWilliams got some relief when Usher F. Linder, an eminent trial lawyer and former attorney general of Illinois, arrived in town and agreed to assist in the prosecution. Linder found himself somewhat hampered but undaunted by the fact that the trial had been ongoing for several days by the time he entered the case. When Linder walked into the courtroom with his pipe clenched firmly in his teeth, Judge Davis took notice. "Mr. Sheriff!" Davis boomed. "You will permit no one to smoke in this courtroom while court is in session—except General Linder!" This remark provoked a good deal of laughter in the courtroom, but it did not deter Linder from smoking. He kept his pipe firmly clenched in his teeth for the better part of the trial.[14]

Despite the much-needed help supplied by Linder, McWilliams's case continued to unravel. It seemed that all of George's relatives took the stand to testify that Jane was the most loving and attentive of wives, that George had the utmost confidence in her, and that Jane had absolutely no opportunity whatsoever to administer poison to him without being detected by some other member of the family. The doctors who testified for the prosecution were none too certain in their opinions, and the doctors who testified for the defense so thoroughly muddied the question of how George died that it was a toss-up whether he had been poisoned or beaten to death.

The defense team offered testimony about foot tracks behind the privy, suggesting that someone could have hidden behind the privy waiting for George to answer the call of nature. According to the defense theory, this someone was the mysterious man in black who had been seen skulking around George's home. Since the man in black definitely was not Jane, this theory completely exonerated her. Theo, on the other hand, needed to prove that he was not the man in black. Lincoln and Logan attempted to do this by having a number of different witnesses attest to Theo's saintly character and by putting on an alibi defense, carefully tracing Theo's movements throughout the night of the murder. From the testimony, we can reconstruct a timeline for May 15, 1856.

MOVEMENTS OF JANE AND THEO ANDERSON ON MAY 15, 1856

8 A.M.   Council Sampson sees Jane talking to a "tolerably young man" at the front gate of the Anderson home.

10 A.M.   Jane leaves home to go to Rebecca Dunning's to work on a dress she is sewing.

10:30 A.M.   Jane arrives at Rebecca Dunning's home, where they work on the sewing project until noon.

12 P.M.   Jane returns home.

12:30 P.M.   Theo eats dinner at Charles Anderson's home.

1 P.M.   Theo goes to livery stable; Jane arrives at Charles Anderson's home.

1:30 P.M.   Theo leaves livery stable.

2:30 P.M.   Jane leaves Charles Anderson's home and is escorted by Abijah Anderson straight to her home, where she begins cutting a pattern for a dress. Charles Pride thinks he sees Theo and Jane walking down street near courthouse; the man must be Abijah Anderson.

3 P.M.   Jane returns to Rebecca Dunning's home to continue work on the dress.

4 P.M.   Jane leaves Dunning home to run to store to buy some material; Theo is at post office.

4–4:10 P.M.   Jane buys material at C. M. Smith's store.

4:10 P.M.   Jane returns to Dunning home.

5 P.M.   Jane leaves Dunning home to return to her own home.

6 P.M.   Abijah Anderson sees Jane and Theo talking in front yard of Anderson home.

6:05 P.M.   Gideon Northerner sees Theo and Jane talking at the front gate of George's yard.

6:30 P.M.   Benjamin Green and Henry Vaughn are with Theo at Charles Anderson's house. They leave Charles's and walk around town with Theo, who is wearing light-colored clothing, until 8 P.M. John Morgan eats supper at George Anderson's home. George returns home and talks with Jane. Morgan leaves and walks around square.

8 P.M.   Benjamin Green parts company with Theo and Henry Vaughn.

8:30 P.M.   Henry Vaughn parts company with Theo, who wanders around town.

9 P.M.   John Morgan arrives home at George Anderson's. George is in bed. Morgan goes to bed. Theo's window of opportunity to commit the murder begins.

9:30 P.M.   Theo arrives home at Charles Anderson's and goes to bed. Theo's window of opportunity to commit the murder ends.

10 P.M.   Phebe Todd locks front door of Charles Anderson's home, after which nobody can enter or leave the house undetected.

10:15 P.M.   William E. Plank passes down alleyway behind George Anderson's home and sees a man in black step out from a lot directly opposite Anderson's lot. Man resembles Theo but is dressed differently from the way Theo dressed.

10:15–11 P.M.   Jane wakes John Morgan and tells him to go look for George. Morgan finds George's body and goes for doctor. On the way back from the doctor's, John wakes Charles Anderson. Charles, Abijah, and Theo Anderson get out of bed and go to George Anderson's home.

11 P.M.   People start arriving at George Anderson's home in response to John Morgan's alarm.

Theo had spent most of the evening wandering around town with his friend Henry Vaughn, but the alibi had holes. Theo separated from Vaughn at 8:30 and did not get back to Charles Anderson's until 9:30. He had a window of opportunity to commit the murder between 9 P.M., when John Morgan came home to George's house to go to bed, and 9:30, when Theo returned home to Charles Anderson's and went to bed. Theo could have immediately gone to George's at 8:30 when he separated from Henry Vaughn, taken up a vigil behind the privy, and brained George at the door of the privy sometime between 9 and 9:30. Only two things tell against this theory: evidence that Theo could have done it does not mean that he did it, and Theo was wearing light-colored clothing. The man in black wore dark clothing, far more appropriate for a nighttime ambush.

Theo possibly had a second window of opportunity between 9:30, when he went to bed at Charles Anderson's, and 10 P.M., when Phebe Todd locked the door. This window presents many problems. During that half hour, Theo would have had to put on dark clothing, sneak out of Charles's house, go the three and a half blocks to George's house, hide behind the privy waiting for George to answer the call of nature, brain him when he went to the privy, sneak back home undetected, and be back in bed before Phebe Todd locked the door. This scenario is possible but not likely.

At noon on Wednesday, November 26, the defense rested. McWilliams began his final argument after the noon meal and argued all afternoon. Judge Davis recessed court when he completed his argument. The next morning, Stuart argued on behalf of Jane until noon, and Edwards argued her case all afternoon. On Friday morning, McWilliams answered the arguments of Stuart and Edwards, and that afternoon, Lincoln argued on behalf of Theo. Saturday morning, Logan gave an argument on behalf of Theo, and that afternoon, Linder closed the arguments on behalf of the prosecution.[15]

Linder's argument may have dealt the final blow to the prosecution case. Having come into the case late, he was not entirely familiar with all the players. He thought Theo was the handsome young man sitting at the defense table next to Jane. The young man's brash attitude irritated Linder, as he "frisked about and got law books and pointed out pages to Lincoln and the rest of the lawyers in defense."[16] Linder resolved to make an issue of the defendant's lack of remorse when his turn came to argue. General Linder described what happened when he unleashed his wrath on the impertinent young man:

> I had no intention to deal with the case but in a serious and solemn manner, and after summing up the evidence and showing how strongly it pointed to the guilt of the woman and her paramour, turned, and pointing my finger to the man I supposed to be her associate in crime, I said: "Gentlemen of the jury, if you wanted any additional evidence of this man's guilt, it would only be necessary for you to recur to his boldness and impudence on this trial;" and pointing to his face said, "you can see guilt written all over his countenance," when he calmly rose from his seat and said, not in an angry tone: "General Linder, you are mistaken; I am not the criminal, but my name is Rosette; I am a lawyer, and one of the counsel for the defendants."[17]

These were the only words young Rosette spoke in the jury's hearing during the entire trial, but they sank home. The press reports describe what happened next: "The General looked somewhat astonished at this piece of information; after recovering himself he said, 'Well, sir, I beg your pardon, but I have taken you to be the prisoner during the whole trial.' It is hardly necessary to say that the gravity of the Court was completely upset; the judge, jury, and everybody else roared with laughter, but General Linder; even the young lawyer thought it a good joke."[18]

In his memoir of the incident, Linder did not mention the gales of laughter, but he did admit, "This unfortunate mistake thoroughly broke me down, and I limped lamely through the remainder of my argument."[19] Linder may have limped, but he limped resolutely. He did not conclude his argument until 9 P.M. After several hours of deliberation, the jury returned a verdict of not guilty for both defendants.[20]

The problem with circumstantial evidence cases is that nobody actually saw the crime occur. The prosecution must therefore piece together a sufficiently incriminating mosaic of circumstances from which it can argue an inferred series of events. Given the circumstances of George's death, the prosecution's case theory should have looked something like this: "Theo procured strychnine for Jane, and she tried to kill George by slowly poisoning him. When Dr. Fowler voiced his suspicions, Jane discontinued the slow poisoning and waited a sufficient period of time for suspicion to die down. She then killed George with a massive dose of poison and enlisted Theo's aid in carrying him to the privy and bashing him in the head to make it look like he had been attacked outside."

This scenario depends heavily on the fact that the head wound did not bleed, which suggests that it was inflicted postmortem, and the presence of strychnine in George's body. The window of opportunity for moving the body outside would have been the 9 to 9:30 hole in Theo's alibi. The fact that the head wound did not bleed and the fact that George had strychnine in his system also tend to militate against his having been ambushed by a mysterious disappearing man in black. The defense, however, was able to raise sufficient reasonable doubt based on the man in black, Jane's highly visible displays of love and affection for George, and the support of George's relatives for Jane and Theo.

The romance of Jane and Theo Anderson, if ever there had been one, died during the criminal proceedings against them. Perhaps it was the stress of standing trial that extinguished any feelings of affection that existed between them, or perhaps it was Jane's discovery that Theo was courting her daughter at the same time he was courting her. Whatever the reason, after the trial they parted ways for good. Theo moved back to New Jersey, and Jane lived on in Springfield as a widow.[21]

12.

PEOPLE versus ISAAC WYANT, April 5, 1857

ON FRIDAY, OCTOBER 12, 1855, AROUND 2 P.M., ASON RUSK STOOD IN THE DeWitt County Circuit Court clerk's office at the courthouse in Clinton, Illinois, warming himself by the stove with Squire McGraw, the clerk, and Harry Kidder. McGraw stepped out of the office for a few minutes, and while he was gone, Isaac Wyant opened the door and stepped in. Rusk, apparently taking no notice, stood unmoving by the stove as Wyant walked over to him and pulled an Allen pepperbox revolver from his pocket. Before Sam Colt's famous revolvers there was the pepperbox—a small-caliber pistol with multiple rotating barrels configured something like the barrels of a Gatling gun or modern mini-gun. Whereas most handguns of that age had to be reloaded each time they were fired, pepperboxes would fire multiple times before they had to be reloaded. The small-caliber, double-action, percussion cap pepperboxes made by Allen and Thurber were the most common. Pepperboxes were point-heavy, inaccurate, and nearly impossible to aim, but they made excellent close-quarter personal defense weapons. Rusk, who had experienced previous difficulties with Wyant, was carrying two pepperboxes himself. Completely unaware of Wyant's entry, Rusk took no defensive actions. He simply stood by the stove with his arms folded across his chest.[1]

Pepperbox revolver similar to the one used by Isaac Wyant. FROM SCHAUBS, "MOUNTAIN MEN AND LIFE IN THE ROCKY MOUNTAIN WEST."

Wyant wasted no time, firing his first shot into Rusk's side. The second shot hit Rusk's shoulder, and the third went into his arm. By this time, Rusk was on the floor with Wyant standing over him. Wyant stooped, put the muzzle of the pepperbox to Rusk's head, and fired again.[2] Harry Kidder, after he recovered from the shock of what he had just seen, grabbed Wyant by the shoulder and told him he could "shoot no more." Wyant asked Kidder if he wanted to take up the fight, and Kidder replied, "No, but you can shoot no more here." Wyant turned and walked out of the office.[3]

Squire McGraw had been walking back to his office when he saw Wyant open the door to the office and walk in. McGraw heard Wyant's gunshots and Rusk's screams. Then the door to the office opened again, and Wyant walked out. He told McGraw, "I have shot the damned rascal that shot my arm off." Wyant left the courthouse, and McGraw went looking for Constable W. W. Williamson. The constable was in Taylor and Bell's store next door to the courthouse when he heard the shots, and he immediately went toward the source of the gunfire. He met McGraw, who demanded that he arrest Wyant.

Williamson caught Wyant a short distance from the courthouse, with the Allen revolver still in his hand. The constable had to wrestle it from his grasp. When Williamson told Wyant he was under arrest for the murder of Ason Rusk, he replied, "If I have killed him, damn his soul, that is just what I came here to do." Williamson searched Wyant and removed a second pepperbox from his person. The revolver in Wyant's hand had four empty barrels, and the one in his pocket had a full load of six balls. At some point during the arrest, Wyant threw up. As Williamson led Wyant back to the courthouse, Wyant begged him, "For God's sake, don't take me where I can see the dead man. His friends will shoot my poor body all to pieces." Williamson placed him in the courtroom in the custody of a jailer named Taylor until an examination could be held before two justices of the peace.[4] When Taylor asked if he wanted a lawyer, Wyant replied that he was a stranger in town and did not know any lawyers. Taylor recommended Leonard Swett.

Dr. Christopher Goodbrake had also heard the shots and immediately went to the courthouse. Wyant was leaving the courthouse and said something to Goodbrake about the shooting, but the doctor was too excited to take note of his words. The next person Goodbrake saw was Squire McGraw, who directed him into the clerk's office, where he found Rusk lying on the floor. Goodbrake made note of the locations of the gunshot wounds. Although he found the head wound to be the immediate cause of death, he believed the wound to the side was also a fatal injury.[5]

Leonard Swett, Lincoln's favorite trial partner. FROM THE ABRAHAM LINCOLN PRESIDENTIAL LIBRARY AND MUSEUM.

Coroner B. F. Hall took custody of the body and decided to leave it in place until the following morning, when an inquest could be held. While Hall was delaying the inquest in the clerk's office, Justices Daniel Robbins and Samuel Phares were going forward with the examination. The record of the examination shows that a lawyer, probably Leonard Swett, appeared on behalf of Wyant and asked for a continuance until the following morning. The justices granted the request.[6]

The next morning, B. F. Hall convened a coroner's jury over Rusk's body in the clerk's office. The verdict found that Ason Rusk "came to his death by four pistol shots, shot by one Isaac Wyant, on the 12th of October, 1855, which caused the immediate death of Ason Rusk."[7] That same morning in the courtroom, Justices Robbins and Phares held their examination, taking the testimony of David Taylor, W. W. Williams, Squire McGraw, Harry Kidder, and Dr. Christopher Goodbrake. At the conclusion of the examination, they ordered Wyant held without bail pending indictment by the DeWitt County grand jury.[8]

Given the bare-bones account of the shooting that came out at the examination, things looked very grim indeed for Isaac Wyant. Leonard Swett
wanted to know much more than what had happened that fatal day, however,
and he would have accompanied his client back to the jail to begin collecting
the facts to weave together into a defense. No record exists of how many
interviews Leonard Swett conducted with his client, but we do know that he
ferreted out every last detail that he could possibly use in the defense of Wyant.

Swett learned that the event that led to the killing had occurred in June
1855, when the Wyant and Rusk clans were embroiled in a heated dispute
over the ownership of a parcel of land in DeWitt County. The dispute had
wound up in the exact place where such disputes should be resolved—the
courtroom. On the evening after the trial, both parties traveled home on the
same road. The Rusk party left for home before the Wyants, but they did not
travel quite as fast, and the Wyants overtook them at a fork in the road where
one group was to go to the left and the other to the right. Recriminations had
flown hot and heavy between Ason Rusk and Isaac Wyant at the hearing, and
Rusk decided that the meeting on the roadway gave him a good opportunity
to have it out with Wyant. He stopped at the fork and waited. As the Wyant
party arrived at the fork, Rusk spoke.

"Ike, I want a word with you," he said. Wyant stopped and came toward
Rusk. "What did you threaten to whip me for?" Rusk wanted to know.

"For meddling in my brother's land," replied Wyant.

"If you want to fight, I can fight you fair right here and now," said Rusk.

Wyant retorted, "You are a God damned rascal, and I want nothing to
do with you."

Rusk threw off his coat, and Wyant did the same. What happened next is
a matter of dispute. According to the Wyant clan's version, as Ike attacked,
Rusk stepped back, pulled a pistol, and fired. The Rusks insisted that Ike
pulled a bowie knife and came at Rusk. Whichever way the fight started, all
agreed that the gunshot ended it. The pistol ball struck Wyant just below the
elbow, shattering the bones of his lower arm.[9]

The next day, three doctors attended Isaac Wyant as his arm was ampu-
tated. Dr. Warner administered chloroform, Dr. Lemon performed the am-
putation, and Dr. Goodbrake observed. Wyant at first refused the chloroform
but later consented. There was some problem with the dosage. The doctors
had trouble putting him under, and he regained consciousness during the
operation. Warner finally administered a dose of ether to render him fully
unconscious. After the operation, Wyant began to act strangely. He seemed
obsessed with two ideas: that Rusk would try to kill him again, and that he

should kill Rusk to avenge the loss of his arm. Recriminations flew back and forth between the two parties, and Wyant began stalking Rusk, who armed himself and went about his business. Rusk relaxed his vigilance, however, when Wyant left Illinois on a trip to Indiana and was unaware of Wyant's return to DeWitt County.[10]

The details of the backstory sowed the seed of an idea in Swett's head; he decided to water it. He held at least one interview with his client that was attended by Dr. Lemon. We know at least part of what was said during that interview because the jailer, Taylor, overheard it. In Wyant's presence, Swett asked Dr. Lemon whether the use of chloroform could have any lasting effect on the brain. Lemon gave him the conventional wisdom of the time: yes, chloroform could cause insanity.[11] Shortly after Swett and Lemon left the jail, Taylor brought Wyant his meal. When he approached Wyant, the prisoner began to engage in what Taylor later testified were "foolish actions." Taylor told Wyant, "You need not feign to be insane with me." Wyant ceased his foolish behavior and behaved normally for the rest of his stay in the DeWitt County Jail.[12]

As luck would have it, Wyant had killed Rusk on a Thursday, and the October term of the DeWitt County Circuit Court convened the following Monday. The first part of the week was occupied with civil trials, as Amzi McWilliams presented the accumulated cases of the past six months to the grand jury. Lincoln attended court defending the Illinois Central Railroad in three cases.[13] He also represented William Dungey, who was suing his brother-in-law Joseph Spencer for slander.[14] Lincoln spent Monday and Tuesday in legal maneuvering on his cases, but on Wednesday he went to trial on one of his railroad cases.

Wilson Allen had sued the railroad for common-law trespass. The declaration filed by his attorney, Leonard Swett, charged that the railroad had removed fifty thousand cubic feet of fill dirt from Allen's land and left it pockmarked with open borrow pits. Allen wanted just compensation for the damage done to his property.[15] The case went to trial on Wednesday (the day after the grand jury indicted Wyant for murder), and the jury awarded Allen $762.50 in damages. Some might say Allen won the case, but viewed from a different perspective, it could also be considered a loss, as he had asked for $5,000 in damages. McWilliams did not arraign Wyant on this day, probably because his lawyer, Leonard Swett, was busy trying the railroad case.

The next day, Lincoln tried the case of *Dungey v. Spencer*. Joseph Spencer had accused his brother-in-law William Dungey, who had a dark complexion, of being "a negro."[16] Dungey took exception to the accusation and hired Lincoln to file a slander suit against Spencer. At the trial, Lincoln single-handedly confronted three lawyers for the defense, one of whom, Clifton H. Moore, had been his co-counsel at the trial the day before. The jury returned a verdict for the plaintiff in the sum of $600.[17] As Swett was not tied up in a jury trial on this day, McWilliams brought Wyant up before the court and had him arraigned.[18]

On Friday, October 19, McWilliams called the Wyant case up for trial. Swett moved for and obtained a continuance of the trial. He also obtained an order that Wyant be housed in the Tazewell County Jail "because the jails of DeWitt, McLean, and Sangamon Counties are each insufficient to safely and comfortably keep the said Isaac Wyant."[19] At the May 1856 term of the DeWitt County Circuit Court, Swett obtained another continuance of the trial by moving for a change of venue to McLean County.[20] When the September term came around, Swett obtained another continuance,[21] meaning that the case would be tried in 1857, after McWilliams left office in the wake of his disastrous prosecution of the Andersons.

Swett's Fabian tactic of delay served two ends: it ensured that the case would be prosecuted by a lawyer who was not nearly as familiar with the case as McWilliams had been, and it gave Swett time to prepare an insanity defense to spring on the unprepared new prosecutor. The law books of the nineteenth century recognized the possibility of raising an insanity defense,[22] but it had been little used in the United States before Swett used it in the Wyant case.

Leonard Swett, dark haired and bushy browed, six feet five inches tall, and razor thin, looked so much like Abraham Lincoln that people often mistook him for Lincoln. They were both active, well-respected lawyers on the Eighth Circuit, but there the similarities ended. Lincoln grew up in poverty, worked hard with his hands, and got his "book learning" largely through self-study; Swett grew up in a wealthy family, attended college, and had an extensive classical education. Lincoln played at being a soldier in the Black Hawk War; Swett nearly died from illness caught while campaigning in Mexico during the Mexican-American War. Lincoln, hale and hearty, arrived in New Salem, Illinois, on a flatboat going to New Orleans and decided to settle there and live; Swett, emaciated from illness, walked into Bloomington, Illinois, coming from New Orleans, trying to get back home to Maine, and decided that he would die there. Lincoln's decision to live in New Salem eventually led him into a thriving career as a lawyer on the Eighth Circuit; Swett's decision to die in Bloomington eventually led him into a thriving career as a lawyer on the Eighth Circuit.[23] Despite their different backgrounds, the two men became fast friends, and with the addition of Judge David Davis, the trio became known as the Eighth Circuit's Great Triumvirate. According to Henry Clay

Whitney, of all the lawyers in the Eighth Circuit, Lincoln preferred Swett as his co-counsel. Whitney declared that Lincoln relied heavily on Swett, seeming to say, "I am alright now that Swett is with me."[24]

Swett had his work cut out for him. He had to learn the current medical knowledge on mental illness, investigate his client's behavior and background, and research the law relating to insanity. His first stumbling block was that Illinois had no law regarding the issue of insanity. The first appellate case to deal with insanity in the criminal setting was *Fisher v. People*,[25] decided by the Illinois Supreme Court two years after Wyant's trial. Swett was thus reduced to going to legal textbooks and the sparse case law cited in them to find his authorities. Swett diligently investigated the state of medical knowledge on the subject of mental health. He visited the Illinois State Lunatic Asylum and traveled to New York and Massachusetts, educating himself on the subject of mental health, and he read the Bible from cover to cover twice looking for scripture to quote in his arguments.[26] When the case came on for trial on March 31, 1857, Swett had taken advantage of the eighteen months since Wyant's arrest to conduct a thorough investigation of the facts of the case, learn what he needed to know about the treatment of mental disease, recruit his expert witnesses, and marshal his authorities. He was ready for trial. His co-counsel would be his partner, William Orme, who later distinguished himself as a general officer during the Civil War but unfortunately died from tuberculosis contracted while in service.[27]

Ward Hill Lamon, on the other hand, was definitely not in an enviable position. Having just taken over the office of state's attorney, and having inherited Amzi McWilliams's full criminal caseload for every county in the Eighth Circuit, Lamon found himself far less prepared than Swett. Lamon also must have realized that he, as merely an average trial lawyer, was badly outclassed by Leonard Swett. Faced with an important case (a murder), an arcane defense (insanity), and a highly competent adversary (Leonard Swett), Lamon needed help. He found that help in the person of three lawyers.

The first, Clifton H. Moore, had practiced in Clinton, DeWitt County, since 1841 and probably had an encyclopedic knowledge of the various lay witnesses who would be called on behalf of both the prosecution and the defense. His skill as a trial lawyer, however, is open to question. Moore was a town-dwelling attorney who did not travel the circuit.[28] He therefore could not have been a top-notch trial lawyer. Also recruited by Lamon to assist in the prosecution was a young attorney by the name of Harvey Hogg, a newcomer to Illinois. A native of Tennessee, Hogg had graduated as class valedictorian from Lebanon Law School (now Cumberland School of Law). Hogg had a well-deserved reputation as an orator, and the consensus of opinion was that he would go far in his profession. Although not an abolitionist, he steadfastly opposed slavery, and when the Civil War broke out, he raised several companies of Union cavalry. On August 30, 1862, Lt. Col. Harvey Hogg was killed in action while leading a cavalry charge at the Battle of Bolivar.[29]

Lamon's final recruit for the prosecution team was Abraham Lincoln, whose credentials as a criminal trial lawyer could not be questioned. His opportunity to prepare, however, can be questioned. Whereas Swett had eighteen months to prepare his case, Lincoln had at most three, and those three months were very busy. On January 4, 1857, the Republican legislative delegation caucused in Lincoln's law office in preparation for the opening of the legislative session the next day. Lincoln then spent the rest of the month shuttling back and forth between Federal Court and the Illinois Supreme Court. On Monday, January 12, he took time off from court to give a speech at the inauguration of Governor William Henry Bissell. During the first week of February, Lincoln spent his days in Federal Court and his evenings attending parties. On February 21, Lincoln departed Springfield for a business trip to Chicago. He returned home by train on March 4 and stayed in Springfield until the end of the week. He then departed to practice law on the circuit. His travels took him first to Clinton in DeWitt County, then to Lincoln in Logan County. From Lincoln he went to Peoria, and from Peoria he went to Metamora. On March 30, he handled a civil case in Metamora and then traveled to Bloomington, where he made the opening statement in the case of *People v. Wyant* on March 31, 1857.[30] At some time during this busy three-month period, Lincoln agreed to assist Lamon and familiarized himself as best he could with the facts of the case. He was woefully unprepared for the case that Leonard Swett had built over the past eighteen months.

Judge Davis spent the morning of March 31 dealing with other matters, but he took up the Wyant case immediately after the noon meal.[31] Jury selection took some time, and the panel was exhausted without seating the required number of jurors. The sheriff had to go out to bring in supplemental jurors before a full complement of twelve could be seated. Lincoln made the opening statement for the prosecution; Swett reserved making his opening until after the close of the prosecution case. Lincoln then called and examined the prosecution witnesses and, as the *Daily Pantagraph* reported, "a clear prima facie case having been made out by the witnesses, the State's evidence closed the same evening."[32]

A prosecutor needs five ingredients to ensure a conviction: (a) an *a*greeable jury, (e) an *e*gregious crime, (i) an *i*nnocent victim, (o) an *o*dious defendant, and (u) *u*ndeniable guilt. Of the five vowels, (a) is the most important, and the next three, (e), (i), and (o), are essential for the prosecutor to have that critical first ingredient. No matter how undeniable the guilt of the accused, if the jurors are not upset about the crime, if they dislike the victim, and if they sympathize with the defendant, the verdict is going to be not guilty. On the face of things, the Wyant case had all the vowels. There was no denying that Wyant had shot and killed Rusk. Rusk was taken unaware with his arms folded and did nothing to either provoke the attack or defend himself. Wyant ambushed Rusk and shot him multiple times, then he walked over, pressed the muzzle of his handgun to Rusk's head, and executed him. When the doctor got there, Rusk's brains were oozing out of his head and onto the floor. Jailer Taylor stood ready to testify that Wyant was faking his insanity.

This seemingly ironclad case led the prosecution team into a grievous error. They put on evidence only of what happened the day that Wyant shot Rusk. The evidence of the prior shooting was clearly relevant to prove motive, but they did not have a single witness testify about the circumstances of the prior shooting. This gave Swett an excellent opportunity to turn the tables on the innocent victim and odious defendant scenario. Swett got to tell the story of the first shooting in the light most favorable to the defendant. The defense version of events was that Rusk had called Wyant out and challenged him to fight, and when Wyant took up the offer, Rusk cravenly shot the unarmed Wyant's arm off. The prosecution responded by putting on rebuttal evidence tending to show that Wyant had attacked Rusk with a knife, but the story would have been much stronger and more believable if it had been told as part of the prosecution's case in chief. As it was told in rebuttal, it sounded like a lame excuse for Rusk's misbehavior. There is an old saying among trial lawyers that whoever tells the best story wins. The way the stories unfolded at trial, it appeared that the prosecution told only half the story to begin with, the defense then added important detail, and the prosecution tried to repair the damage by making excuses. If the prosecution had begun with a story of the dastardly Wyant repeatedly attacking Rusk until Wyant finally killed him, then the defense would have been the side that appeared to be making excuses.

Seizing the opportunity to be the first to tell the story of the initial encounter between Rusk and Wyant, Swett transformed Rusk from victim to villain. After erasing the innocent victim, Swett set about to erase the odious defendant. Swett called witness after witness to testify to Wyant's changed behavior after the first shooting: his throwing up immediately after the shooting, his fear of seeing Rusk's dead body, his depression, his paranoid fear that Rusk would kill him, his fixation on his missing arm, his insisting that his severed arm be exhumed so that he could inspect it, his feelings of sensation in his missing fingers, his picking at his head, his accusing his sister of shooting his arm off. One after another, the relatives of Isaac Wyant took the stand and painted as bleak a picture as they possibly could of the grievous injury Wyant had suffered at Rusk's hands.

Having erased the odious defendant and transformed his client from villain to victim, Swett's final step was to erase the egregious crime. It was time for a parade of doctors to take the stand and testify that Wyant was insane. Swett had recruited an impressive array of medical men to take the stand and render that opinion. Probably the most impressive of the lot was Dr. Andrew McFarland, the director of the Illinois State Lunatic Asylum. It cannot be said that Lincoln was blindsided by Swett's defense, but he was completely taken aback by the number and quality of the witnesses. Lincoln put on a spirited rebuttal, but Swett had told a much better story for the defense than Lincoln had told for the prosecution. The jury had been persuaded by Swett's portrayal of a villainous victim and a victimized defendant. With their sympathies in favor of the defendant, they merely needed an excuse to vote for acquittal, and the insanity defense provided that excuse. Once they had the excuse to return the congenial acquittal, the prosecution would be hard-pressed to move them back toward an uncongenial conviction.

The evidence closed on Thursday, April 2, and Judge Davis adjourned court at 6 p.m. The next morning, Harvey Hogg gave the prosecution's opening final argument. His argument lasted three hours, after which Judge Davis recessed court for the noon meal. That afternoon, William Orme spoke on behalf of the defense for three hours, and then Swett took the stage. Judge Davis stopped him at 6 p.m. and recessed court for the day. He said Swett could conclude his argument on Saturday morning. The next morning, Swett spoke until noon. After the noon meal, Lincoln closed for the prosecution, finishing his speech a little before 6 p.m. Of the arguments of counsel, the *Daily Pantagraph* said, "We are sorry that we cannot furnish a sketch of the speeches of the several counsel. They were all eloquent and powerful. Those of the senior counsel on either side [Lincoln and Swett], in particular, were models of forensic eloquence."[33]

Judge Davis then instructed the jury on the law, and here again Swett scored a marked victory, persuading Davis to give jury instructions that were very favorable to the defense. The jury deliberated until 1 A.M. on Sunday, April 5,[34] when they returned a verdict finding Wyant not guilty by reason of insanity and "earnestly recommend[ing] that the Honorable Court take the necessary steps to have him the said Isaac Wyant removed immediately to the State Lunatic Asylum at Jacksonville."[35]

The very next day, Lincoln was back in his law office in Springfield writing a legal opinion for J. K. DuBois on the duties of an auditor under the newly enacted banking laws.[36] Leonard Swett was still in court in McLean County. He presented Judge Davis with a pleading stating that his client Isaac Wyant was insane and requesting that the judge begin legal proceedings to have Wyant committed. Davis convened a jury of six men, and evidence was presented. At the close of the evidence, this second jury returned a verdict finding Wyant insane and recommending that he be committed.[37]

Davis committed Wyant to the Illinois State Lunatic Asylum, where he became a guest of the star witness for his defense, Dr. Andrew McFarland. After the passage of two or three years, Wyant was declared sane and released. He returned to DeWitt County but did not stay long. He moved to Indiana, much to the relief of those witnesses whom he had threatened to kill for testifying against him. For years afterward, however, the witnesses feared that Wyant might come back and make good on his threat.[38]

In the latter part of April 1857, when the circuit court had come to Danville, Attorney Joseph E. McDonald overheard Lincoln and Swett discussing a murder trial that Lincoln had prosecuted and Swett had defended on a plea of insanity. McDonald asked them the name of the defendant, and they replied that his name was Isaac Wyant. "Why, when I practiced law in Indiana, I represented him for every crime on the calendar," said McDonald. The next day, Lincoln approached McDonald and asked if he thought Wyant might have been "possuming" insanity. Lincoln suspected this but was not sure and did not want to punish a man who was really insane. McDonald told this story to Jesse W. Weik in August 1888, when Weik was helping William Henry Herndon do the research for a biography of Lincoln. We cannot be sure of the precise words that passed between McDonald and Lincoln, because McDonald was telling the story thirty years after the fact, and Weik was not taking good notes on the interview. Weik made no record of McDonald's response as to whether he thought Wyant was "possuming."[39] What we can be sure of, however, is that Swett mounted such a good defense that he had Lincoln questioning whether Wyant might not really be insane.

It was probably at the same term of court when Lincoln and McDonald discussed Wyant that Lincoln received a letter from an old and dear friend of his, Colonel James G. Sloo, a powerful leader of the Democratic Party in southern Illinois. Sloo had a bitter enemy, John E. Hall, the clerk of the circuit court in Shawneetown. The colonel was a candidate for public office, and someone had written an unflattering letter about him to the local newspaper. The writer signed his name "Vindex," but it was assumed that Hall had written the letter. Sloo's son, Robert, was incensed because the letter did not just assault his father; it libeled his sisters as well. In what was almost a reenactment of the Wyant-Rusk killing, Robert C. Sloo went to the clerk's office, where he found Hall standing, dictating an official document to his deputy clerk, Robert G. Ingersoll. There in the clerk's office, in front of Ingersoll, Sloo shot Hall to death with a pepperbox revolver.[40] The defense was going to be insanity, and Colonel Sloo wanted Lincoln to come to Shawneetown to join his son's defense team.

Lincoln was in the company of a group of lawyers when he received the letter. He read the letter in their presence, and he usually read aloud. He immediately turned to Leonard Swett and said, "Mr. Swett, I want you to go in my place."

"I am unknown to the parties," Swett protested, "and they would not be satisfied with the change."

"Mr. Swett," Lincoln said earnestly, "if I can get you to go, it is not fair to that young man and his family that I should go." Swett agreed to go if Lincoln would pave the way with a letter of recommendation.[41]

Lincoln wrote the letter; Sloo accepted Swett as counsel for his son; and Lincoln's instincts proved correct. The trial lasted over a month during the summer of 1857 and more than one hundred witnesses testified. One key witness for the defense was Dr. Andrew McFarland of the Illinois State Lunatic Asylum. The jury found the defendant not guilty by reason of insanity, and he was committed to the asylum under McFarland's care. The trial received nationwide newspaper coverage,[42] and the *American Journal of Insanity* devoted thirty-five pages to describing the testimony at the trial.[43] The next time Lincoln and Swett tried a homicide case, they were on the same side.

13.

PEOPLE versus JOHN BANTZHOUSE, October 2, 1857

THIS IS THE FIRST IN A STUDY OF THREE CASES THAT LINCOLNOCLASTS HAVE
cited as examples of underhanded tactics employed by Lincoln. In this first
case, he supposedly used pretrial maneuvering to delay a murder case past the
expiration of the speedy trial deadline, and thus freed a stone-cold killer; in
the second, he purportedly aided and abetted the escape of another murderer;
and in the third, he allegedly manufactured evidence, suborned perjury, and
made an inflammatory argument to trick a jury into finding a murderer not
guilty. At least, those are the charges leveled against him by his critics. This
and the next two chapters delve into the facts of these three cases and examine
how badly Lincoln may have misbehaved in them.

January 1, 1857, began a new era in Sangamon County. The legislature
had removed the county from Lincoln's beloved Eighth Circuit and put it in
a newly created Eighteenth Circuit. This meant that the county had a new
circuit judge, E. Y. Rice, and a new state's attorney, James B. White. The
Illinois State Journal recognized White's youth and inexperience but said
that he "has application and industry, and we presume will discharge the
duties of his office with ability and propriety."[1] The *Journal* went on to say
that the grand jury would take up the case of "People v. John Brunthouse,"
charged with murder for the shooting death of Walter Clark. The misspelling
of Bantzhouse's name in the newspaper proved to be merely the first of a
series of literary errors that dogged the case.

The events leading up to the case began when John Bantzhouse entertained
a group of men at his house on Friday evening, February 20, 1857, and the
party got out of hand. A disagreement degenerated into a brawl, and someone
knocked over an oil lamp, throwing the room into darkness. Despite the lack
of light, the brawl continued. Bantzhouse decided on an ill-advised method of
breaking up the fight: he snatched up his shotgun, stepped outside, and fired
it through a window into the room filled with combatants. Twenty-five lead
pellets hit Walter Clark in the chest and side, killing him instantly.[2]

On Sunday, February 22, Young M. Hudson and George M. Maxwell swore out an affidavit before Justice of the Peace H. M. Harmon seeking Bantzhouse's arrest for murder. Harmon issued the warrant, and the constable arrested Bantzhouse that same day.[3] Bantzhouse sat in jail until May 2, when the Sangamon County grand jury returned an indictment purportedly charging him with two counts of murder. Stripped of its redundancies, the first count alleged, "The Grand chosen selected and sworn . . . present that on the twenty third day of February [1857]," John Bantzhouse made an assault on Walter Clark with a shotgun and "shot and sent forth as aforesaid the Walter Clark in and upon the breast and side of him the said Walter Clark," inflicting a mortal wound four inches deep. Thus the first count said the grand something or other, possibly the grand jury, charged that one day after being arrested for murdering Clark, Bantzhouse killed Clark by performing the impossible feat of shooting Walter Clark out of the barrel of the shotgun "in and upon the breast and side of him the said Walter Clark." The second count charged Bantzhouse with murdering Clark on February 22, one day after Clark's death. It did, however, properly identify the grand jury as the charging body and said that Bantzhouse shot Clark with buckshot.[4] White had fumbled the drafting of the indictment. Would Bantzhouse's lawyers take advantage of the blunder?

Bantzhouse hired a stable of defense lawyers: John A. McClernand, Elliot B. Herndon, George W. Schutt, Wilford D. Wyatt, William Henry Herndon, and Abraham Lincoln.[5] Of Lincoln's co-counsel, McClernand had the most talent. A colleague of Lincoln's in the Illinois legislature, a congressman, soon to become a distinguished Civil War general, McClernand was a man to be reckoned with.[6]

With six sets of eyes studying the indictment, the defense team should have readily discerned the issues with its sufficiency. But if Bantzhouse's team of lawyers noticed the deficiencies, they did not immediately take advantage of them. Instead, they moved for a continuance, which Judge Rice granted. When the case came up for trial the following August, the *Illinois State Register* erroneously reported that jury selection began on Wednesday of the first week of the term.[7] The next day, the *Register* ran a correction: "In our yesterday's paper we were somewhat mistaken in relation to the case of the People vs. Barnshousel. Instead of taking up the afternoon of Wednesday in procuring a jury in this case; the defendant took a change of venue, and he will be sent to Macoupin county for trial."[8]

When the case came up for trial in Macoupin County, Judge Rice dismissed the indictment and ordered Bantzhouse released from jail. White tried to get Bantzhouse rearrested, but according to the *Journal*, "before another indictment

John A. McClernand, a formidable trial lawyer and one of many lawyers who attained the rank of general during the Civil War. PHOTOGRAPH COURTESY OF THE LIBRARY OF CONGRESS.

could be framed, he had made use of leg-bail and taken to the woods."[9] In a maneuver reminiscent of the one attempted in the Fraim case, the defense team got the venue changed, got the indictment dismissed, and got their client freed. Their client then fled the jurisdiction before the state's attorney had an opportunity to go back to Sangamon County and get him reindicted.

Almost everything written about the Bantzhouse case declares that Lincoln got the case dismissed for violation of his client's right to a speedy trial.[10] This misinterpretation of the evidence comes from the paucity of the original records, which merely say that the judge quashed the indictment without saying why.[11] In casting about for an explanation, nonlawyer historians hit upon the following provision from the Illinois habeas corpus statute: "If any person shall be committed for a criminal, or supposed criminal matter, and not admitted to bail, and shall not be tried on or before the second term of the court having jurisdiction of the offence, the prisoner shall be set at liberty by the court, unless the delay shall happen on the application of the prisoner."[12]

Applying the statute to Bantzhouse, it seemed obvious that he got released because he was not tried quickly enough. This leads to the conclusion that with a motion to continue and a motion for change of venue, Lincoln maneuvered the inexperienced White into letting the speedy trial time run. There are two problems with that interpretation: First, the provision comes from the habeas corpus statute, and therefore the remedy for failure to try Bantzhouse within the prescribed time would be a writ of habeas corpus, not a dismissal of the indictment. And second, the statute does not apply when the accused causes the delay. Bantzhouse's motion to continue delayed the case. His motion for change of venue further delayed the case. He had no right to relief under the statute.

White got outmaneuvered, but speedy trial had nothing to do with it. A close study of the judge's docket for the September term of 1857 tells the tale of what really happened. Nine cases are listed on the page of the docket where Bantzhouse's case appears, and the space in the judge's docket for each case was limited. The disposition of eight of those cases is described in very few words, but so much happened with Bantzhouse's case that the entry for his case fills all the space available.

The first entry in the Bantzhouse case was made on October 1. The September term of court convened on the fourth Monday, September 28. This means that White waited four days to call up the Bantzhouse case. This is odd, because murder cases usually take precedence over other cases. White had made his witnesses post bond swearing they would appear to testify on the fourth Monday in September,[13] indicating that was when he intended to start the trial. He must have had a good reason for delaying the Bantzhouse case, and the judge's docket shows us what it was: a key witness failed to appear to testify.

Looking at the docket entry by entry, the first one reads, "Oct 1 Motion to quash second count sustained." This means that the defense indeed recognized the problems with the wording of the indictment and chose to attack the legal sufficiency of the second count. At first blush, this seems strange, because White actually did a better job of pleading the second count than he did the first. Why attack the better pleaded count and let the more poorly pleaded count stand? There was method in the defense team's madness, and it is revealed in the docket.

The second entry reads, "deft arraigned and pleads not guilty." Now the defense attorneys, by entering a plea of not guilty, waived the right to contest formal defects in the indictment. They moved to dismiss the second count before pleading because it contained only formal defects. They believed that the first count was so poorly worded that it was fatally defective, and entry of a plea would not waive the defendant's right to raise its defects at a later time, possibly on a motion to arrest judgment after the defendant was convicted.

They would thus get two opportunities to free their client: one opportunity on a not guilty verdict and one opportunity to arrest judgment if the jury found him guilty. It was about this time that White realized he had been outmaneuvered.

The third entry in the docket reads, "States atty moves to nolle pros." By entry of a nolle prosequi, the state's attorney dismisses the charge. This entry tells us that White realized his error and asked permission to drop all charges so he could reindict Bantzhouse with a properly worded indictment. In making this motion, White almost made an even bigger error, but Judge Rice saved him by taking the motion under advisement without immediately ruling on it. Then White asked that a writ of attachment be issued for the arrest of the key witness who had failed to appear. That ended the maneuvering for October 1, but Judge Rice revisited the case the next day.

The first docket entry for October 2 says, "Motion to nolle pros withdraw by states atty." It seems that during the overnight recess, White realized that the Macoupin County grand jury had no authority to indict Bantzhouse. He had to go back before a Sangamon County grand jury to get an indictment. This could not be done until the next term of court in Sangamon County. If Judge Rice had allowed the nolle prosequi on October 1, Bantzhouse would have been released from jail and would be long gone before another indictment could be filed.

When the defense saw that White was not going to bring the case on for trial but was going to let Bantzhouse sit in jail until he got a new indictment at the next term of Sangamon County Circuit Court, it moved to dismiss the indictment. The final two entries of the docket read, "Motion to quash indictment sustained. Prisoner discharged." White had bungled his first murder prosecution. The *Illinois State Journal* described what happened in the following words: "Upon motion the indictment was quashed for informality; the prisoner was discharged under some statutory provision, and before another indictment could be framed, he had made use of leg-bail and taken to the woods. It is probable that he will not be heard of very speedily in this part of the country."[14] Bantzhouse was never heard from again.

Under the common law, when an indictment was dismissed for "informality," it meant that something was wrong about the way the indictment came to be filed—either some impropriety with the grand jury or some impropriety with the wording of the indictment. Courts were quicker to dismiss an indictment for informality than they were to arrest judgment for informality, because on a dismissed indictment, the defendant could be retried; on an arrested judgment, he could argue that he was protected from prosecution by former jeopardy. For example, in *State v. Noblett*,[15] the North Carolina

Supreme Court reversed a trial court that arrested judgment in a murder case where the indictment charged that the defendant had inflicted a mortal "blow" upon the victim rather than a mortal "wound." Had the defense moved to dismiss before arraignment, the court probably would have upheld the trial court's ruling.[16]

The defense team outmaneuvered the rookie prosecutor and set a killer free without punishment using tactics that modern courts condemn as a "gotcha maneuver."[17] Lincoln, however, deserves no censure—he was not there. Apparently someone decided that with six lawyers, Bantzhouse had an overabundance of attorneys, and Lincoln dropped out of the case. On Monday, September 28, when Bantzhouse was scheduled to go to trial, Lincoln was in Springfield drafting a mortgage.[18] He was likewise in Springfield on September 29 and 30, tending to personal business.[19] It is barely possible, but highly unlikely, that after finishing his personal business on September 30, Lincoln dashed the forty-five miles to Carlinville so that he could attend court. For all Lincoln knew, the Bantzhouse case was already over by October 1. Although at the beginning of his career, Lincoln may have attempted a similar maneuver in the Fraim case, he had nothing to do with White's defeat in the Bantzhouse case. The credit, or blame, for the sharp maneuver that freed the killer should be laid at the feet of John A. McClernand.[20]

14.

PEOPLE versus MELISSA GOINGS, October 10, 1857

ROSWELL GOINGS, A "QUARRELSOME AND BIBULOUS" OLD FARMER WHO LIVED in Worth Township, Woodford County, wanted his wife to shut up.[1] Melissa Goings wanted to keep talking. It was a silly argument over whether a kitchen window should be up or down, but it would cost Roswell Goings his life. When Melissa disobeyed his order to be quiet, Roswell got out of his rocking chair at the kitchen table and hobbled to the window where she stood. Seventy-seven years old and somewhat unsteady on his feet, Roswell spent most of his time sitting and drinking. When he got within arm's reach of Melissa, he grabbed her by the throat and began to choke her. She struggled and was able to free herself from his stranglehold. Satisfied that he had taught Melissa proper respect, Roswell hobbled back to his rocking chair. Melissa went to the stack of firewood by the kitchen stove and chose a stout piece of stove wood about the length of a man's arm. She was not through talking. "Come back here and try that again," she challenged. Roswell got up and went over to her again. As he came close to her, she drew her arm back to strike with the club. Roswell turned away, and Melissa's first blow landed on his back. He fell to the floor on his face, and her next two blows landed on the back of his head.

Josephus Goings heard the commotion from another room and rushed into the kitchen to find his father lying on the floor and his mother standing over Roswell with a bloody stick in her hand. Melissa said simply, "I struck him." Josephus saw that Roswell was trying to get back up but not having much success. He went over to his father and helped the injured man to his rocking chair. Josephus washed the blood from Roswell's head and ministered to the wounds as best he could. Roswell remained conscious for a few hours but eventually slipped into a coma from which he never recovered. He was dead within a week.

Word spread about the incident, and a number of people gathered at the house. Although Josephus insisted that his father never spoke after being injured,[2] James Brady reported hearing Roswell make statements that could arguably be considered dying declarations. According to Brady, who saw

Roswell about two hours after the incident, Roswell confided that he and his wife were having words about the window, and he had put his hands on her and told her to hush. She dared him to do it again; he went over and she struck him. Roswell concluded by saying, "I expect she has killed me."[3] Chapter 1 discussed the four requisites for a dying declaration to be admissible in evidence: (1) the prosecution must be for unlawful homicide; (2) the declarant must know that he is dying; (3) the statement must relate to the cause of his death; and (4) the declarant must die. To these four requirements, a qualification must be added: Simon Greenleaf, the leading authority on evidence in Lincoln's time, held that "where it appears that the deceased, at the time of the declaration, had any expectation or hope of recovery, however slight . . . , the declaration is inadmissible."[4] Although Roswell said, "I expect she has killed me," Roswell Hibbs, another visitor, testified that Roswell Goings told him, "If I get over it I will have revenge."[5]

When Coroner Benjamin Kindig arrived at the Goings farm to conduct the inquest, he found that the family had already buried Roswell. Since it was essential that the coroner's jury examine the body, Kindig ordered Constable John Lane to exhume Roswell's body and return it to the scene of the killing.[6] At the inquest, the coroner's jury learned that Melissa and Roswell "lived rather disagreeable,"[7] and that two days before the incident, Melissa had told Joshua Van Wilson, "If I ever have to strike Roswell I mean to kill him if I can."[8] After hearing all the evidence, the coroner's jury returned the following verdict:

> We, the undersigned, jurors impaneled and sworn on the 21st day of April, in the year 1857, in the township of Worth, in the county of Woodford, in the state of Illinois, by Benjamin W. Kindig, Coroner, to inquire & true presentment make, in what manner & by whom Roswell Goings, found suddenly deceased on the 18th of the present month, came to his death. After having examined the said body & hearing the evidence, we do find, that the deceased came to his death by violence; & that said body has on it the following marks & wounds inflicted by Malisa Goings, the wife of the deceased; a bruise on the back, & a long deep cut on the head & the skull much fractured, & the brains injured, & which the jury find did cause the death of said person in five days from their infliction.[9]

Two days later, Melissa Goings appeared at an examination before Justices of the Peace Robert T. Cassell and Joseph Morley, who took evidence and found probable cause to believe that Melissa Goings had unlawfully killed her husband. They did, however, set bail in the amount of $1,000. Under Illinois law at the time, defendants charged with murder could not be released on bail unless it was shown that the "proof is [not] evident and the presumption [is not] great."[10] This means that they believed that the prosecution had, at best, only a weak case of murder against Melissa. Another sign that the prosecution had a questionable case was that Armstrong Goings, a blood relative of the victim, posted bail for Melissa.[11]

Melissa went free on bail, but State's Attorney Hugh Fullerton had other ideas. On October 8, 1857, Fullerton had the Woodford County grand jury indict Melissa for murder. When the grand jury returned the indictment in open court, Fullerton asked that Judge James Harriott order a capias issued for the arrest of Melissa Goings.[12] There is some confusion over whether she was actually taken into custody on this capias. Although some authorities say that she was,[13] a careful reading of the court minutes seems to indicate that the capias had not yet been served on her. The capias itself, which could give a definitive answer to the question, seems to have disappeared from the court records.

On October 10, Melissa Goings appeared before Judge Harriott for arraignment. Fullerton intended to immediately begin Melissa's trial, but Lincoln asked for a brief recess to speak privately with his client. The court minutes described the proceedings as follows:

> This day came the people by Hugh Fullerton states attorney as well the defendant in her proper person attended by [Henry] Groves & [Abraham] Lincoln her attorneys. A copy of the indictment, list of jurors & witnesses having been furnished & given to defendant. The defendant being arraigned and called on for a plea & for plea herein says she is not guilty.
>
> [Brief recess].
>
> And now afterwards on the same day this cause coming on further to be heard the defendant being called came not and also Armstrong Goings & Samuel Beck her sureties being called came not to produce the body of Melissa Goings.
>
> It is therefore ordered by the court that the recognizance in this cause be forfeited and that scire facias issue herein returnable to next term of this court.[14]

Thus Melissa appeared before the court with her lawyers, and after pleading not guilty, she was free to accompany them out of the courtroom. Had she been arrested on the capias, she would most likely have remained in the custody of the sheriff during the recess. When the recess was over and she did not appear, the judge ordered her $1,000 bail forfeited. If she had been under arrest, the sureties on her bail would have already been discharged from their obligation of producing her in court, and their money would have already been returned to them.

What happened to Melissa Goings during that recess? In the village of Metamora, the scene of the Goings trial, the oral history gives two versions. In one version, Lincoln and Melissa went outside the courthouse and walked in the park across the street. Only Lincoln returned from that walk. The old courthouse still stands in Metamora, having been converted into a museum, and it still faces on Village Square Park. On August 22, 2009, the village of Metamora unveiled two statues in the park to commemorate this first version of the tale. One statue depicts Lincoln, tall and thin, wearing a stovepipe hat, and the other Melissa Goings, small and frail, wrapped in a shawl. As he walks, Lincoln gestures with his hand as if making a point, and Melissa turns her head as if to make sure she understands what he has to say.[15] The second version says that the two simply retired to a private room downstairs in the courthouse. Lincoln departed the room through the door, but Melissa left through an exterior window.

Ambrotype of Lincoln, taken as he rode the circuit around the time he represented Melissa Goings. PHOTOGRAPH COURTESY OF THE LIBRARY OF CONGRESS.

The two versions agree that Lincoln came back to the courtroom alone. Judge Harriott was supposedly prejudiced against Melissa in some way, and Lincoln feared his bias might result in Melissa being hanged. Melissa's disappearance might have disappointed some in the packed courtroom who had come to see the spectacle of a murder trial defended by Lincoln, but others may have been gladdened that she had fled. According to oral history, sympathy for Melissa ran high in the county, and few wanted to see her prosecuted. When Melissa failed to appear, the bailiff accused Lincoln of "running her off," and Judge Harriott allegedly demanded that Lincoln come forward and explain what had happened. Lincoln is supposed to have replied in a clear voice, "Your honor, I did not chase her off. She simply asked me where she could get a good drink of water, and I said Tennessee has mighty fine drinking water." At this remark, the courtroom erupted in laughter.[16] Our best evidence for the proposition that this exchange in open court between judge and lawyer never happened is the fact that Harriott did not hold Lincoln in contempt of court.

The story of the Tennessee drinking water did not become current until June 1921, when it was told at a retirement supper for Judge George W. Patton. William L. Elwood, a member of the Woodford County bar, related the story, which had been told to him by the court bailiff, Robert T. Cassell. According to Cassell, who also served as a justice of the peace:

> Mrs. Goings was brought into court that Lincoln might talk to her. After a while I was told by the state's attorney to bring her up for trial, but she could not be found. I asked Lincoln about her and he said he did not know where she was.
>
> I replied, "Confound you, Abe, you have run her off."
>
> "Oh, no, Bob," replied Lincoln, "I did not run her off. She wanted to know where she could get a good drink of water, and I told her there was mighty good water in Tennessee."[17]

Some have suggested that there might have been collusion with law enforcement to help Melissa escape. The only evidence of this is the fact that she was seventy years old and had only a few minutes' head start. Law enforcement officers in the prime of life ought to have easily caught a seventy-year-old woman on foot before she got to the county line. Collusion is less likely than simple lack of enthusiasm for the hunt. It would not be the first time, or the last, that a law enforcement officer pursued a fugitive at a leisurely pace because he felt more sympathy for the suspect than the victim. Melissa Goings never returned to Woodford County, and the charges against her were eventually dropped. She was last heard from in 1865 in Tehama County, California, where she executed a deed selling her interest in the Goings homestead in Woodford County to Frank Joseph Sikle.[18]

Now, back to the question of whether Lincoln counseled his client to flee. We can discount the story for two good reasons: First, the story is based on secondhand hearsay related sixty-two years after the fact. This hardly constitutes proof of anything unless some corroboration can be found for it. And second, Hugh Fullerton had none of the five ingredients a prosecutor needs to ensure a conviction: (a) an agreeable jury, (e) an egregious crime, (i) an innocent victim, (o) an odious defendant, and (u) undeniable guilt. The jury was not likely to be agreeable, as it was going to be drawn from a county where sympathy ran high for the defendant. The crime was hardly egregious—a battered spouse killed an abusive husband who was in the act of trying to strangle her. Roswell Goings, a quarrelsome drunk, was by no means an innocent victim. Melissa, a seventy-year-old victim of spousal abuse, was not an odious defendant. And guilt was far from undeniable, because Melissa had a colorable claim of self-defense. The justices of the peace admitted Melissa to bond, demonstrating that they thought the case against Melissa was weak. Why would Lincoln counsel his client to run when he was almost assured of victory if he stood and fought? Even if Melissa got convicted, it would be for manslaughter at most, and with Lincoln's record for getting pardons, he should have had her freed before she could be transported to prison.

In trying to discern how the story came to be told at all, we can infer a possible source from two unrelated literary references: Lincoln's secretary, John Hay, and his colleague, Usher F. Linder. In his diary for July 18, 1863, Hay recorded an anecdote Lincoln had told him about Linder: "He told one good story about U. F. Linder getting a fellow off who had stolen a hog, by advising him to go and get a drink, suggesting that the water was better in Tennessee."[19] Linder told the story on himself in *Reminiscences of the Early Bench and Bar of Illinois*. After the prosecution had rested its case, Linder and his co-counsel, Anthony Thornton, conferred with their client and told him that he was almost certainly going to be convicted.

"Shall I take to the brush?" asked the hog thief.

"Oh, no," Linder replied sarcastically, "I should be very loath to give you such advice as that; but this is a very warm day, and you must be thirsty, and the water here is about as bad as any I ever drank." Linder then turned to his co-counsel and said, "Anthony, don't you think the water in Kentucky is a great deal better than here?" Thornton enthusiastically agreed.

Linder turned back to his client and said, "If you are dry, go and get a drink; your presence is not particularly needed here during the argument, and we will make that consume the rest of the day." To give their client a good head start, they prolonged their arguments as much as possible, and it was several hours before the prosecutors noticed that the defendant was missing. The jury returned a verdict of guilty, but the client was long gone. Major Poor, one of the prosecutors, confronted Linder: "Your client has 'cut sticks,' and I am inclined to think you advised it."

Linder replied:

Oh, no, Major. I hope you don't entertain such an opinion of me. I didn't advise him to run away. During the trial he asked me if he should take to the brush and I told him no; "but," said I to him, "as the day is hot, and you are perhaps thirsty, and being out on bail, you have a right to go and get a drink of water," and that was all I said to him; but I asked Mr. Thornton in his presence, Major, if he did not think the water in Kentucky was much better than in Illinois, and he said it certainly was. Now, Major, if my client should have taken this as a hint to leave and jump his bail, I shall feel exceedingly sorrowful.

"The Devil take you and your sorrow!" the prosecutor replied. Linder decided to skip that county during the next term of court.[20]

Although Linder gives no indication of when this incident occurred, we can date it to sometime before 1853. Kirby Benedict, one of the prosecutors, was appointed to the federal bench in that year. Lincoln surely remembered the incident when Melissa Goings disappeared. His recollection of Linder's comical misbehavior may have inspired him to make the quip to Cassell, but it is unlikely that he made such a suggestion to Melissa Goings.

15.

PEOPLE versus WILLIAM DUFF ARMSTRONG, May 7, 1858

OPEN-AIR REVIVALS WERE POPULAR EVENTS IN ANTEBELLUM ILLINOIS. WOR-
shipers would set up a temporary tent village at some rural location, build a
stage, and hold religious services. Sometimes these camp meetings, as they
were called, lasted two or three weeks. Inevitably, some of the worshipers
got thirsty for something stronger than water, and drunken rowdies would
plague the camp meetings. Laws prohibited the selling of intoxicating li-
quors within a mile of any camp meeting, but this did not solve the problem.
Wherever there was a camp meeting, at a mile distance there would be a
whiskey camp.

On the evening of August 29, 1857, at a whiskey camp just outside a camp
meeting in Walnut Grove, Mason County, Illinois, James Preston Metzker
got into a fight with William Duff Armstrong. Armstrong later claimed that
Metzker, who was armed with a loaded whip, bullied him beyond endurance,
and he struck Metzker a mighty blow with his fist. Metzker, being a bigger
man, then overpowered Armstrong and took him to the ground. William
A. Douglas and George Dowell intervened and pulled Metzker off Armstrong. According to Douglas, "We could not tell how badly Metzker was
hit. His eye was fearfully blackened and we washed him. I said 'George, his
skull is cracked.'"[1] Metzker may have received a grievous injury, but he was
not through fighting. Later that night, he tangled with James H. Norris and
received another mighty blow to the head. After this, Metzker went home,
took to his bed, languished for several days, and died.

The Mason County grand jury indicted Armstrong and Norris for murder
on November 5. Judge Harriott appointed William Walker to defend Norris,
but Armstrong's widowed mother scraped together enough money to hire
a young attorney named Caleb Dilworth, who later distinguished himself
in the Civil War, achieving the rank of brevet brigadier general.[2] Dilworth
immediately moved for a change of venue, but Walker took Norris to trial.
The jury found Norris guilty of manslaughter and set his punishment at

eight years. Judge Harriott then granted Dilworth's motion and transferred the case to Cass County.

On November 16, the circuit court convened in Beardstown, the seat of Cass County, and State's Attorney Hugh Fullerton called up the Armstrong case for trial—but he could not go forward. The record had not been transferred from Mason County. Fullerton asked that a writ of certiorari issue commanding the Mason County Clerk to forthwith deliver the necessary papers. Because Caleb Dilworth had only one case, Armstrong's, before the court for that term, he went home. On November 19, Fullerton realized that he had not formally moved to continue the Armstrong case, so he called Armstrong before the court to make the motion. Abraham Lincoln happened to be in court that day on another matter and stepped in for the limited purpose of representing Armstrong at the hearing. He asked Judge Harriott to release Armstrong on bail. After a spirited argument, Judge Harriott granted the motion for continuance and denied bail to Armstrong.[3]

When the hearing ended, nobody, not even Lincoln himself, realized that Lincoln would actually try the case at the next term of court, but Armstrong's widowed mother was determined that he take the case. Hannah Armstrong and her deceased husband were two of Lincoln's oldest and dearest friends in

Courtroom of the old Cass County Courthouse, the only courtroom in which Lincoln practiced that is still in use today. PHOTOGRAPH TAKEN BY THE AUTHOR.

Illinois, and when Armstrong got arrested, she immediately began lobbying Lincoln to represent her son. She first wrote him a letter, then sent an emissary to Springfield to plead on her behalf, and finally went there herself.[4] Lincoln was noncommittal. This may surprise some readers, who are familiar with the story of Lincoln writing and volunteering to defend Armstrong. Some readers may have even seen a copy of the letter Lincoln purportedly wrote, but Lincoln scholars have pronounced the letter a forgery.[5]

The trial of Duff Armstrong for the murder of James Preston Metzker was set to begin on May 2, 1858. Hugh Fullerton appeared in court, accompanied by local attorney J. Henry Shaw, who had been hired by the Metzkers to assist him. On the other side, Caleb Dilworth had the assistance of William Walker, who had defended Norris the year before. Lincoln was nowhere around.

Fullerton had problems. His two most important witnesses—Dr. B. F. Stevenson, who rendered the opinion as to Metzker's cause of death, and Charles Allen, the only eyewitness who had seen Duff Armstrong with a weapon in his hand—had not answered their subpoenas. Fullerton could not proceed to trial without these two essential witnesses. At Fullerton's request, Judge Harriott issued a writ of attachment for the arrest of the two men.[6] Fullerton had other matters to present to the court, but the defense team and the other witnesses who were under subpoena could do nothing but wait patiently from day to day hoping that Allen and Stevenson could be brought into court.

Lincoln arrived in Beardstown on May 6, four days after the trial of Duff Armstrong had been scheduled to begin.[7] Having come to assist Shaw in the trial of a divorce case, he went to Shaw's office, where they discussed the divorce matter and another case involving a land transaction. Lincoln made no mention of any intent to participate in the Armstrong trial.[8] After Lincoln left Shaw's office, Hannah Armstrong buttonholed him. Would he help defend her son? Lincoln said he would—if Caleb Dilworth would agree. Lincoln approached Dilworth to offer his assistance, and Dilworth gladly welcomed him onto the defense team. That evening, Dilworth, Walker, and Lincoln met with the witnesses and went over Walker's notes from Norris's trial.[9] According to Dilworth, this was Lincoln's first introduction to the facts of the case.[10] Lincoln thus had one night to assimilate the evidence, assess its significance, and assemble a defense for Armstrong. The next morning, May 7, Fullerton had rounded up Stevenson and Allen and was ready to go to trial—and so was Lincoln.

A judicious study of the numerous and often conflicting accounts of the trial can reveal a full picture of the defense Lincoln assembled in a single night. We have the accounts of Dilworth and Walker for the defense, Shaw the assistant prosecutor, juror John T. Brady, jury foreman Milton Logan, Judge James Harriott, witness William A. Douglas, a young lawyer named Abram Bergen, and Duff Armstrong himself.[11] They differ in the details of the case, but they all agree that Charles Allen was a key witness and that Lincoln cross-examined Allen, used an almanac to undermine his testimony, and gave a rousing final argument. This gives rise to the question as to whether Lincoln won the case with a brilliant cross-examination or with an eloquent final argument.

Careful study of the sources gives us the answer: Yes, with those two means and more. Lincoln's conduct of the trial provides us with an exemplary model of how to analyze, present, and argue a criminal case, and we would do well to study his methods. Over the years, second-guessers have questioned almost everything Lincoln did in the Armstrong trial and have advanced all sorts of negative interpretations of Lincoln's tactics. Because these criticisms have been thoroughly investigated and refuted elsewhere,[12] this chapter will simply report the events of the trial as they unfolded.

Lincoln learned that Metzker had fought with Armstrong and received a mighty blow to the face. After Douglas and Dowell separated them, Metzker and Armstrong shook hands and made up. Metzker then left, walking across the grounds of the whiskey camp. James H. Norris, who had a grudge against Metzker, saw him coming, picked up a wooden neck yoke about three feet long, and hid behind a tree. When Metzker walked by, Norris stepped out from behind the tree and clubbed him on the back of the head.[13] Most witnesses had not seen Armstrong hit Metzker with anything other than his fist, except the missing Charles Allen, who had sworn that he saw Armstrong hit Metzker with a weapon. The severity of the wound to Metzker's face—a compressed skull fracture with the bone driven into the brain—suggested that he had been hit with something more than an empty fist.

There seems to be confusion among our sources as to the identity of the weapon, but this confusion is more apparent than real. Jurors John T. Brady and Milton Logan called it a "slingshot," but Duff Armstrong himself and prosecutor J. Henry Shaw, who kept the weapon as a souvenir, called it a "slungshot."[14] Carl Sandburg gives us the best description of the weapon. Sandburg wrote that the maker "put an eggshell into the ground, filled it with lead, poured melted zinc over the lead . . . ; then he had cut a cover from a calfskin bootleg, sewed it together with a squirrel-skin string, using a crooked awl to make the holes; and he had then cut a strip from a groundhog skin that he had tanned, and fixed it so it would fasten to his wrist."[15] This made a heavy weight on the end of a cord, useful as a flexible club to inflict serious injury—definitely not a modern slingshot.[16]

In the nineteenth century, "slingshot" and "slungshot" appear to have been synonyms. Old criminal cases often used the terms interchangeably.[17] The term "slungshot" will be used when referring to the weapon described by Sandburg.

Allen's failure to appear left the prosecution without any proof that Armstrong had used a deadly weapon, but it left the defense without some important proof as well. Allen was the only person who had seen Norris hit Metzker.[18] Without Allen's testimony, the evidence would show Metzker being struck by only one person—Armstrong. Whether he hit Metzker with a slungshot or his fist would be irrelevant; Armstrong would have been the only possible source of the injuries to Metzker's head. With Allen's testimony, the defense would have someone else (Norris) to blame for inflicting the mortal injuries to Metzker's head. On balance, the defense might be better off with Allen's testimony than without it.

Sometime during the evening, Lincoln learned why Allen had not answered his subpoena. The Armstrongs had talked him into hiding out in the town of Virginia, about thirteen miles away.[19] On discovering what had happened to Allen, Lincoln persuaded the Armstrongs to go get him and bring him back. Rather than explain how important Allen's testimony might be to the defense, Lincoln simply told the Armstrongs that if Allen did not show up for trial at this term of court, then Duff would sit in jail another six months awaiting trial.[20]

Now if there were only some way to weaken Allen's testimony about seeing Armstrong with a slungshot. Dilworth had a witness who could do just that. The morning after the fight, a slungshot had been found lying on the ground at the whiskey camp, and someone—probably Allen—had picked it up. Allen had identified the slungshot as the one used by Armstrong at Norris's trial, but the slungshot did not belong to Armstrong. It belonged to Armstrong's cousin Nelson Watkins, who had brought it to the whiskey camp in his pocket. At the end of the evening's festivities, Watkins had crawled under a wagon to go to sleep, and the slungshot had been uncomfortable in his pocket. He took the slungshot out of his pocket and set it down, intending to put it back in his pocket the next morning. Apparently his morning-after hangover prevented him from remembering to retrieve the slungshot, and he walked off and left it where Allen could find it.[21]

In talking with Watkins that evening, Lincoln learned that Armstrong could not possibly have used the slungshot to hit Metzker. It was in Watkins's pocket when Armstrong and Metzker fought. Although Watkins was Armstrong's cousin, and he could prove Armstrong did not use the slungshot, Watkins assured Lincoln, "You don't want to use me as a witness." And why was that? "Because I know too much. Let me tell you what I know . . ."

Lincoln stopped him. "All I want to know is this: Did you make that slung-shot? And did Duff Armstrong ever have it in his possession?"

Watkins protested, "On cross-examination they may make me tell things I do not want to tell!"

"I will see to it that you are not questioned about anything but the slung-shot," Lincoln promised.[22] He was referring to the rule that cross-examination cannot exceed the scope of the direct examination. As early as 1840, the U.S. Supreme Court had recognized the "well established" rule that "a party has no right to cross-examine any witness except as to facts and circumstances connected with the matters stated in his direct examination."[23] And that is how the testimony of Nelson Watkins played out. At trial, Lincoln questioned Watkins only about the slungshot, asking nothing about what Watkins saw of the fight, which confined the prosecution's cross-examination to questioning only about the slungshot. Watkins did not have to tell the things he did not want to tell, and Lincoln never learned that Watkins had seen Armstrong hit Metzker in the face with a wagon hammer.[24] Choosing to remain willfully ignorant of Watkins's harmful information, Lincoln crafted a direct examination that kept it concealed.

The story of the wagon hammer is secondhand hearsay. Years after the trial, juror John T. Brady told an interviewer that he had gotten the story from Nelson Watkins a few weeks after the trial. Secondhand hearsay is inadmissible in a jury trial, but historical investigation is not a forensic endeavor, and if secondhand hearsay has indicia of reliability, it should be credited. The indicia of reliability for the wagon hammer story are as follows: First, neither Brady nor Watkins was a lawyer, so they were not likely aware that Lincoln's refusal to allow Watkins to give him bad information was in keeping with the behavior of some trial advocates who did not want their minds cluttered with harmful information. And second, neither Brady nor Watkins displayed any awareness of the significance of what Lincoln told Watkins about how he was going to prevent the prosecution from asking the questions Watkins feared. It is possible that Brady or Watkins could have made up a story, but it is highly unlikely that either one of them could have made up a story that cohered so closely with two subjects about which they were ignorant, evidence law and trial tactics.

The next morning, with all his witnesses present, Fullerton was prepared to go forward with his case against Armstrong—just as soon as he had tried another case. Lincoln, Walker, and Dilworth had no choice but to sit and wait for the completion of the first trial. One newly christened young attorney, Abram Bergen, had no cases to handle that day, but he spent the day in court observing the other trials and trying to learn as much as he could by watching the more experienced attorneys trying cases. He wanted to see one lawyer in particular—Abraham Lincoln. Decades later, Bergen reminisced about that day in a speech to the Kansas Bar Association:

> In the courtroom, while waiting for the Armstrong case to be called for trial, I watched and studied his face for full two hours. . . . He sat among the lawyers for these two hours with his head thrown back, his steady gaze apparently fixed on one spot of the blank ceiling, without the least change in the direction of his dull, expressionless eyes, and without noticing anything transpiring around him, and without any variation of feature or movement of any muscle of his face. I suppose he was thinking of his coming case.[25]

When the jury on the first case retired to deliberate, the trial of Duff Armstrong began. The most complete near-contemporary account we have of the trial comes from the typewriter of J. McCan Davis, who worked as an investigator for Ida M. Tarbell while she was writing her biography of Lincoln. Davis interviewed all the surviving participants he could find and wrote a six-page report on the case for Tarbell. He described the prosecution case in the following words:

> The jury empaneled, the [cross-]examination of witnesses seems to have been conducted, on behalf of the defense, chiefly by Lincoln. Many of the witnesses bore familiar names; . . . and Lincoln had known their fathers. "The witnesses were kept out of the court-room until called to testify," says Wm. A. Douglas. "I happened to be the first witness called and so heard the whole trial." . . .
>
> The testimony was of a most conflicting character. Apparently no two persons had observed precisely the same incidents of the fight. Most of Armstrong's witnesses (he had twenty-five in all) were sure he had no weapon in his hand when he struck Metzker; some acknowledged the night too dark to see the affray with distinctness. Witnesses varied widely as to the precise hour of the encounter. Some said it was as early as nine o'clock; others as late as eleven; while most of them fixed it between ten and eleven o'clock. So much uncertainty was favorable to the defense. Yet there were circumstances pointing strongly to Armstrong's guilt. A sling-shot found on the grounds near the scene of the fight was produced. . . . Yet it was not traced to Armstrong's hands by any positive evidence. But now came a witness who seemed not to have

participated in the general spree of the fateful night, and who was able to recall with great distinctness and particularity all that happened. His name was Charles Allen, and he was the most formidable witness produced by the prosecution.

He had, according to his story, stood by and watched the fight; he had seen Armstrong strike Metzker with the terrible sling-shot, "because," he declared "the moon was shining brightly.["][26]

According to the legend of the Almanac Trial, Lincoln destroyed Allen's credibility on cross-examination by confronting him with an almanac that showed that there was no moon at all that night. Some versions of the legend even go so far as to claim that Allen broke down on the witness stand and confessed to the murder himself. None of this happened. This fanciful version of the trial's climax originated in a novel about Lincoln published in 1887 by Edward Eggleston.[27]

The first problem with the legend is that the moon was in fact out that night. When Lincoln produced the almanac and demonstrated that the moon was on the horizon going down, the prosecution objected, saying that the almanac showed the moon to be on the horizon coming up. Juror John T. Brady later recalled Lincoln's reply that it did not matter, "for if it was just going down or just coming up, it was not overhead where the sun would be at 1 P.M., according to Allen's testimony."[28]

The second problem with the legend is that Lincoln did not confront Allen with the almanac. If he had done so, Allen might just have remembered something that Duff Armstrong later disclosed to a newspaper reporter: "It was light enough for everybody to see the fight. The fight took place in front of one of the bars and each bar had two or three candles on it."[29] The safer course of action was to firmly commit Allen to the moon being high overhead, and then contradict him later, after he had left the stand and could not testify to a remembered or invented alternative source of light. Lincoln did just that. He firmly committed Allen to the position of the moon. Of Lincoln's cross-examination, Davis wrote, "Under Lincoln's questioning he repeated the statement until it was impossible that the jury should forget it."[30] After the prosecution rested, Lincoln nonchalantly remarked that he supposed the judge would take judicial notice of an almanac. The judge would. Just to make sure either side could refer to it if needed, Lincoln asked the judge to mark the almanac into evidence. The judge did. That was all that happened with the almanac during the presentation of the evidence. Lincoln did not mention what the almanac said about where the moon was that night until he made his final argument,[31] and it threw the prosecution into such a panic that when they gave the closing final argument, they had no answer for it.[32]

Nor can we accept the contention that Lincoln accused Allen of perjury. First, it would have been counterproductive. Allen alone among all the witnesses testified to seeing Norris hit Metzker with the neck yoke. Lincoln would make the task of shifting guilt away from Armstrong much more difficult by branding Allen a perjurer. As Judge James Harriott later recalled, "Lincoln's theory was that [the] neck yoke killed Metzker and that it cracked the skull in front."[33] Juror John T. Brady later described the cross-examination of Allen in the following words: "Lincoln was very good to him, encouraging him by supplying words as he hesitated for them and telling him not to get excited, but keep quiet and tell everything just as he saw it."[34] This is hardly the cross-examination one would expect of a lawyer preparing to accuse a witness of perjury.

Lincoln needed to explain how the skull came to be cracked in both front and back, and he got that explanation from a Beardstown physician named Charles Parker. Using a skull as a demonstrative aid, Parker explained that a blow to the back of the head could have caused a contrecoup fracture on the opposite side of the head. Parker went on to say that he had actually treated three such contrecoup fractures in his practice.[35] According to the best medical science of the time, a blow to the back of the head from the neck yoke would not cause a contrecoup fracture. The most likely cause of such a fracture would be a fall where the back of the head was hit over a large area. With such a large area hit, the back of the head would not be fractured, but the force of the blow would transfer to the front of the head and fracture the fine bones around the eye.[36] Parker suggested that Metzker could have sustained such a fracture by falling from his horse when he rode home after the fight. There was a slight problem with Parker's diagnosis, however. According to the literature, a contrecoup fracture "is never depressed."[37] To get a depressed fracture of the fine bones around the eye would require the thrust of a stick, umbrella, or other blunt-ended body[38]—perhaps a wagon hammer or the metallic weight at the end of a slungshot.

Lincoln asked Judge Harriott to instruct the jury "that if they believe from the evidence that Norris killed Metzker, they are to acquit Armstrong, unless they also believe beyond a reasonable doubt that Armstrong acted in concert with Norris in the killing,"[39] and Harriott agreed to do so.[40]

After all his adroit legal maneuvering during the trial, Lincoln gave a final argument that moved even one of the prosecutors. J. Henry Shaw recalled Lincoln's argument in the following words:

There were many witnesses, and each one seemed to add one more cord that seemed to bind him down, till Mr. Lincoln was something in the situation of Gulliver after his first sleep in Lilliput. But when he came to talk to the jury (that was always his forte) he resembled Gulliver again. He skillfully untied here and there a knot and loosened here and there a peg, until, getting fairly warmed up, he raised himself in his full power and shook the arguments of his opponent from him as though they were cobwebs. He took the jury by storm. There were tears in Mr. Lincoln's eyes while he spoke. But they were genuine. His sympathies were fully enlisted in favor of the young man, and his terrible sincerity could not help but arouse the same passion in the jury. I have said it a hundred times, that it was Lincoln's speech that saved that criminal from the gallows.[41]

We thus see that Lincoln won the Almanac Trial by using a number of strategies: surgically cross-examining Charles Allen, supported by a judicious use of the almanac, which weakened but did not destroy the witness's testimony; making a well-crafted direct examination of Nelson Watkins,

"Lincoln Defends Armstrong." The drawing is inaccurate in that Lincoln wore a white suit and had no beard. DRAWING COURTESY OF THE LIBRARY OF CONGRESS.

which dissociated Armstrong from the slungshot without revealing the incriminating information Watkins had; presenting expert medical testimony to give another explanation for the wound to Metzker's face; writing the jury instruction, which facilitated his laying the blame for Metzker's murder completely at Norris's feet; and analytically destroying the prosecution's case in final argument.

He did something else in final argument that has caused some to call his ethics into question. After he "shook the arguments of his opponent from him as though they were cobwebs," Lincoln reminisced about how the Armstrong family had welcomed him into their home when he was a penniless young man, how he had rocked Duff Armstrong as a baby, and how his great love for the Armstrongs had led him to take the case without charge. This sort of argument would be highly improper today, but Lincoln was giving the argument over one hundred years ago, when the rules were different. As a matter of fact, Hugh Fullerton invited Lincoln's comments when, on final argument, he told the jury that the Metzkers had tried to hire Lincoln to assist him in the prosecution of Armstrong.[42]

The claim has been repeatedly made that Lincoln used a faked almanac and that the moon was really high in the heavens where Allen said it was. That claim has repeatedly been refuted. Not rebutted, refuted.[43] Lincoln biographers William Barton, Albert Beveridge, and J. McCan Davis all investigated the faked almanac story and found it wanting.[44] Even Edgar Lee Masters, who never missed a chance to say something derogatory about Lincoln, concluded that "the story of the forged almanac which persisted in Illinois for years was preposterous to the last degree."[45] The story probably derives its vitality from Lincoln's campaign for president in 1860. His campaign literature mentioned the trial and overdramatized the story by claiming there was no moon at all on the night of the killing.[46] This played into the hands of his opponents, who could claim Lincoln had committed fraud by pointing to any almanac and showing that the moon was indeed out that night.

16.

PEOPLE versus TOM PATTERSON, APRIL 21, 1859

TOM PATTERSON OPERATED A GENERAL STORE IN SADORUS, CHAMPAIGN County, Illinois. He tried to be a good neighbor and often extended credit to his customers. One of his customers, Samuel DeHaven, a man whose thirst for alcohol seemingly knew no bounds, tested the limits of Patterson's generosity on March 24, 1858, when he staggered into the store and drunkenly demanded that Patterson sell him a hatchet on credit. Patterson said he would extend credit on the hatchet as soon as DeHaven settled up his currently pending bill. DeHaven, who had a reputation for becoming violent when drunk, did not like Patterson's answer. He loudly expressed his dislike, and Patterson ordered him out of the store.[1]

Within a few minutes DeHaven returned, accompanied by some of his cronies. He picked up a spade and threatened to hit Patterson. The storekeeper picked up a two-pound weight from a balance beam scale sitting on the counter. Concealing the weight by his side, Patterson held it ready to defend himself. The two men stood confronting each other until DeHaven raised the spade as if to strike. The face-off ended when DeHaven became distracted and looked away from Patterson, who then threw the weight with all his might. His coattails flew up over his shoulders from the force of the throw, and the weight embedded itself behind DeHaven's ear to the depth of an inch in his skull.

DeHaven collapsed, and the onlookers pronounced him dead. A cursory examination proved otherwise, and Patterson went from combatant to first responder. He took DeHaven into his home and rendered first aid. He summoned two physicians, but all his efforts proved futile, and DeHaven died the next day. Patterson got arrested, and State's Attorney Ward Hill Lamon indicted him for manslaughter. Patterson hired two local lawyers, Henry Clay Whitney and William G. Coler, who secured his release on $3,000 bond.

Of the five ingredients that will ensure a conviction—(a) an agreeable jury, (e) an egregious crime, (i) an innocent victim, (o) an odious defendant, and

(u) undeniable guilt—it would appear that Lamon's case lacked ingredients (i), (o), and (u). If anything, Lamon appears to have had an odious victim, an innocent defendant, and very deniable guilt. As to ingredient (e), killing a belligerent deadbeat drunk armed with a deadly weapon hardly qualifies as an egregious crime. Most juries confronting this fact pattern would be predisposed to acquit, and Patterson's lawyers had only to raise a reasonable doubt as to whether their client had acted in self-defense.

The Patterson case demonstrates the importance of ingredient (a). De-Haven was a longtime resident of Champaign County, Patterson a relative newcomer. DeHaven may have been a drunk, but he was Champaign County's drunk; Patterson was a carpetbagger who had swooped down on the poor farmers of the county and was getting rich off the sweat of other men's brows. Since the jurors would come from among the citizens of Champaign County, Lamon had a high likelihood of seating an agreeable jury that would view the case as the egregious crime of a money-grubbing capitalist killing a lovable drunk. If Lamon seated such a jury, it would never listen to even a valid self-defense claim. No matter how innocent Patterson might be, to stand trial in Champaign County could be tantamount to suicide.

Whitney and Coler apparently realized Patterson's predicament and called for reinforcements. They recruited the two best criminal defense attorneys they could find—Leonard Swett and Abraham Lincoln. Unfortunately, when the case came up for trial in October 1858, neither Lincoln nor Swett was in court. Lincoln was in the midst of a whirlwind railroad tour of Illinois, making campaign speeches at every whistle stop as he strove to get elected to the U.S. Senate.[2] Swett was one of Lincoln's staunchest political allies, so he was probably on the campaign trail with Lincoln. The election was to be held on November 2. After that day, Lincoln would be back to the practice of law. If they could just get the case put off until the next term of court, Lincoln and Swett would certainly be able to attend and help try the case. But Patterson's lawyers could expect vigorous opposition to any motion to continue. They had already gotten a continuance in the April term,[3] and neither the judge nor the prosecutor would be eager to continue the case yet again.

They could use a simple tactic without having to actually move for a continuance, however: they could move for a change of venue. Patterson certainly needed one, and a change of venue would automatically put the case off until another day. Nevertheless, Whitney and Coler, two experienced attorneys, did something that on the face of it appears to be a monumental blunder. They did not move for a change of venue; they moved for a continuance. Not

Ambrotype of Lincoln,
taken the year before he
tried the Patterson case.
PHOTOGRAPH COURTESY OF
THE LIBRARY OF CONGRESS.

only that, but they agreed that if they got the continuance, they would forever
waive their right to a change of venue.[4] This maneuver might not have sealed
Patterson's fate, but it put the defense in a deep hole.

How could they have made such a bad decision? With a little study, we
can understand the dilemma they faced. They needed a continuance until
Lincoln and Swett could join them, but they were unlikely to get one because they had already received a continuance. A change of venue would
automatically continue the case—but not long enough. In 1857, the Illinois
legislature had reconfigured the Eighth Circuit, reducing it to five counties
and setting the terms of court for those counties.[5] According to the schedule
set by the legislature, the fall term of the Champaign County Circuit Court
began on Monday, October 18, 1858. It was the next-to-the-last county in the
fall rotation, and the term of the Vermilion County Circuit Court began on
November 1. If the defense team got a change of venue, the case would go to
trial two weeks later in Vermilion County, and Lincoln would still be on the
campaign trail. The defense attorneys had two options, neither of which was
satisfactory: they could take a change of venue and try the case in Vermilion

County without Swett and Lincoln, or they could waive a change of venue in return for a continuance and try the case in Champaign County with Swett and Lincoln present. They chose option two. Obviously they expected that, as in "The Devil and Daniel Webster," even a hostile jury would be swayed by the eloquence of such a talented defense team. Hindsight suggests that they made the wrong decision. When the case was finally tried on April 21, 1859, both Lincoln and Swett were in court, but Daniel Webster had more success than they did.[6] Although things turned out well for the fictional Jabez Stone, Tom Patterson got convicted.

Over a dozen witnesses testified at the well-attended trial, and it became clear that the issue was whether Patterson's action was necessary to defend against death or great bodily harm. In such a case, the jury instructions have great importance. Judge David Davis agreed to give the defense's requested jury instructions, which Lincoln wrote in his own hand, as follows:

The Court instructs the jury:
1. If they believe from the evidence that when Patterson threw the weight, he had a reasonable and well grounded fear that he was in immediate danger of his life, or of great bodily harm, from Dehaven, with the spade, they are to find Patterson "Not guilty"—
2. That if they have any reasonable doubt whether Patterson then was in such reasonable and well grounded fear, they are to find him "Not guilty"—
3. That if, upon the whole case, they have any reasonable doubt of Patterson's guilt, as charged in the indictment, they are to acquit him—

Beneath Lincoln's written instructions, Judge Davis added the following language in his own hand:

The Jury are not to decide the question of the Defendant's guilt or innocence by a preponderance of testimony, or by the probabilities of the defendant's guilt or innocence.

In a criminal case, the Jury will not convict if they entertain a reasonable doubt of the defendant's guilt.[7]

These instructions were good for the defense, but Ward Hill Lamon also had four written requests for instructions. They were not as well-worded as Lincoln's, and Judge Davis declined to give one of them, but the instructions Davis did give damaged Patterson. If we clean up Lamon's language to make it more coherent, the instructions told the jury the following:

3rd. Unless the Jury believes from the evidence ... that the danger was so urgent and pressing from an attack made upon him by Dehaven that in order to save his own life, or to prevent great bodily harm, the killing of Dehaven was absolutely necessary; and unless the Jury believe from the evidence that ... the Defendant had really in good faith endeavored to decline any further struggle before the mortal blow was given, then the law is against the Defendant, and the jury will find him guilty.

4th. Unless the Jury believe from the evidence that Defendant and Dehaven were engaged in a personal conflict, and that without any fault of Defendant, and that the Defendant did all that a reasonable man ought to do, under like circumstances, to avoid such conflict before striking the mortal blow, then the law is against the Defendant and the Jury will find him guilty.[8]

The prosecution's instructions suggested to the jury that the defense had a burden of proving that the mortal blow was absolutely necessary and that Patterson had done everything he could to avoid using deadly force before he struck the blow. Of course, the defense did not have to prove anything, but Lamon's instructions could certainly have misled the jury into thinking that it did.

Leonard Swett gave the opening final argument for the defense, Lamon argued for the prosecution, and Lincoln closed for the defense. The defense team obviously thought that the one-two punch of Swett and Lincoln arguing the case would ensure a victory. It did not. The jury convicted Patterson and recommended a sentence of three years in prison. Judge Davis sentenced accordingly, and Patterson was shipped off to Joliet.

There is an old saying that victory has a thousand fathers, but defeat is an orphan. That was not the case with Tom Patterson's conviction of manslaughter. The participants at the trial almost unanimously blamed Lincoln. In an interview with Lincoln biographer William Henry Herndon, Judge Davis said that Swett did a good job, but Lincoln not so much. Whitney told Lincoln biographer Jesse Weik that Lincoln made a line of argument that contained "very damaging" admissions.[9]

Two stories have come out of the Patterson trial, neither of which rings true. The first is that Patterson murdered DeHaven and was lucky to be charged only with manslaughter. This story probably originated with Whitney, who later claimed that Patterson was guilty and should have been charged with murder. According to Whitney, Patterson was a worthless saloonkeeper, and his victim was nothing more than a harmless, lovable lush. When the

villainous Patterson demanded that DeHaven pay his bill, the put-upon De-
Haven ineffectually waved a spade at Patterson, and Patterson maliciously
murdered him.[10] In reality, Patterson ran a general store, not a saloon (De-
Haven came into Patterson's store to buy a hatchet, not something usually sold
in a saloon), and when DeHaven attacked him with a spade, Patterson should
have been within his rights to defend himself. Why, then, would Whitney
say Patterson was guilty? Could it be that he was reluctant to admit that he
defended an innocent man and got him convicted?

As the second story goes, Lincoln decided Patterson was guilty and simply
quit in the middle of the trial. Judge Davis told Lincoln biographer William
Henry Herndon that Lincoln decided midtrial Patterson was guilty and told
his co-counsel, "Swett, you defend him. I can't."[11] Ward Hill Lamon per-
petuated the second version in his biography of Lincoln, writing that when
Lincoln determined his client to be guilty, he became "morally paralyzed"
and said "Swett, the man is guilty. You defend him. I can't." Lincoln then
refused to take a cent of the fee, insisting that Swett take it all.[12] In his study
of Lincoln's law practice, Brian Dirck suggested that Lincoln may have quit in
the middle of the case because he was exhausted by his recent senatorial campaign against Stephen A. Douglas.[13] Henry Clay Whitney, however, denied the
charge that Lincoln abandoned their client midtrial. "I note that Lamon and
other biographers state that he declined his fee and wouldn't argue it. I know
he did argue it, and that he and Swett and I, each got two hundred dollars."[14]
Whitney did, however, blame the defeat on Lincoln, and it is quite likely that
fatigue from the Senate race contributed to a poor performance by Lincoln.

According to Whitney, Swett gave a rousing final argument that left Whitney "full of faith that our client would be acquitted entirely." Court recessed
for the day, and Lincoln was to argue the next morning. Whitney remembered
that Lincoln "made some good points" but also engaged in a "line of argument
and admission, that was very damaging." One thing Lincoln did that Whitney
regarded as "especially atrocious" was to criticize one of Swett's arguments
to the jury. Swett had painted a heartrending picture of how Patterson's poor
wife and children would be devastated if their protector were sent to prison,
but Lincoln pointed out that such considerations should be immaterial to a
jury, which must decide cases on the evidence rather than emotion.[15] Whitney
believed Lincoln's argument "brought disaster to some of our effective—but
illegitimate—arguments."[16]

Lincoln's misstep might not have mattered before an impartial jury, but
before a Champaign County jury composed of friends of the deceased, it
sealed Patterson's fate. What hamstrung Lincoln in his argument was most

likely a quality that Whitney praised in another setting: Lincoln's "infallible and remorseless logic." In the Patterson case, however, Whitney criticized Lincoln for that very same quality, writing that his "merciless logic drove him to the belief that the culprit was guilty."[17] Lincoln's "merciless logic" more likely drove him to the conclusion that Swett's arguments were specious, and he refused to adopt them as his own. It may well have been that had either Lincoln or Swett alone argued, Patterson would have stood a better chance of gaining an acquittal. Two good arguments in isolation often make one atrocious argument when put together. For this reason, when multiple counsel try a case, they must all speak with one voice.

It cannot be denied that Lincoln turned in a subpar performance in the case, but he partially redeemed himself by obtaining a pardon for his client after Patterson had served one year of the three-year sentence. A group of Patterson's friends got up a petition to have him pardoned, and they enlisted the aid of Judge David Davis. Davis wrote a letter to Governor John Wood recommending a pardon, and Lincoln endorsed it with the following words at the bottom of Davis's letter: "Considering the absence of previous bad character of Patterson himself, the necessities of his family, the excellent character of all his family connections, and the very numerous signed petition of his neighbors, I recommend that he be pardoned at once."[18] Patterson received his pardon on August 30, 1860. Governor Wood could hardly ignore the recommendation of the Republican nominee for the presidency of the United States.

17.

PEOPLE versus SIMEON "PEACHY" QUINN HARRISON, September 3, 1859

IT SHOULD BE CLEAR BY NOW THAT RECONSTRUCTING THE COURSE OF LIN-coln's criminal trials has proven somewhat tricky. No transcripts survive from any of the cases studied so far, and the court records give scant information about what went on in the courtroom. Contemporary news accounts of some of the more celebrated cases are available, but for most of Lincoln's trials, it is necessary to rely on the reminiscences of the participants. Most of these were recorded years and even decades after the events, and they suffer from inaccuracies introduced by fallible memory and the all-too-human tendency to embellish the facts to make the story better.

People v. Harrison, the last of Lincoln's murder cases, serves as an example of how fallible memory coupled with the tendency to embellish can lead to an account that, although accurate in its basic outline, is far from being com-pletely true. The traditional account of the trial comes from four sources, all people who attended the trial: Thomas W. S. Kidd, the court crier (a minor court official); Newton Bateman, a lawyer who was in court on another matter; Shelby M. Cullom, one of Lincoln's co-counsel in the trial; and William Henry Herndon, Lincoln's law partner. Only Kidd gives any detail as to the facts of the case. In an undated letter to Lincoln biographer Ida M. Tarbell, Kidd wrote:

> On July 16th 1859 Greek Crafton a bright young man and a law student in the office of Lincoln & Herndon was engaged in an altercation upon some political question with Peachy [Quinn] Harrison, in a drug store in the village of Pleasant Plains in Sangamon Co. Both of the young men were hot blooded and nearly of equal physical proportions. Ac-cusations of a personal character passed between them followed with angry words and threats of personal injury when Harrison pulled a knife and stabbed Greek between the short ribs of the left side from which he died on the 19th.[1]

William Henry
Herndon, Lincoln's
last law partner
and biographer.
FROM LAMON, *LIFE
OF LINCOLN*, 376.

Kidd told Tarbell that the turning point of the trial came when Lincoln called the Reverend Peter Cartwright, Harrison's grandfather, to the stand. Cartwright testified that Crafton had told him, "I am dying, I will soon part with all I love on earth and I want you to say to my slayer I forgive him. I want to leave this earth with a forgiveness of all who have in any way injured me."[2] When Lincoln argued the case to the jury, he used this testimony to make an emotional appeal to the jury to honor the dying wish of Greek Crafton and join him in forgiving Harrison. Kidd was certain that the pathos of Lincoln's appeal was the only thing that saved Harrison from the gallows.

Herndon writes of Lincoln's epic struggle to get Crafton's deathbed statement into evidence. The battle took place over two days. The judge, a Democrat, had ruled against Lincoln on almost every point of law up to the moment he tried to get the deathbed statement into evidence. The prosecution objected, and after an extended argument, the judge committed error by ruling the statement inadmissible. Over supper that evening, Lincoln told Herndon that he knew he was right and was going to "crowd the judge" in an effort to get the judge to see reason. The next morning, Lincoln made a passionate but well-reasoned argument, coming very close to getting himself held in contempt of court. Eventually the judge relented and allowed the statement into evidence.[3]

Although Herndon assures his readers that the evidence was obviously admissible, almost every lawyer who has voiced an opinion since that time has branded the testimony as improper and wondered how Lincoln could bamboozle a judge into allowing the statement into evidence. John J. Duff called the testimony "hearsay of the rankest sort" and said it was a "deep mystery" how Lincoln could slip such evidence past the judge and prosecutor.[4] Albert J. Beveridge observed, "How Lincoln ever induced the court to admit such evidence does not appear."[5] Based on Kidd's account of the evidence, Duff and Beveridge were right: a deathbed statement may not be admitted into evidence. But a dying declaration may. Although a dying declaration is certainly a deathbed statement, it is more. As discussed in chapter 1, there are four requisites for a dying declaration: (1) the prosecution must be for unlawful homicide; (2) the declarant must know that he is dying; (3) the statement must relate to the cause of his death; and (4) the declarant must die. For example, this statement is a dying declaration: "It's getting dark! I'm dying! Arthur Livingston shot me!"[6] This statement is not: "I want you to say to my slayer I forgive him."

We have no direct evidence of what Shelby M. Cullom had to say about the trial,[7] but Newton Bateman's version of the trial appears in the published transcript of a speech he gave to the Cadmus Club of Galesburg, Illinois, in 1899. As Bateman tells the story, the prosecuting attorneys saw how Lincoln's passionate speech had sunk home with the jurors, and they knew they must do something to counteract it or lose the case. In Bateman's words, here is what happened when the lead prosecutor made his closing final argument:

"Well, gentlemen," said he, "you have heard Mr. Lincoln—'Honest Abe Lincoln,' they call him, I believe. And I suppose you think you have heard the honest truth—or at least that Mr. Lincoln honestly believes what he has told you to be the truth. I tell you, he believes no such thing. That frank, ingenuous face of his, as you are weak enough to suppose, those looks and tones of such unsophisticated simplicity, those appeals to your minds and consciences as sworn jurors, are all assumed for the occasion, gentlemen; all a mask, gentlemen. You have been listening for the last hour to an actor, who knows well how to play the role of honest seeming, for effect."

At this moment, amid breathless stillness, Mr. Lincoln arose, and with deep emotion, and an indescribable expression of pain upon his gaunt features, said: "Mr. ——, you have known me for years and you know that not a word of that language can be truthfully applied to me;" and sat down.

The lawyer hesitated a moment, changed color, and then his better nature regaining the mastery, he turned to Mr. Lincoln and said calmly and with much feeling: "Yes, Mr. Lincoln, I do know it, and I take it all back."[8]

These strands of oral tradition became woven together into the commonly accepted narrative of the trial: Two equally matched young men from prominent families became embroiled in a political quarrel at a drugstore. The quarrel degenerated into fisticuffs. One of the men pulled a knife, and soon the other lay dying on the floor. Lincoln took the case and freed his obviously guilty client by talking the judge into admitting an improper deathbed statement and using that statement as the basis for an emotional plea to the jury urging it to forgive the killer. As a sidelight to the trial, one of the prosecutors called Lincoln a liar, and Lincoln protested so vehemently that the prosecutor retracted his statement in front of the jury.

For this story to be true, Lincoln had to have had a Jekyll-and-Hyde personality that rendered him incapable on April 21, 1859, of arguing effectively for Tom Patterson, who had a good self-defense argument, because his extreme allegiance to truth led him to reject Leonard Swett's fallacious emotional appeal to pardon a murderer because of the man's wife and children, yet fully capable on September 3 of defending Quinn Harrison, whom he knew to be guilty, by hoodwinking the judge into admitting improper evidence and then using that evidence to make a blatant emotional appeal to the jury to ignore the evidence and pardon a murderer. It does not make sense, and that is because it is not true.

A more realistic history of the case became accessible in 1988 with the discovery of a verbatim transcript of the trial. Court reporters were scarcer than hen's teeth in antebellum Illinois, and it was a rare case where the parties were able to afford one.[9] Both Harrison and Crafton came from wealthy families, however, and not only could they afford one, but they hired one—Robert R. Hitt, the court reporter who transcribed the Lincoln-Douglas debates. They came to hire him in a roundabout way. The *Illinois State Journal* initially hired Hitt so it could publish a daily verbatim transcript of the trial,[10] but after the first day of publication, the two teams of lawyers hired him away from the *Journal*.[11] He made a good profit from the switch in employers. Instead of one fee for one transcript, he was able to charge three fees for three transcripts. The Harrison family paid him $25 for a transcript, as did the Crafton family. Lincoln paid an additional $27.95 for a third transcript.[12] As a result, counsel for both sides of the case got something that twentieth-century lawyers rarely did—a daily copy of the transcript of testimony.

When Harrison was acquitted, there was no need for the transcript, and it became a family heirloom stuffed into a box. By the 1980s, it had come into the possession of Mrs. William Harrison, the widow of Quinn Harrison's grandson. In 1988, she allowed the document to be photocopied, and two years later, she donated the transcript to the Lincoln Presidential Library, where it is now part of the Papers of Abraham Lincoln collection.[13] The account that follows has been reconstructed in large part from the transcript of the trial.

Simeon "Peachy" Quinn Harrison and Greek Crafton were about the same age, both in their early twenties; but Crafton was a strong, robust man, and Harrison was not. Crafton weighed about 145 pounds to Harrison's 125.[14] Harrison had been sickly for years, suffering from numerous childhood illnesses, which left him with a slight frame and a weak constitution. Crafton's brother, William, had married Harrison's sister, Elizabeth Catherine.[15] The fact that the two men were in-laws did not mean they were fast friends, however. Harrison did not approve of Crafton's lifestyle or that his younger brother Peter had come under Crafton's influence. He counseled with his brother about consorting with such a ruffian, but Peter continued his association with Crafton. Unfortunately, Peter told Crafton what Harrison had said about him, and this angered Crafton.

On July 4, 1859, Harrison and his friend Frederick Henry attended a picnic at Clary's Grove. Henry met Harrison at his father's house, and the two got into a buggy to ride to the picnic. About a mile and a half from Pleasant Plains, they ran into Greek Crafton and his brother John. They pulled up the buggy, and the four talked pleasantly for a few minutes, until Harrison asked where his brother Peter was.

"He's down at the wagon getting some ladies," replied Crafton. Then he went on to say, "I understand you have been giving Peter a lecture about the company he has been keeping."

"I don't know," Harrison said. "I may have said something about it."

"At some convenient time I shall settle this," Crafton told him.

"It doesn't make a damn bit of difference whether you settle it or not," responded Harrison.

Crafton pulled off his coat, stepped forward, and said, "We can settle it right now."

"I don't want to fight," said Harrison.

"You can't fight," interjected Henry.

"If you ever cast any reflections on my character," Crafton warned, "I'll whip you."

"You damned son-of-a-bitch!" said Harrison. "I'll shoot you and pay you for it!"

Crafton charged into the buggy, but Henry pushed him out. Crafton picked up a clod of dirt and threw it at Harrison, but his aim was bad. He hit Henry instead. Crafton charged the buggy again, and Henry again pushed him out. Henry started the buggy on its way, but Harrison grabbed the reins, stopping it.

"Damn you, you speckle-faced son-of-a-bitch!" said Harrison. "If you ever lay hands on me I'll . . ." When Henry later testified at the trial, he could not remember whether Harrison had said he would shoot Crafton or kill Crafton. After voicing his threat, Harrison let go of the reins, and Henry drove the wagon on to the picnic.

John C. Bone saw both Quinn Harrison and Greek Crafton at the picnic, and he vividly recalled a private conversation he had with Harrison, who took him aside to ask a favor.

"Have you got your tools with you?" Harrison wanted to know.

"No," replied Bone, "I never carry them to such a place."

Harrison said he had a run-in with Crafton that morning and was expecting more difficulties before the day ended. Harrison pulled a silver-handled bowie knife from under the breast of his coat and showed it to Bone. It had a sharpened blade about four and a half to five inches long.

"I borrowed it and the man wants it back," said Harrison. "That's why I need a tool from you. If I give the knife back, I won't have any way to protect myself. I don't want to fight. I can't fight Greek, but if he jumps on me, I'll hurt him if I can."

Bone reassured him, "Quinn, we are all here and you and Greek shall have no difficulty here today. There are other times you can settle the difficulty."

Later that afternoon at the picnic, Harrison spoke to William Purvines about his difficulties with Crafton. Harrison said he did not want to fight Crafton and had armed himself with a knife for protection. "If Greek jumps on me, I'll cut his gut out," he said. "I would as soon kill Greek as kill a dog."

Before the picnic ended, Harrison and Crafton had a second confrontation. Crafton came to Harrison and tried to make up. Harrison, fortified with the knife under his coat, told Crafton they had nothing to make up. Crafton said, "You insulted my parents when you called me a son-of-a-bitch." Harrison assured Crafton that he did not mean for the insult to apply to anyone other than Crafton. And with that nonapology, the two parted ways.

Before he left the picnic, Crafton told his friend James Zane that he was going to whip Quinn Harrison. "He reproved his brother Peter for keeping company with such as me, and he called me a damn son-of-a-bitch. I'll whip him and his brother, too. I'll knock Quinn down and stamp him in the face. I'll stamp his guts out and beat him till he can't go." Zane reported this conversation to Harrison.

The next day, Harrison went to Edmund Crafton's place to settle a pasture bill. Edmund was Greek's uncle, and Greek had apparently given Edmund an embellished account of their encounter on July 4. After settling up their business, Edmund said, "Quinn, I understood last night that you should have said yesterday going to the picnic that you should have damned the name of Craftons and that you would shoot or kill them all and pay for them and if you weren't worth enough money, your father was. I want to know whether you meant to include me and my family or any?"

Harrison replied, "I didn't include anyone except Greek Crafton."

Greek Crafton attended a picnic at Indian Creek some four days later, and he was spoiling for a fight with Harrison. In the presence of three men, Crafton announced his intention to "whip" Quinn Harrison if he came to the picnic that day. Addressing one of the men, David Purvines,[16] Crafton asked if he knew whether Quinn Harrison was at the picnic that day. Purvines asked why he was looking for Harrison.

"Are you a friend of mine?" asked Crafton.

"Yes, I'm your friend," replied Purvines.

"I intend to whip Quinn Harrison, for I have it from Wiley Crafton to do it," said Crafton. "I know he's carrying pistols and bowie knives for me. He carries six pistols. That's how much difference there is between him and me." Crafton rubbed his fists together and continued, "I have used these fellows every night for six months in Springfield."

"Greek, you shouldn't do that," warned Purvines. "This is no place to have difficulties." Although Harrison did not go to the picnic that day, he became aware of the threat, as Thomas White overheard Crafton's threats and warned Harrison about what Crafton was saying. It would be hard in such a small community as Pleasant Plains for Harrison not to hear about Crafton's threats. From July 4 until their fatal confrontation on July 16, Crafton continued to threaten Quinn Harrison.

During the week leading up to the fatal stabbing, Crafton spent a lot of time at Turley's Store in Pleasant Plains, seemingly lounging around and telling people how he was going to whip Quinn Harrison. Turley's Store doubled as the town's post office, and it may be that Crafton was lying in wait for Harrison to come in for his mail. Thomas Turley, the owner of the store, replied to Crafton's boastful threats by saying, "Don't do it. You are bigger and stronger than Quinn. You will get no honor from whipping him, and you might get yourself hurt in the process."

On either the Friday or the Monday before July 16, a gentleman by the name of P. M. Carter came into Turley's Store and saw Greek Crafton there. Crafton announced his intention to whip Harrison and went on to say Harrison was "a-carrying a bowie knife down there for me," as he ran his hand down beneath the front of his shirt. "He will be down here this evening and I am going to give him a chance to use them."

Carter drew Crafton over to the side for a private talk away from the others in the store. "Greek, you need to let Quinn alone. If you do, I'll go Quinn's bail that he won't even speak to you. If ever you attack Quinn, I believe he is determined to kill you as he told you. If you take the advice of a friend you will let him alone."

Crafton replied, "If he is here this evening he has got to try it on." Harrison did not go into Turley's Store that evening.

On the morning of July 16, John Allen sat outside the doorway at Henry Smith's grocery store in Pleasant Plains waiting for the mail to arrive. As he sat there, two things happened. The mail boy came by, headed toward the post office, and Greek Crafton walked into the grocery store. Allen called out to the mail boy that he was early today, and the boy replied that he was trying to get his route done before it got too hot. In a moment, Crafton walked out of the store and announced his intention to go to the post office. Allen decided to accompany him.

As they walked toward the post office inside Turley's Store, Crafton remarked, "John, I allow to whip Quinn Harrison today."

"Greek, what's that about?"

Crafton made no direct reply but said, "I allow I will do it this day if I get a chance."

"You had better let that alone, Greek," said Allen. Again, Crafton made no direct reply. Instead, he said that he expected Harrison to come into Turley's after his mail. When they got to Turley's, Crafton took off his hat and coat and stationed himself beside the door so as not to be visible to anyone coming in from the outside. He stood on the west side of the door, the side that Harrison would have come from if he were coming from his home. Crafton lay in wait for a while but soon tired of his vigil. He put his hat and coat back on and left Turley's.

Short and Hart's Drugstore had no paying customers that morning. Benjamin Short, the co-owner, sat at the counter on a stool near the front door, sharing the newspaper with Quinn Harrison. Harrison sat on a stool next to Short, reading the paper with him. John Crafton, Greek's brother, had come in earlier to inquire whether a friend had kept his promise to leave some money with Hart at the drugstore. Hart had not yet arrived, so John went to the back of the store, lay down on the back counter, and promptly went to sleep. The morning passed quietly until Greek Crafton entered the store. Short, who was sitting nearest the door, noticed Greek taking his coat off as he came through the front door but thought little of it until Greek walked around Short and grabbed Harrison by the arms. Harrison gripped the counter and held on for dear life. The stools toppled to the floor as Short and Harrison stood up, and Short tried to insert himself between the two men to stop the fight. Harrison yelled, "Let go of me! I don't want to fight!" but Greek said nothing. Greek pulled on Harrison, Short pulled on Greek, and Harrison clung to the counter. Greek let go of one of Harrison's arms long enough to strike a mighty blow to his temple, and Harrison let go of the counter. By this time, John Crafton had awakened and joined the fray, trying to get Short off Greek as Short continued to try to get Greek off Harrison.

John called out, "Let Greek go! He can whip him!"

Short replied, "They shan't fight!"

Short and the two Craftons were all pulling in about the same direction, and Harrison was pulling in the other direction, trying to escape. Three strong men were too much for one weak man to overcome, so the fight moved to the back of the store instead of going in Harrison's preferred direction—out the front door. The four men scuffled across the floor to the far corner at the rear of the store, where they collided with a stack of boxes. When they hit the boxes, the neat stack became a pile and they fell partially over it. Greek then let go of Harrison's arm long enough for Harrison to get his hand into the breast of his coat. He stabbed backward, hitting Greek in the stomach. Greek let go of Harrison and staggered out of the drugstore.

Seeing that Greek was injured, John attacked Harrison and Harrison cut him on the arm, seriously wounding him. John continued the fight with missile weapons instead of fisticuffs. He ran to the balance beam scales to pick up the weights to throw at Harrison but could not find them. He threw the scales. By this time, something of a crowd had gathered in the store. One of the bystanders asked John whether he was hurt. John replied, "My God, I am ruined!" John stumbled against a chair, picked it up, and threw it. He saw some glasses on the counter, picked them up, and threw them. Harrison stood his ground, neither advancing nor retreating, and weathered the hail of missiles.

When he ran out of handy missiles, John left the store and went to Dr. Million's office for treatment. His brother Greek was already there. When all was clear in the drugstore, Harrison left and went to lawyer Shelby M. Cullom, who helped him find a hiding place pending legal action on the brawl. Greek Crafton languished for several days and finally died, and a warrant was issued for the arrest of "Peachy" Quinn Harrison for the murder of Greek Crafton. Cullom promised that as soon as a preliminary hearing was scheduled, Harrison would surrender; and the lawyer was as good as his word.

The citizens of Sangamon County took great interest in the progress of the case against Harrison. Both he and Greek Crafton came from large, prominent, and powerful families, and the local newspapers reported every scrap of information they could glean about the case. The two main Springfield papers, the *Illinois State Journal* and the *Illinois State Register*, competed with each other to provide the fullest coverage, and when they ran out of things to say about the case, they each critiqued the other's coverage of the prosecution.

On the morning of August 2, 1859, Quinn Harrison gave himself up to Constable William Perce, and Perce took him to the courthouse, where a huge crowd had gathered to attend the preliminary hearing. James B. White, the elected state's attorney, appeared for the prosecution, assisted by two lawyers whom the Craftons had retained to assist him, John A. McClernand and Norman M. Broadwell. Justices of the Peace Lucien B. Adams and William Hickman presided, and four lawyers appeared on behalf of Harrison: Lincoln, his partner Herndon, Lincoln's old partner Stephen A. Logan, and Milton Hay. Seventy-five witnesses had received subpoenas to appear and testify, but the prosecution asked for a continuance on grounds that their two most important witnesses, Silas Livergood and John Crafton, had not appeared. After much discussion, the justices adjourned court until 8 the following morning. They remanded Harrison to the custody of the county jail.[17]

The next day, the justices heard the case in a courtroom packed with spectators. Only sixteen of the seventy-five subpoenaed witnesses testified, eight for the prosecution and eight for the defense. The testimony took up the entire day. At 6 P.M. the justices adjourned court until 8 the following morning, when the lawyers would be allowed to sum up the case.[18] An interesting relic of the preliminary hearing can be found among the Papers of Abraham Lincoln—a notebook in which one of the defense lawyers made notes of the testimony of the witnesses at the hearing.[19] Although Lincoln's name is written in the book, the handwriting is not his.

The third day of the preliminary hearing was completely consumed by the speeches of the lawyers. That morning, Broadwell opened for the prosecution, and Logan responded for the defense. After the noon meal, Lincoln argued for the defense, and McClernand closed the case for the prosecution.[20] The prosecution argued vehemently for a finding of probable cause for the crime of murder, which would have denied the defendant bail as a matter of right. The defense attorneys, on the other hand, did something very unusual: they strongly contended that Harrison had acted in self-defense, but they suggested that the court nevertheless enter a finding of probable cause for the crime of manslaughter, "lest his release might appear like too hasty a disposition of so serious a matter."[21] The judges found probable cause for the crime of manslaughter and released Harrison on $10,000 bail.

When the defense suggested a finding of probable cause for manslaughter, it gave the justices a face-saving escape from the horns of a dilemma—either to offend the politically powerful Harrison clan by finding probable cause for murder or to offend the politically powerful Crafton clan by finding no probable cause. Given the weakness of the case, the politically independent grand jury could be expected to completely exonerate Harrison by finding no true bill.

Lincoln probably thought the case was over. Otherwise, he would have spent the next few weeks preparing for the upcoming murder trial rather than traveling. He left on a business trip for Iowa shortly after the preliminary hearing concluded and did not return to Springfield until August 18, just before the term of court was to begin.[22] He must have been astonished when the grand jury returned an indictment for murder against Harrison. The *Journal* certainly was. It wrote, "By what mode of precedence they made up their minds to such an indictment is a mystery. If there ever was a case of killing in self-defense, we think the testimony at the preliminary examination of Harrison, showed one."[23]

The *Register* wasted no time in writing a blistering critique of the *Journal*, saying, "It is not for the public press now to express an opinion in justice to either party." The *Register* went on to accuse the *Journal* of playing politics and ended by characterizing the *Journal*'s article as "foolish."[24] The *Journal* could not let such an insult go unanswered. It immediately published a reply, and that reply might give some insight into how the grand jury could have indicted in such a one-sided case as the Harrison case:

> It sounds rather laughable in the *Register* to talk about our lugging politics into the courts, when it is notorious that the very Grand Jury, which that sheet apologizes for, is a packed political machine, made up entirely of the very strongest Democratic partisans, for a particular purpose. If the *Register* is sincere in its deprecation of partisanism in judicial proceedings, let it begin by venting a small vial full of indignation at the composition of its present Grand Jury, before it presumes to arraign others on the charge.[25]

The *Journal* made an allusion to some other political controversy then current, suggesting that the grand jury had been packed with Democrats to gain a political advantage in that squabble. The *Journal* may have been mistaken in its allegation of jury tampering, but such things were not beyond the realm of possibility. Although juries are supposed to be chosen by a random selection process, court officials have been known to manipulate the process in order to stack a jury for political purposes. The *Register* fired off one more article characterizing the *Journal*'s accusation of a handpicked grand jury as a "lame excuse,"[26] and that ended the war of words between the Republican *Journal* and the Democratic *Register*.

If the *Journal*'s accusation were true, or even if the luck of the draw had caused the grand jury to be made up predominantly of Democrats, that may explain the grand jury's action. The fact that State's Attorney James B. White was also a Democrat may have contributed to the indictment of Harrison. Whatever the reason, Harrison was indeed indicted for murder, arraigned, and remanded to the county jail pending trial. Unlike most of the murder cases that Lincoln tried, the defense asked for no change of venue or continuances.

There is some reason to question State's Attorney White's enthusiasm for the case against Harrison. The evidence supporting this comes from the contemporary news accounts and the transcript of the trial. The news reports of Harrison's preliminary hearing were full of references to White's role in the hearing,[27] but he was strangely inactive during the actual jury trial. White declined to make the opening statement for the prosecution because he was "engrossed in other business."[28] The trial transcript also reflects that he declined to conduct the direct examination of any prosecution witnesses or the cross-examination of any defense witnesses. Nor does the transcript reflect that he engaged in the argument of any motions or made a final argument to the jury.[29] The transcript does not identify the lawyer who made the closing final argument for the prosecution, but the newspapers do: John M. Palmer. Palmer "spoke with marked ability for three hours, evincing great ingenuity in handling the testimony, interspersing many remarks upon human nature and human passions, and the duties of citizens and the spirit of the law."[30] White apparently just sat back and let the lawyers hired by the Craftons handle the case. Possibly White was so convinced of Harrison's innocence that he told his co-counsel, "You prosecute him. I can't." More likely he decided that he was not equal to the task of contesting a marginal murder case against two such accomplished attorneys as Lincoln and Logan. Palmer and Broadwell were much more talented lawyers, and White may have simply decided to turn the prosecution over to them.

John M. Palmer, the
lead prosecutor in
the Harrison case.
He later served as a
general during the
Civil War and as a
governor of Illi-
nois. PHOTOGRAPH
COURTESY OF THE
LIBRARY OF CONGRESS.

An additional factor in White's curious inactivity might have been that
he had his hands full at that particular term of court. The Harrison case
concluded on Saturday, September 3, and another sensational murder case,
People v. Branch, began the following Wednesday. White tried the Branch
case with the assistance of another lawyer, but he took an active part in the
prosecution, making the opening statement, examining witnesses, and giving
the closing final argument. The jury found Branch not guilty.[31]

At the Harrison trial, Palmer served as lead counsel, actively assisted by
Broadwell and nominally assisted by White. McClernand had apparently
withdrawn from the case. The defense team consisted of Lincoln, Logan, and
Cullom. Logan and Lincoln split the duties of examining the witnesses, and
Lincoln assumed the task of arguing the admissibility of evidence. Cullom
was responsible for giving the opening final argument for the defense. After
a lengthy voir dire examination of over one hundred potential jurors,[32] a jury
was seated and the case began. Broadwell made the opening statement for
the prosecution by simply reading the indictment and the murder statute.
Logan gave a brief reply, and the witnesses were excused from the courtroom.

Palmer called Dr. J. L. Million as his first witness. Million had been standing outside the drugstore when Crafton staggered out. He went to Crafton,
who collapsed in his arms. Million took Crafton to his house, about one

hundred yards away, and examined the wound. He found it to be a knife wound between the eleventh and twelfth ribs, large enough for the intestines to protrude. He pushed the intestines back into the stomach and sewed the wound up with two or three stitches. Crafton languished from 8 A.M. on July 16 until 8 P.M. on July 18.

Palmer's next witness was Silas Livergood, who had walked into the drugstore in the middle of the fight. When he walked in, he saw Harrison hanging on to the counter for dear life, telling Crafton he did not want to fight. Crafton was trying to pull Harrison off the counter, and Short was trying to pull Crafton off Harrison. Livergood saw John Crafton come from the back of the store and grab Short, saying to let Greek go so he could whip Harrison. He then saw Harrison let go of the counter and the four men scuffle across the floor to the back of the store. When they stumbled into the boxes, Greek was leaning over, and Harrison was able to get his knife out and do the cutting. Greek let go of Harrison, and Short and John Crafton pulled Greek to the front of the store. The entire time, Harrison had his back to Greek. Sometime after Greek got cut, John made his way toward Harrison, and Harrison cut him too. Harrison's knife had a blade about four inches long. To illustrate Livergood's testimony, Palmer drew a rough floorplan of the drugstore on the floor of the courtroom and had the witness point to the various places around the drugstore where the action occurred.[33] Livergood testified that when Greek had Harrison over the boxes, he let go of one of Harrison's arms and struck Harrison in the face. When Greek let go of his arm, Harrison was able to get the knife out, stabbing Greek after his adversary had struck him in the face.

This is the sort of testimony that might prompt a judge to ask, "Mr. Prosecutor, when are you going to start calling the prosecution witnesses?" The other witnesses were not much better. Daniel Harnett, another latecomer to the drugstore, testified to what he had seen of the fight, and it was pretty much the same as Livergood's testimony. Other witnesses were Frederick Henry, who had prevented Greek from jumping onto Harrison at the July 4 picnic; John Bone, from whom Harrison had tried to borrow a knife; Edmund Crafton; and William Purvines, whom Harrison had told that although he did not want to fight Greek, he would cut his guts out if he had to. The prosecution got some help from the testimony of Peter Livergood, who had gone and talked to Harrison while he was hiding from the law. Harrison asked Peter whether the Craftons were hurt badly, and Peter told him, "I don't know how bad John is, but I don't think Greek will live until sundown."

"There is no danger," replied Harrison. "You couldn't kill a hound. If my knife had been longer I could have done quicker work."

The star witness for the prosecution was John Crafton, the victim's brother, who had sustained a severe cut on his arm when he came to the aid of his brother. Lincoln did a masterful job of neutralizing John's testimony with what is sometimes called concession-based cross-examination. Lincoln's main strategy was to portray Greek as the aggressor. He intended to do this by getting John to repeat admissions he had made at the preliminary hearing. There was no court reporter at the preliminary hearing, but Lincoln had the notes of John's testimony taken at the hearing. Lincoln also wanted to try to get John to admit favorable facts that had already been proven by other prosecution witnesses or that he intended to prove by defense witnesses. This sort of cross-examination is seldom flashy, but it can be devastating. Lincoln's cross went like this:

Q: About that time [when the fight began] did you hear either of the parties say anything?

A: No, sir. I don't remember any such thing. I think I said the first thing spoken in the room. I told Mr. Short to let them loose, that Greek could whip him.

Q: You did not add that "Greek should whip him?"

A: No, sir, but I told him he could whip him.

Q: Did you see anything about the beginning or for a little while of Harrison holding on to one of the counters?

A: No sir . . . I did not see any holding on. [This reply had to have hurt John's credibility with the jury. Everyone else testified to seeing Harrison holding on to the counter.]

Q: Were they so far from the counter as to leave no question about it in your mind?

A: I suppose if a man had tried, he could reach the counter from where they were. . . .

Q: And then you pulled on him [Benjamin Short], rather to pull him out of the fight?

A: I could not say whether I pulled him or not. I caught his arm and told him to let them loose. I held on until he pushed me backwards over this south counter. . . .

Q: You did not see the knife when the blow was given?

A: I did not see the knife go into him. . . .

Q: I suppose when you told Short to let him alone—that Greek could whip him, that you had the ordinary meaning and wanted Greek to whip him?

A: I thought after they got into the fight that Greek could whip him.

Q: And you wanted him to?

A: Well, certainly I did.[34]

Palmer called a few more witnesses after John Crafton, who simply testified to facts already covered by other witnesses, and then he announced that
the prosecution rested its case. It would not be an overstatement to say that
the prosecution case was underwhelming. According to the prosecution evidence, Harrison had been sitting at a counter in a drugstore minding his own
business when Greek Crafton walked up behind him and grabbed his arms.
Harrison announced that he did not want to fight and hung on to the counter
for dear life. Others joined in the scuffle as Crafton assaulted Harrison and
Harrison tried to escape. Crafton let go of one of Harrison's arms to strike
Harrison in the face, and Harrison pulled a knife. Harrison, who never faced
Crafton during the melee, stabbed backward, inflicting the fatal wound. The
defense now had an opportunity to present evidence in Harrison's defense;
and if Palmer expected that the case against Harrison would get even weaker
than it already was, his expectations would soon be fulfilled.

It is a testament to the weakness of the prosecution case that Palmer did
not call the only witness who saw the fight from start to finish. Benjamin
Short had testified for the prosecution at the preliminary hearing, but between the preliminary hearing and the trial, the prosecution team decided
that his testimony had more negatives than positives. They were not going to
prevent the defense from calling Short as a witness, but they could weaken the
negative aspects of his testimony by making the defense call him. Evidence
favorable to the defense takes on much greater weight when it is extracted
from prosecution witnesses on cross-examination. It also works the other way
around. Evidence favorable to the prosecution takes on greater weight when it
comes from the mouth of a defense witness. It frequently happens that a weak
prosecution witness can be turned into a good witness for the prosecution if
the defense can be maneuvered into calling him. This is probably what the
prosecution hoped to accomplish by declining to call Short.

Logan called Short as the first defense witness. He testified to the familiar
scenario of Crafton's sudden attack, Harrison's attempt to avoid the fight,
Crafton's manhandling of Harrison, and Harrison's eventual stabbing of Crafton. When Logan turned Short over to Palmer, Palmer performed a textbook
example of how not to conduct a cross-examination. Lincoln's cross-examination of John Crafton had consisted of questions seeking helpful facts that
Crafton had to admit. If Crafton did not admit the facts, other evidence was

available to prove him wrong. Palmer's cross-examination of Short consisted of one question after another in an attempt to get him to say things that he could safely deny without fear of contradiction from anyone. Palmer asked a particularly harmful series of questions about the time before John Crafton awoke and entered the fray. As Short was the only wakeful witness in the drugstore at that time, there was nobody to contradict him.

Q: Is it not true that as Crafton came up Harrison rose to his feet?

A: He rose to his feet when Crafton took hold of him. . . .

Q: Did he say to Crafton that if he laid his hands on him he would kill him?

A: I think not—nothing about killing or defending himself, I think. I think he said he didn't want to fight or wouldn't fight him and to keep off. I don't recall anything else. . . .

Q: Did he curse Crafton?

A: He did not.[35]

Not only were these facts helpful to Harrison, but neither Logan nor Lincoln had brought them out on direct examination. Palmer would have been better off asking no questions than asking these questions. Palmer also attempted to shift some of the blame for Crafton's death by suggesting that if Short had tried harder to separate the men, he could have prevented the death. This may have been true, but it was also irrelevant.

Q: Wasn't there plenty of time for you to have placed yourself between them [when you saw Greek was going to attack Harrison]?

A: I suppose I might have put myself between them if I had been in a pretty smart hurry. . . .

Q: Can you give any reason why you could not separate these men?

A: I suppose if I had laid out all my strength I might. I didn't try very hard.

Q: Why didn't you try very hard?

A: I thought we could get them to stop without it.[36]

When Palmer finished the cross-examination of Short, he had accomplished very little other than to reemphasize those portions of Short's testimony favorable to Harrison and bring out additional testimony favorable to Harrison. Lawyers sometimes refer to this sort of ineffectual cross-examination as "supplemental direct examination."

The defense of Quinn Harrison had four objectives: to establish from eyewitness testimony that Crafton was the aggressor and Harrison tried to avoid the fight, to establish by "earwitnesses" that they had heard Crafton make numerous threats to seriously injure Harrison, to establish that Harrison was physically incapable of fighting Crafton hand-to-hand, and to prove that Crafton made a dying declaration accepting responsibility for his own death. Short's testimony went a long way toward accomplishing the first objective, but they had more than just the testimony of Benjamin Short.

John Allen testified that when he came into the drugstore, he saw Harrison holding on to the counter and Crafton trying to pull him off. Allen saw the counter slide two or three feet out of place before Harrison finally let go of it.[37] With the testimony of John Allen, the defense had established the first objective of the defense and was ready to move on to the second. Allen had heard Crafton make threats against Harrison, but he could not recall ever having told Harrison about the threats. Palmer objected to Allen's testimony about the threats, and Judge E. Y. Rice sustained the objection. It was this ruling, and not the ruling on Crafton's dying declaration, that so incensed Lincoln. Lincoln knew he was right and the judge was wrong.

In almost any freshman course on criminal law in almost any law school, students learn that threats by a deceased against his killer, if communicated to the killer, are relevant on the issue of whether the killer reasonably feared the deceased when he used deadly force in self-defense. If the defendant never heard the threats, they could have no bearing on whether the defendant reasonably feared the deceased. This was the common law, but at the time of the Harrison trial, courts were beginning to expand the admissibility of threat evidence to circumstances where the defendant never heard the threats. In fact, the Illinois Supreme Court had recently widened the admissibility of threat evidence. *Campbell v. People* was a case where the defendant killed a man who had attacked him with a hatchet.[38] The defendant claimed self-defense and tried to introduce evidence of threats the deceased had made against him. The trial court ruled the threat evidence inadmissible because the threats had never been communicated to the defendant, but the Supreme Court reversed for a new trial, saying, "Although they may never have come to the knowledge of the defendant . . . [if] the deceased had made threats against the defendant, it would be a reasonable inference that he sought him for the purpose of executing those threats, and thus they would serve to characterize his conduct towards [the defendant], that he had attempted to accomplish his declared purpose, and if so, then the prisoner was justified in defending himself."[39]

Lincoln probably did not get as angry as Herndon said he did, but he did get angry enough for his co-counsel to step in and try to make peace. Hitt's transcript notes at this point that Logan "said that, as there was now a good deal of feeling excited on the subject at the moment, he would propose that the other evidence proceed, & this matter be postponed for further argument tomorrow morning."[40] They agreed to this course of action, and the defense proved up several threats by Crafton that had been communicated to Harrison. Palmer did not object to these threats coming into evidence. This partially established the second objective of the defense, but Lincoln still wanted to get all the threats into evidence, not just the ones that Harrison heard.

Lincoln and Logan established the third objective of the defense with two witnesses: Dr. Albert Atherton, Harrison's personal physician, and the Reverend Peter Cartwright, Harrison's grandfather. Cartwright testified about Harrison's many childhood sicknesses and his frailness as a youth and a young man, and Dr. Atherton attested to Harrison's ill health and inability to do manual labor for at least the past three years.

When Lincoln and Logan moved to the fourth objective of the defense, the dying declaration, they hit another snag. Palmer vehemently objected to the evidence on the grounds that it did not go to prove how the deceased was killed. Judge Rice expressed the opinion that the testimony about the dying declaration should be proffered outside the presence of the jury so that he could make a preliminary ruling on its admissibility. Today this is a common practice when one side or the other offers evidence of questionable admissibility. The evidence is proffered outside the presence of the jury, and if the judge rules it inadmissible, the jury never hears it. Lincoln, probably still smoldering from the judge's ruling on the threat evidence, exclaimed that he "had never heard of such a law."[41] Despite Lincoln's objection, Rice decided that he was going to rule on the testimony about the dying declaration outside the presence of the jury. He recessed court for the day.

The next morning, with the jury out of the courtroom, they proffered Cartwright's testimony. Lincoln was not happy about the exclusion of the jury and took an exception to the judge's ruling. This meant that in the event Harrison got convicted, Lincoln intended to appeal the conviction on grounds that the judge improperly excluded the jury for the proffer. Lincoln would have lost that point on appeal. Despite his never having heard of such a law, it was well settled at the time that the judge was to make a preliminary ruling on the admissibility of a dying declaration before a jury could hear it.[42] Sometimes, when balked in one effort, an attorney becomes unduly passionate about other efforts. It seems that this is what happened with Lincoln. Stymied by the judge's refusal to allow the threat testimony, Lincoln became somewhat unreasonable over the proffer of the dying declaration.

With the jury absent, Cartwright told a pitiful tale of woe, recounting how he had just returned home from a trip and was suffering from an injured hip he had sustained in a riding accident. His wife told him of the "dreadful affair," which Cartwright said "shocked me exceedingly." Cartwright then told how he was called to the dying man's sickroom to pray for him. Despite intense suffering from his injured hip, Cartwright rushed to Greek Crafton's bedside. According to Cartwright, when he knelt by the bed, he took Crafton by the hand and expressed his deepest sorrow over such a fatal calamity. Crafton replied, "The honest hour has come upon me, and in a few moments I expect to stand before my final Judge; do you think there is any mercy for me? Will you pray for me?" Cartwright repeated his deep regret, and Crafton said, "Yes, I have brought it on myself, and I forgive Quinn." By this time, the pain in Cartwright's hip was unbearable, so he stood and was offered a chair. After sitting in the chair, he distinctly heard Crafton repeat, "I have brought it upon myself. I forgive Quinn, and I want it said to all my friends that I have no enmity in my heart against any man; and if I die I want it declared to all that I die in peace with God and all mankind."[43]

After hearing the arguments of the lawyers, Judge Rice ruled the dying declaration admissible. As noted earlier, a deathbed statement forgiving the killer is not a dying declaration, because it does not relate to how the fatal wound was inflicted.[44] If we take the traditional story as true, Lincoln led Rice into error. As is often the case, however, the earliest Lincoln biographers remembered the sensational but forgot the significant. They recalled the pathos of Crafton's supposedly forgiving Harrison but forgot the significant portion of the statement—Crafton's admission that "I have brought it [my death] upon myself."

Palmer by this time was fighting a rearguard action, trying to stave off defeat by any means possible. He argued that the only part of Cartwright's testimony that the jury should hear was the dying declaration, and that the other testimony about the heartrending attendant circumstances should be held inadmissible. Unfortunately for Palmer's position, the attendant circumstances were necessary for the jury to decide whether Crafton really thought he was going to die. The bedrock theory on which the dying declaration was first ruled admissible was the theory that the dying declaration "derives the value of its sanction from the religious sense of the party's accountability to his Maker," and someone who was about to "render to Him the final account" would not run the risk of eternal damnation by telling a lie on his deathbed.[45]

The jurors came back in, and when they had taken their seats in the jury box, Cartwright repeated his story for their ears. The *Journal* noted a difference between the way he testified while the jury was out and the way he testified before the jury. While the jury was out, he testified in "a characteristic and forceful manner," but before the jury, he testified "in a voice tremulous with age and feeling."[46] The reverend had preached at hundreds of revivals, and his sermons had won thousands of souls to the church. He knew how to motivate an audience, and it appears that he made full use of his oratorical skills before the jury. Palmer did not ask Cartwright a single question on cross-examination.

It would be easy to discount Cartwright's testimony as highly untrustworthy, coming from the mouth of the defendant's grandfather, but the defense followed Cartwright with the testimony of his son Madison, who testified that he had heard Crafton tell his father, "I brought it upon myself,"[47] and the testimony of Dr. John Slater, who said he had heard Crafton tell Cartwright, "The honest hour is upon me. I am a dying man and in a few minutes or hours at most I shall have finished my earthly existence," and then go on to tell Cartwright "I forgive Quinn."[48]

Palmer did not cross-examine Madison Cartwright, and he should not have cross-examined Dr. Slater. His cross-examination of Slater brought out a second dying declaration made after Cartwright left the room:

Q: Have you now detailed all he said in reference to the manner of his death & Harrison?

A: All he said at that time. He remarked after the Dr. stepped out of the room.

Q: Dr. Cartwright?

A: Yes.

Q: Was it a continuation of the same conversation?

A: It was not continued to Mr. Cartwright. He was not in the room. . . .

Q: State what he said in that continued conversation?

A: . . . that he had brought this upon himself & that he wished all the world to understand that he died in peace with God & man.[49]

It seems clear that, as implausible as it may seem on the face of it, Greek Crafton did in fact tell Cartwright that he was responsible for his own death. Four things tell us that, although Cartwright certainly embellished and dramatized the deathbed statement, he spoke the truth: Palmer's lack of cross-examination of the Cartwrights, his bungled cross-examination of Dr. Slater, his failure to call anybody else who was in the crowded room at the time to contradict Cartwright, and his examination of the rebuttal witnesses, Jacob Epler and Dr. Million. The discussion of the prosecution's case on rebuttal below will show how the fourth point validates the dying declaration.

When Cartwright concluded his testimony, Judge Rice took up the issue of admissibility of the evidence of Crafton's uncommunicated threats. Broadwell opened the argument of the law on behalf of the prosecution, followed by Logan, and then Lincoln. Palmer made the closing argument for the prosecution. Hitt recorded that "the arguments of the counsel were learned, elaborate & eloquent."[50] The argument being concluded, Judge Rice recessed court for dinner (the noon meal).

After dinner, Judge Rice ruled that evidence of all threats, whether communicated to Harrison or not, was admissible. The defense called P. M. Carter, Thomas Turley, John Allen, John Purvines, Abijah Nottingham, and James Zane, all of whom testified to various threats that Greek Crafton had made, saying he intended to do serious bodily injury to Quinn Harrison. After these witnesses testified, the defense rested.

At this stage of the trial, Lincoln and his associates had to have felt good about the way the case had gone. The prosecution had put on a weak case, and they had responded with powerful evidence from four sources: Benjamin Short's account of the fight, the evidence of Crafton's threats against Harrison, the evidence of Harrison's frail health, and Crafton's deathbed statement exonerating Harrison. They could not, however, be content to rest on their laurels. The defense team could feel confident that if the jury did what it should, it would acquit. Juries, however, do not always do what they should. The defense still had much work to do in order to shepherd the jury to a favorable verdict.

At this stage, Palmer was grasping at straws. He tried to call two witnesses, Jacob Epler and Dr. J. L. Million, in hopes that they would testify to having heard Crafton say quite different things about Harrison from his deathbed. The last few pages of the transcript have deteriorated, so we do not have all of Epler's testimony, but we can piece together what he most likely said from the legible portion together with the *Journal's* report of his testimony and the attorney's notes of his testimony from the preliminary hearing. He did not contradict Cartwright so much as add to what Cartwright said. After Cartwright left Crafton's bedside, Benjamin Short came to see the dying man. Crafton blamed Short for his injury, saying he would not have gotten cut if Short had not interfered. After Short left, he repeated the statement and then asked if Harrison had been arrested yet. When told no, he said that it was about time Harrison should be arrested. This time Lincoln did not object when Judge Rice announced that he would hear the testimony on proffer outside the presence of the jury before ruling on its admissibility. After hearing the proffer, Rice ruled it admissible.

Apparently Epler had been present when Crafton made his dying declaration to Harrison, heard the dying declaration, and could have testified to hearing it. Palmer, of course, did not ask Epler whether he heard the dying declaration. Not only did he decline to ask about the dying declaration, but he was very careful to prevent Lincoln from asking Epler about it. He used the same stratagem that Lincoln had used with the witness Nelson Watkins in *People v. Armstrong*, and it worked just as well for Palmer as it had for Lincoln. At that time, there was a well-established rule that "a party has no right to cross-examine any witness except as to facts and circumstances connected with the matters stated in his direct examination."[51] All Palmer had to do to prevent Lincoln from asking about the statement was to make it clear that he was not asking anything about what had been said when Cartwright was in the room:

Q: State if you heard Mr. Crafton say anything about the connection of Mr. Harrison with his death, *after* the time Mr. Cartwright was there & held his conversation with him.
A: It was after the conversation with Mr. Cartwright.
Q: State what you heard him say about the connection of Mr. Harrison & his death *after* Mr. Cartwright was there.[52]

Because Lincoln was prevented from asking the most important question that anyone could have asked Epler—whether Crafton had really made those statements to Cartwright—we can say with a high degree of probability that he would have answered, "Yes, Greek really said that to Mr. Cartwright." Palmer attempted the same ploy with his next witness, Dr. Million, but things did not work out quite as well:

Q: State whether you had any conversation with Greek Crafton *after* Mr. Cartwright had the interview, about the connection of Mr. Harrison with his death.
A: Not after, before Mr. Cartwright had the interview.[53]

Palmer withdrew Million as a witness and rested. What Crafton may have said before he talked to Cartwright was irrelevant.

It was now time for final arguments. Broadwell opened for the prosecution and spoke for approximately one hour. When he finished speaking, Judge Rice took an hour-and-a-half evening recess for supper. After supper, Shelby M. Cullom spoke his first words during the trial by making the opening final argument for the defense. Because of the September heat in the crowded courtroom, Cullom fell ill and had to cut his argument short. It now came

Logan's turn to argue, and he spoke for an hour and a quarter. Hitt reported that he spoke "with great ability, discussing the facts with the most impressive earnestness & eloquence."[54] Judge Rice recessed court in the middle of Logan's speech, saying he could conclude his argument the next morning.

The next morning, a Saturday, Logan spoke for another hour and a half before turning the floor over to Lincoln. The page of the transcript that records Lincoln's remarks is probably the most badly deteriorated portion of the entire transcript, which means we have lost the sense of most of what he said. His main arguments can be pieced together, however, by reading the transcript along with the description of his remarks in the *Journal*. Hitt reported that Lincoln "dwelt principa[ll]y [on] . . . various facts in evidence as to the act . . . between deceased & the prisoner on the 16."[55] The *Journal* said that Lincoln made "a speech of two hours, examining the evidence with great skill and clearness, discussing the law and replying to the positions assumed by the counsel for the prosecution with a subtle and resistless logic, and frequent illustrations of singular fitness. It was delivered in an earnest, natural and energetic manner."[56]

Neither source makes any mention of the emotional plea Lincoln is supposed to have made for the jury to ignore the fact that Harrison had murdered Crafton and honor Crafton's dying wish that Harrison's crime be excused. Either Lincoln never made such an argument or, if he did, it was not nearly as melodramatic as memory came to paint it. He likely used the dying declaration to make a logical argument—that Crafton knew better than anyone else whether Harrison acted in self-defense, and if he admitted that he had brought his misfortune on himself and was willing to forgive Harrison, then he surely believed Harrison acted in self-defense. All of this leads to the inescapable conclusion that Harrison had acted in self-defense and should be acquitted. This is the sort of "merciless logic" that Lincoln was renowned for as a practicing lawyer.[57]

At the conclusion of his speech, Lincoln made a remarkable suggestion: he announced that the key witness in the case was Silas Livergood and suggested that Hitt read back Livergood's testimony to the jury before it retired to consider its verdict. To announce that one of the main prosecution witnesses was the key witness in the case and suggest that his testimony be read back indicates that Lincoln was supremely confident Livergood's testimony would exonerate Harrison. Since Lincoln had previously shown a distaste for doing things outside the presence of the jury, we can also be sure that he made the suggestion in its hearing. Palmer first consented to the procedure, but then objected.

Palmer stumbled when he opposed the reading back of Livergood's testimony. Livergood was a prosecution witness. The prosecution should have
been proud of his testimony and glad to have the jury hear it again. To act
otherwise was to admit that Livergood's testimony hurt the prosecution more
than it helped. When Palmer prevented the jury from rehearing Livergood's
testimony, he hurt his case at least as much as if the jury had actually reheard
the testimony.

By the time Lincoln concluded his remarks, the noon hour was upon them.
Judge Rice recessed court for dinner, and when court reconvened in the afternoon, Palmer spoke. Hitt did not write anything about Palmer's speech,
but the *Journal* described it: Palmer "spoke with marked ability for three
hours, evincing great ingenuity in handling the testimony, interspersing many
remarks upon human nature and human passions, the duties of the citizens
and the spirit of the law."[58] The *Journal* said nothing about Palmer calling
Lincoln a liar, and it is highly unlikely that Palmer ever did such a thing.

When Newton Bateman told the Cadmus Club the story of Palmer calling
Lincoln a liar, he took care to conceal Palmer's name. By the time Bateman
made his speech in 1899, three things had happened: Palmer had distinguished
himself as a Civil War general, he had served as governor of Illinois, and
Bateman's memory had been dimmed by the passage of forty years. Couple
those facts with the oral historian's natural tendency to embellish, and we have
good reason to doubt Bateman's story. We have another good reason to discount Bateman, and it comes from T. W. S. Kidd, the crier of the court. In his
letter to Ida M. Tarbell, Kidd gave a much different account of the incident: "In
the Harrison murder case the prosecuting attorney stated that such a witness
made a certain [untrue] statement, when Mr. Lincoln rose and made such
a plaintive appeal to the attorney to correct the statement, that the attorney
actually made the *amende honorable* [a satisfactory apology], and afterwards
remarked to a brother lawyer that he could deny his own child's appeal as
quickly as he could Mr. Lincoln's."[59]

As with most divergent stories of an incident, the less dramatic version
has the greater claim to plausibility. Which seems more likely: that Palmer
simply misstated the facts of the case and Lincoln corrected him, or that he
called Lincoln a liar and Lincoln shamed him into an apology? In deciding
between the two versions, remember that Palmer and Lincoln were political
allies, and a mere month after the trial, Lincoln wrote to Harrison urging
him to support Palmer in an upcoming election.[60] It is odd enough that a
defense attorney would write to a former client saying, "Please vote for the
man who just prosecuted you for murder," but it is outlandish to think that

a lawyer would write to his client saying, "Please vote for the man who just prosecuted you for murder and just called me a liar."

The jury was out for one hour and nine minutes and came back with a verdict finding Harrison not guilty. The large crowd in attendance at the trial greeted the verdict with thunderous applause. Either there were no Democrats on the jury or the Democrats on the jury were fair-minded men who would not allow party politics to cloud their judgment.

The Craftons were not satisfied with the verdict. They swore out a warrant for the arrest of Benjamin Short, accusing him of having aided and abetted Quinn Harrison in committing the murder of Greek Crafton. Constable Hamilton arrested him on Friday, September 9, and the town of Pleasant Plains erupted in anger. On the evening of September 9, a citizens' committee met at the public hall for the purpose of drafting a resolution condemning the arrest of Short. The committee duly adopted a five-paragraph resolution decrying Short's arrest, expressing full confidence in his innocence, and protesting any further agitation of the affair. On Monday, September 12, Justices Adams and Hickman held a preliminary hearing in the matter. William Henry Herndon appeared for the defense, but White declined to appear for the prosecution. As nobody was there to present evidence on behalf of the prosecution, the justices dismissed the case against Short.[61]

Quinn Harrison had a checkered career after his prosecution. His feud with the Craftons continued until, several years later, he again knifed John Crafton in a brawl. He eventually went west, where he lived a peripatetic life. He had been roaming the West for some twelve years when he received news that his father had died. Harrison then returned to Illinois to claim his inheritance. Either Harrison's ill health had been exaggerated at his trial or life in the Far West agreed with him, as Harrison returned to Springfield a powerful man. He soon demonstrated his strength in an argument with his sister over the division of their father's estate. Harrison seized his sister, lifted her up in the air, and slammed her to the floor. She was severely injured and confined to her bed in critical condition. Her husband, Amos Ely, immediately swore out a warrant for Harrison's arrest. With Harrison sitting safely in jail, Ely then retained counsel and filed suit against Harrison for $5,000 in damages. The result of those proceedings is unknown, but they probably prevented him from enjoying anything of his father's inheritance.[62]

This investigation of the trial of "Peachy" Quinn Harrison has shown the traditional story of the trial to be true in broad outline: Harrison killed Crafton in a scuffle; Lincoln defended Harrison; Harrison's grandfather testified to a dying declaration by Crafton; and Harrison was acquitted. It has also shown the traditional story to be false in almost every detail: The fight was not over politics; it was over Harrison's disapproval of Crafton's influence on his younger brother. Harrison was not a murderer; he acted in self-defense. Lincoln did not hoodwink the judge into allowing inadmissible evidence; the dying declaration was properly admitted into evidence. Lincoln did not make an emotional final argument urging the jury to ignore Harrison's guilt and honor Crafton's dying wish. And Palmer did not call Lincoln a liar.

18.

The Legacy of Lincoln the Lawyer

ON DECEMBER 7, 1912, JOSEPH BENJAMIN OAKLEAF ADDRESSED THE BANQUET held at the conclusion of the Illinois District Attorneys' Association's annual session. Oakleaf, a lawyer and Lincoln biographer, had been asked to speak on the subject of Abraham Lincoln as a criminal lawyer. He opened his speech by voicing the conventional wisdom that Lincoln "abhorred criminal practice" and handled only the cases of the innocent and destitute. Oakleaf then spent the rest of his speech talking about anything but Abraham Lincoln's criminal law practice.[1] This survey has shown that there actually is much to be said about Lincoln's criminal trial practice, and it has challenged the commonly held beliefs that Lincoln "abhorred criminal practice" and was not very good at it.

The first exhibit in the case against Lincoln as a competent criminal lawyer is that only a small percentage of his practice was devoted to criminal law. Some have accounted for this small percentage by speculating that the loss of the Fraim case, coming so early in Lincoln's career, soured him on criminal law, and thus he afterward avoided criminal cases in general and murder cases in particular. Simple case count does not tell the story. In Aesop's fable of the lioness and the vixen, when the vixen boasted of her litter of cubs and noted that the lioness had only one, the lioness replied, "But that one's a lion." In civil cases, the litigants argue about money; in criminal cases, the issues are life and liberty. Because of the stakes, Lincoln's criminal practice, especially in homicide cases, took on an importance far beyond what mere numbers suggest. One murder case is not the equivalent of one debt collection case. The depth and breadth of Lincoln's criminal trial experience cannot be gauged by merely counting cases, nor can the significance of his criminal practice be gauged by a mere case count. Lincoln tried homicide cases at the rate of approximately one per year for his entire career, not a shabby number for a general practitioner in a sparsely populated jurisdiction.

The next exhibit in the case against Lincoln's competence is his win-loss ratio. By one author's count, Lincoln tried seventeen murder cases and lost ten of them.[2] One problem with counting "trials" is that there are many different ways to count them. A more revealing way to count Lincoln's trials would be not to count a proceeding as a trial unless a jury returns a verdict. How many murders did Lincoln defend by this count? He litigated, but did not try, eighteen murder cases. He tried two of the eighteen murder cases (Isaac Wyant and James Denton) as a prosecutor, leaving fifteen murder defenses. In one of those murder defenses (Edward B. Tinney), he got the murder charge dismissed, and his client stood trial for manslaughter. Of the remaining fourteen murder cases, one of his clients (Melissa Goings) disappeared from the courtroom just before the trial began, one trial (David Longnecker) resulted in a hung jury, one defendant (Edward Barrett) entered a plea bargain, and one case (Archibald and William Trailor) was dismissed after the preliminary hearing.

That leaves ten murder defenses that went to a jury verdict (table 18.1). Of those ten, two defendants (William Fraim and William Weaver) were convicted as charged of murder, and three (William D. Davis, Moses Loe, and David Thompson) were convicted of manslaughter. The remaining five defendants were acquitted. The two murder convictions came early in Lincoln's career, when he was relatively inexperienced. His last three murder trials (Jane and Theo Anderson, Duff Armstrong, and "Peachy" Quinn Harrison) were spectacular victories. Most criminal defendants facing the prospect of death by hanging would count a conviction of manslaughter as a victory, but for the sake of argument we will count them as losses. By this ungenerous count, Lincoln won fifty percent of his murder cases. A baseball player with a .500 batting average would be bound for the Hall of Fame at Cooperstown. By that measure, Lincoln deserves a place in the pantheon of great American criminal defense attorneys.

The deciding item of evidence on the question of Lincoln's competence as a criminal trial lawyer is not practice percentage, win-loss ratio, or the opinions of historians. It is the opinions of his colleagues at the bar. Time and again, his colleagues sought him out to assist them in criminal trials. The most telling example of this comes from the Anderson case, when Amzi McWilliams offered Lincoln $200 to help prosecute the case, while the members of the defense team each contributed one-fourth of their fee to jointly hire Lincoln to come on board and assist in the defense.

The question is not whether he was a good criminal trial lawyer; the question is just how good was he? But first, some other myths must be dismissed. That he never read a law book through in his life is patently absurd in light of the reading program he recommended to an aspiring young lawyer: "Begin

TABLE 18.1. Lincoln's Murder Defenses Tried to Verdict

Client	Year	County	Verdict
Henry B. Truett	1838	Sangamon	Not guilty
William Fraim[1]	1839	Hancock	Guilty as charged
Spencer Turner	1840	DeWitt	Not guilty
William Weaver[2]	1845	Champaign	Guilty as charged
William D. Davis[3]	1850	Clark	Guilty of lesser, manslaughter
Moses Loe[4]	1853	DeWitt	Guilty of lesser, manslaughter
David Thompson[5]	1856	Champaign	Guilty of lesser, manslaughter
Jane and Theo Anderson	1856	Sangamon	Not guilty
William Duff Armstrong	1858	Cass	Not guilty
"Peachy" Quinn Harrison	1859	Sangamon	Not guilty

[1] Fraim was executed.
[2] Weaver escaped before his execution.
[3] Davis was sentenced to three years. His pardon petition was denied.
[4] Loe was pardoned after serving four years of an eight-year sentence.
[5] Thompson was pardoned after serving two years of an eight-year sentence.

with Blackstone's Commentaries, and after reading it carefully through, say twice, take up Chitty's Pleading, Greenleaf's Evidence, & Story's Equity &c. in succession."[3] In this regard, Lincoln practiced what he preached. He never darkened the door of a law school, but he taught himself by reading law. That he did not know legal technicalities is refuted by his alternative pleading in the Delny rape case, his well-crafted direct examination of Nelson Watkins in the Armstrong case, and his hypertechnical attack on the indictment in the Fraim case. Contrary to his popular image as a lawyer who refused to rely on technicalities and argued the equities rather than the intricacies of a case, Lincoln showed in the Fraim case that he was capable of engaging in sharp maneuvering with the attempt to withdraw Fraim's general plea of not guilty and enter a plea in abatement. His motion for arrest of judgment also shows that he was quite capable of raising hypertechnical objections. The Truett case gives the lie to the canard that Lincoln was incapable of defending a guilty client.[4]

Lincoln's reputation for giving up on cases in which he had lost faith comes in the main from the Denton and Patterson cases. Despite the myriad problems with the Denton case, Sandburg was wrong about Lincoln abandoning the case. He stuck with it to the bitter end, and when he could not attend the retrial, he sent his partner. Moreover, Duff was wrong about Lincoln talking Lamborn into dropping the case. Most of all, the case does not support Sandburg's assertion that Lincoln was not a good prosecutor. When Lincoln assisted the prosecution, the jury hung, but when the prosecution was deprived of Lincoln's assistance, the jury acquitted.

Lincoln never abandoned Tom Patterson either. He had different ideas than his trial partners about how to try the case, and that difference of opinion helped scuttle the case, but the loss certainly had nothing to do with Lincoln's abandoning the defense. His "inability" to argue the case for Patterson stemmed from his refusal either to misstate the facts or to make disingenuous arguments. Lawyers in Lincoln's day were not so scrupulous as the modern rules of professional conduct require,[5] as evidenced by the words of the nineteenth-century rhetorician Richard Whately, who recommended that when making a persuasive speech, everyone except lawyers should "keep on the side of what he believes to be truth; and, avoiding all sophistry, to aim only at setting forth that truth as strongly as possible."[6] Lincoln, unlike his contemporaries, seems to have tried to adhere to Whately's principle.

The Patterson case does disclose a weakness Lincoln developed after becoming a mature trial lawyer. Although Lincoln was easy to work with, he had his own ideas about how a case should be tried. Whitney wrote that Lincoln's tendency to march to his own drumbeat never caused any friction with co-counsel, "but it did not infrequently occur that his carrying out of the part assigned to him, was inharmonious with the general plan, and sometimes unfortunately so."[7] Whitney cited the Patterson trial as an example of Lincoln's disastrous refusal to follow his co-counsel's lead when he disagreed with them.

Another apparent chink in Lincoln's armor can be found in his court-appointed representation of indigent clients, a service for which antebellum Illinois lawyers received no fee. It seems that when he did not get paid for his services, he sometimes did not exert the same level of effort as on cases where he was compensated. For example, Lincoln tried the Armstrong case without fee, and that case was finished in a little over half a day. He was handsomely compensated in the Harrison case, a case of similar complexity, and that case took almost an entire week to try. Lincoln also merits criticism for his handling of the Weaver case. He asked for a change of venue in the Dorman case, where his client would almost certainly have been found not guilty, but even if found guilty, Dorman would have suffered at most an eight-year prison sentence. Lincoln did not ask for a change of venue in the Weaver case, where his client not only faced the hangman's noose but also was believed to be a "drunken, reckless wretch" by the community from which his jury was drawn. Could it be that Lincoln did not exert himself for Weaver because he believed the man was guilty and deserved to be hanged? Or was it because Weaver did not have $50 to pay for Lincoln's services? In Lincoln's defense, he acted as any other contemporary Illinois lawyer would have done in the same situation. Cases like Weaver's demonstrate the wisdom of our modern public defender system.

The discussions of the cases have dealt with many of the allegations of wrongdoing by Lincoln as they have arisen, and there is no need to reiterate them here. Suffice it to say that Lincoln was an ethical lawyer, and the allegations of misconduct are unfounded. The allegations that seem to have the greatest merit are those questioning the ethics of arguments made by Lincoln. Most of those allegations are based on faulty "facts," such as Lincoln's purported argument to the Harrison jury, asking it to ignore the law and join Crafton in forgiving his murderer. Those that do have a basis in fact arise from using a twenty-first-century yardstick to measure nineteenth-century ethics. The prime example of this second fallacy comes in the critique of Lincoln's reference to his friendship with the Armstrong family when he defended Duff Armstrong. Such remarks are certainly improper today, but the critics overlook two facts: State's Attorney Fullerton invited the comments when he told the jury that the Metzkers had tried to hire Lincoln to assist the prosecution, and Assistant Prosecutor Shaw spoke of Lincoln's argument in glowing terms and never once complained about anything Lincoln had said.[8]

One other allegation against Lincoln's performance in the Armstrong case merits comment. It has been asserted that Lincoln committed witness tampering, suppression of evidence, and possibly subornation of perjury with the handling of the witness Nelson Watkins.[9] This allegation is completely groundless. First, assuring a witness that he will not be asked questions he does not want to answer is not witness tampering. Second, artfully constructing a direct examination to preclude cross-examination on an uncongenial topic is not suppression of evidence; it is a time-honored trial tactic, which John M. Palmer used against Lincoln in the Harrison trial. Finally, the assertion that Lincoln suborned perjury makes no sense. Watkins said, "I may be asked some questions I don't want to answer," and Lincoln said, "I'll make sure those questions aren't asked." Where in that conversation has Lincoln asked Watkins to lie? To suggest that Lincoln did something wrong in the handling of Watkins's testimony betrays a profound misunderstanding of the role of the defense attorney in a criminal trial.

Lincoln was not just a competent, ethical criminal lawyer in the mold of David B. Campbell. He was an excellent criminal lawyer. When he drafted an indictment, as he did in the Delny case, it was a model of brevity, clarity, and lucidity. Unlike some of the prosecutors he faced, he drafted his indictments to meet all contingencies. Recall that David Campbell could have convicted Spencer Turner of assault and battery with a deadly weapon, but he charged Turner only with murder and lost. Lincoln indicted Delny on two different theories of rape, covering all possibilities and ensuring a conviction. The first count charged forcible rape, and the second count charged rape of a child. One element of the crime of rape as charged in the first count was that the victim did not consent. The second count, as drafted by Lincoln, did not require proof of consent. Under Illinois law, if the victim was under ten and the defendant over fourteen, consent or lack of consent was irrelevant. Lincoln therefore gave himself two ways to prove the crime, a reasonable precaution given the problems inherent in taking testimony from a child as young as Jane Ann. Both forms of rape carried a potential life sentence.[10]

When Lincoln confronted a seemingly impossible situation, he devised an imaginative way of dealing with it. He quite likely had a hand in the unique agreement for George Denton's testimony in the first trial of James Denton, and he devised an inventive way of getting the testimony of an unavailable witness (Deborah Ater) before the prosecutor and getting the charges dropped against his client James H. Hollingsworth.

In the Armstrong case, Lincoln fully assimilated the facts, assessed their significance, and assembled his defense in a single evening, and then performed admirably the next day at the trial. Few defense attorneys have the mental acuity to digest the facts of a case, divine the weaknesses in the prosecution, and devise a defense within the brief time that Lincoln had. Although Lincoln's cross-examination of the witness Charles Allen was not the dramatic total destruction of legend, his skill at cross-examination was nonetheless on full display. He weakened Allen's testimony just enough, but not too much, and in the process proved the truth of the maxim that when cross-examining, it is not necessary to examine crossly. The statement of juror John T. Brady sums up Lincoln's technique quite well: "Mr. Lincoln was careful not to cross Mr. Allen in anything, and when Allen lacked words to express himself, Lincoln loaned them to him."[11] After having committed Allen to the position of the moon, Lincoln later contradicted him with the almanac. Of Lincoln's use of the almanac, Brady said, "The almanac evidence led the jury to the idea that if Allen could be so mistaken about the moon, he might have been mistaken about seeing Armstrong hit Metzker with a slung-shot, although Allen impressed me with the idea that he was telling what he believed to be the truth."[12]

In the Harrison case, Lincoln employed another technique of cross-examination by both forcing helpful concessions from John Crafton and discrediting him when he refused to concede the obvious. We did not see a dramatic knockout blow being landed in this series of questions, but that happens more in fiction than it does in an actual courtroom. What we did see was Lincoln asking short, closed, leading questions that asserted facts favorable to his client. He thereby maintained tight control over the witness. If the witness admitted the facts, it advanced Lincoln's case. If he denied the facts, Lincoln had the contradictions ready at hand for impeachment. Lincoln put in a workmanlike effort that demonstrated his mastery of the art of cross-examination.

Because Lincoln was the author of such oratorical masterpieces as the Gettysburg Address and Cooper Union Speech, little time need be spent discussing his consummate skill as a courtroom orator, an ability that his colleagues recognized so early in his career that he was trusted with delivering the closing final argument in his first murder case. In summary, Lincoln was a competent, diligent attorney who combined knowledge of the law with profound powers of analysis, the courage to make hard decisions, the creativity to use innovative strategies, the ability to quickly respond to a rapidly changing tactical environment, and the rhetorical skill to be an effective communicator, a deadly cross-examiner, and a persuasive speaker. These abilities not only served his clients well as he traveled the Eighth Judicial Circuit of Illinois but also served his nation well as he led it through the Civil War.

Appendix

Notes

Bibliography

Index

Appendix:
Counties and County Seats of Lincoln's Eighth Judicial Circuit

County	Dates	County Seat
Livingston	1839–47	Pontiac
Menard	1839–47	Petersburg
Christian	1839–53	Taylorville
Macon	1839–53	Decatur
Sangamon	1839–57	Springfield
Tazewell	1839–57	Tremont (1839–51); Pekin (1851–present)
DeWitt	1839–61	Clinton
Logan	1839–61	Pottsville (1839–47); Mount Pulaski (1847–53); Lincoln (1854–present)
McLean	1839–61	Bloomington
Mason	1841–45	Havana
Shelby	1841–45; 1847–53	Shelbyville
Moultrie	1843–53	Sullivan
Piatt	1841–53	Monticello
Woodford	1841–57	Versailles (1841–42); Metamora (1843–96)
Champaign	1841-61	Urbana
Vermilion	1845–61	Danville
Edgar	1847–53	Paris

Notes

Introduction: The Legend of Lincoln the Lawyer

1. Harold Holzer, "Reassessing Lincoln's Legal Career," in Billings and Williams, *Abraham Lincoln, Esq.*, 6, 10; Brian Dirck, "A. Lincoln, Respectable 'Prairie Lawyer,'" in ibid., 73–74.
2. Mark E. Steiner, "Does Lawyer Lincoln Matter," in Billings and Williams, *Abraham Lincoln, Esq.*, 46.
3. Hay and Nicolay, *Abraham Lincoln*, 1:303; Sandburg, *Abraham Lincoln*, 2:60; Steiner, *Honest Calling*, 12.
4. Burlingame, *Abraham Lincoln*, 1:312.
5. Barr, *Loathing Lincoln*, 10–11.
6. See, e.g., Gaetke, "Lessons in Legal Ethics"; Walsh, *Moonlight*; Ram, *Treatise on Facts*, 269n1, 505.
7. Russell, *Edgar Lee Masters*, 277.
8. On Lincoln hating criminal cases, see Oakleaf, *Lincoln as a Criminal Lawyer*, 3; Duff, *A. Lincoln*, 51; and Peterson, *Lincoln in American Memory*, 339. On his being a poor criminal lawyer, see Hill, *Lincoln the Lawyer*, 235–38, Dirck, "A. Lincoln, Respectable 'Prairie Lawyer,'" 72; and Lupton, "A. Lincoln Esquire," 40. On his lack of talent, see Masters, *Lincoln the Man*, 130–36. On his lack of "intellectual unscrupulousness," see Duff, *A. Lincoln*, 52n1.
9. Oakleaf, *Lincoln as a Criminal Lawyer*, 4.
10. Stowell, *Papers of Lincoln*, 2:338.
11. Dirck, *Lincoln the Lawyer*, 116.
12. Stowell, *Papers of Lincoln*, 2:339.
13. See Barton, *Life of Lincoln*, 1:228–29; DiLorenzo, *Real Lincoln*, 10; Brown, *Authentic Individualism*, 105.
14. E.g., Major General John A. McClernand, who served as Grant's second in command at Vicksburg; Major General John M. Palmer, who distinguished himself at Stones River and Chickamauga; Brigadier General William Orme, who contracted tuberculosis at Vicksburg; Brevet Brigadier General Caleb Dilworth, who distinguished himself at Kennesaw Mountain, Chickamauga, and the Siege of Atlanta; Edward D. Baker, who declined an appointment as major general to serve as a colonel, killed in action at the Battle of Ball's

Bluff; and Colonel T. Lyle Dickey, who served as chief of cavalry for the Army of Tennessee.

15. Lincoln, "To George B. McClellan," February 3, 1862, *Collected Works*, 5:118–19.

16. Ibid., 5:121–24.

1. PEOPLE versus HENRY B. TRUETT, *October 13, 1838*

1. King, "Case That Made Lincoln," 786–90.

2. H. B. Truett & Co. v. Ransdell, Benner and Davis, et al., *Law Practice of Abraham Lincoln*, file L04740 (hereafter cited as *LPAL*).

3. Pratt, "Lincoln's First Murder Trial," 244–45.

4. The description of this confrontation comes in the main from the contemporary news articles "Deplorable Catastrophe," *Illinois State Journal*, March 17, 1838, *LPAL* doc. 84698; and "The Springfield Affair," *Galena (IL) Gazette*, March 24, 1838, *LPAL* doc. 123271.

5. Curtenius v. Wheeler, 5 Gilman 462, 10 Ill. 462, 1849 WL 4217 (1849); Greenleaf, *Evidence*, 14th ed., 1:427.

6. Starkey v. State, 17 Ill. 17, 21 (1855).

7. Palmer, *Bench and Bar of Illinois*, 2:881.

8. Linder, *Reminiscences of Bench and Bar*, 65–67.

9. Selby, *Anecdotal Lincoln*, 110–13.

10. Jurors § 6, *Statute Laws of Illinois* (1839), 396.

11. Court Minutes, People v. Truett, *LPAL* doc. 90362. See "People v. Henry Truett: A Transcript of the Court File from Lincoln's First Murder Case," http://almanac-trial.blogspot.com/2016/03/people-v-henry-b-truett-transcript-of.html.

12. Court Minutes, People v. Truett, *LPAL* doc. 90375.

13. "Truet's Trial," *Illinois State Journal*, October 20, 1839, *LPAL* doc. 123274. See "Lincoln's First Murder Case: The News Reports," http://almanac-trial.blogspot.com/2015/06/lincolns-first-murder-case-news-reports.html.

14. Spiegel and Kavaler, "Lincoln Defends the Murderer of a Physician," 318.

15. Dekle, *Prosecution Principles*, 167.

16. Burlingame, *Abraham Lincoln*, 1:133.

17. Spiegel and Kavaler. "Lincoln Defends the Murderer of a Physician," 319.

18. "People vs. Henry B. Truett," *Peoria (IL) Register*, October 20, 1838, *LPAL* doc. 123275.

19. Ibid.

20. Court Minutes, People v. Truett, *LPAL* doc. 90404.

21. King, "Case That Made Lincoln," 787.

2. PEOPLE versus WILLIAM FRAIM, *April 23, 1839*

1. Selby, *Anecdotal Lincoln*, 60.

2. Conger, *History of the Illinois River Valley*, 1:152.

3. Ibid., 1:168.

4. "Murder," *Illinois State Journal*, March 3, 1838, *LPAL* doc. 120858.

5. Indictment, People v. Fraim, *LPAL* doc. 58289. See "People v. William Fraim: A Transcript of the Court File from Lincoln's Least Successful Murder Defense,"

http://almanac-trial.blogspot.com/2016/03/set-forth-below-is-transcript-which-i.html.

6. Caton, *Early Bench and Bar of Illinois*, 135–38.

7. Palmer, *Bench and Bar of Illinois*, 2:62–63.

8. Oaks and Hill, *Carthage Conspiracy*, 3.

9. Plea, People v. Fraim, April 23, 1839, *LPAL* doc. 58301.

10. Clark, *Criminal Procedure*, § 131.

11. Blackstone, *Commentaries, Book Four*, 334–35.

12. Indictment, People v. Cordell, *LPAL* doc. 92492.

13. Court Minutes, People v. Cordell, *LPAL* doc. 92499.

14. Fraker, *Lincoln's Ladder*, 23.

15. Archbold, *Criminal Procedure*, 110.

16. Verdict, People v. Fraim, *LPAL* doc. 58302.

17. "The Only Murderer, Defended by Lincoln, Who Was Hanged for His Crime," *Lincoln Lore*, no. 1459 (September 1959).

18. Motion for Arrest of Judgment, People v. Fraim, *LPAL* doc. 58310.

19. Duff, *A. Lincoln*, 65; Joel E. Ferris, "Timely Letter about Lincoln File in County," July 6, 1953, Abraham Lincoln's Important Cases: Fraim Murder Case.

20. Order, People v. Fraim, *LPAL* doc. 58308.

21. Beam, *American Crucifixion*, 140.

22. Bateman, Selby, and Currey, *Encyclopedia of Illinois and History of Hancock County*, 2:765.

23. Ibid.

24. Ibid., 766.

25. "Abraham Lincoln Defended Slayer in this County," February 8, 1940, Abraham Lincoln's Important Cases: Fraim Murder Case.

3. PEOPLE versus SPENCER TURNER, *May 23, 1840*

1. Also see "Counties and County Seats of Lincoln's Eighth Judicial Circuit," http://almanac-trial.blogspot.com/2016/04/counties-and-county-seats-of-lincolns.html.

2. Woldman, *Lawyer Lincoln*, 88.

3. Fraker, *Lincoln's Ladder*, 95.

4. Verdict of the Jury upon Coroner's Inquest, People v. Turner, *LPAL* doc. 3104. See "People v. Spencer Turner: Transcript of the Court File in Lincoln's Third Murder Case," http://almanac-trial.blogspot.com/2016/03/people-v-spencer-turner-transcript-of.html.

5. Offenses against the Persons of Individuals § 52, *Statute Laws of Illinois* (1939), 206.

6. Palmer, *Bench and Bar of Illinois*, 1:174.

7. Fraker, *Lincoln's Ladder*, 96.

8. Complaint, Lincoln v. Turner and Turner, *LPAL* doc. 1992.

9. Linder, *Reminiscences of Bench and Bar*, 196.

10. Caton, *Early Bench and Bar of Illinois*, 52–53.

11. Linder, *Reminiscences of Bench and Bar*, 203.

12. Plea, Pratt v. Lowry, *LPAL* doc. 40995.
13. Pratt, *Personal Finances of Lincoln*, 41.
14. Duff, *A. Lincoln*, 71.
15. Verdict, People v. Turner, *LPAL* doc. 3112.
16. Palmer, *Bench and Bar of Illinois*, 2:897–98.
17. Plea, Lincoln v. Turner and Turner, *LPAL* doc. 5376.
18. Replication, Lincoln v. Turner and Turner, *LPAL* doc. 5377.

4. PEOPLE versus ARCHIBALD AND WILLIAM TRAILOR, June 18, 1841

1. Lincoln, "To Joshua F. Speed," June 19, 1841, *Collected Works*, 1:255.
2. Lincoln, "The Trailor Murder Case," April 15, 1846, *Collected Works*, 1:373–74.
3. Duff, *A. Lincoln*, 85.
4. "Public Notice," *Sangamo Journal*, June 4, 1841, People v. Trailor & Trailor, *LPAL* doc. 127588. The brothers' surname is spelled three different ways in the sources—"Trailor," "Trailer," and "Traylor." I have preferred Lincoln's spelling of the name.
5. Linder, *Reminiscences of Bench and Bar*, 258.
6. Duff, *A. Lincoln*, 84.
7. Lincoln, "To Joshua F. Speed," June 19, 1841, *Collected Works*, 1:255.
8. Lincoln, "The Trailor Murder Case," April 15, 1846, *Collected Works*, 1:373–74.
9. Ibid., 1:375.
10. Lincoln, "To Joshua F. Speed," June 19, 1841, *Collected Works*, 1:257.
11. Ibid., 1:257–58.
12. Ibid., 1:258.
13. "Public Notice," *Illinois State Journal*, June 25, 1841, People v. Trailor & Trailor, *LPAL* doc. 125913.
14. Angle, *Here I Have Lived*, 120.
15. Lamon, *Life of Lincoln*, 318.
16. Lincoln, "The Trailor Murder Case," April 15, 1846, *Collected Works*, 1:376.
17. Ford, "Crime That Baffled Lincoln," 15.
18. Power, *History of Sangamon County*, 720–24.
19. Ibid., 721.
20. Ibid., 723.
21. Lincoln, "The Trailor Murder Case," April 15, 1846, *Collected Works*, 1:376n3.
22. Baggini and Fosl, *Philosopher's Toolkit*, 209–11.

5. Various Criminal Cases, 1845–46

1. Palmer, *Bench and Bar of Illinois*, 2:627.
2. See "People v. Edward B. Tinney: Transcript of Murder Case Defended by Lincoln," http://almanac-trial.blogspot.com/2016/03/people-v-edward-b-tinney -transcript-of.html.
3. Indictment, People v. Tinney, *LPAL* doc. 43137.
4. Stewart, *History of Champaign County*, 1:146.
5. Whitney, *Life on the Circuit*, 476.
6. Ibid., 476–77.

7. Lamon, *Life of Lincoln*, 326.

8. Stewart, *History of Champaign County*, 1:179.

9. See "People v. William Weaver: The Transcript of the Court File of a Murder Case Lost by Lincoln," http://almanac-trial.blogspot.com/2016/03/people-v-william-weaver-transcript-of.html.

10. Stewart, *History of Champaign County*, 1:179.

11. Ibid., 1:161.

12. Indictment, People v. Dorman, *LPAL* doc. 92306. See "People v. James Dorman: Transcript of the Court File of a Murder Case Defended by Lincoln," http://almanac-trial.blogspot.com/2016/03/people-v-james-dorman-transcript-of.html.

13. Capias, People v. Dorman, *LPAL* doc. 12726.

14. Indictment, People v. Parker, *LPAL* doc. 12916. See "People v. Peter Parker: Transcript of the Court File from a Manslaughter Case Defended by Lincoln," http://almanac-trial.blogspot.com/2016/03/people-v-peter-parker-transcript-of.html.

15. Bateman, Selby, and Currey, *Historical Encyclopedia of Illinois*, 1:222.

16. Minutes, People v. Page, *LPAL* doc. 7153.

17. Pardon Petition, People v. Parker, *LPAL* doc. 89428.

18. Verdict, Powell v. Worth, *LPAL* doc. 13646.

19. Minutes, Powell v. Worth, *LPAL* doc. 13636.

20. Indictment, People v. Denton and Denton, *LPAL* doc. 12665.

6. PEOPLE versus JAMES AND GEORGE DENTON, June 12, 1846

1. Indictment, People v. Denton and Denton, *LPAL* doc. 12665. See "People v. George & James Denton: Transcript of the Court File of a Murder Case Which Lincoln Prosecuted," http://almanac-trial.blogspot.com/2016/03/people-v-george-james-denton-transcript.html.

2. Court Minutes, People v. Denton and Denton, *LPAL* doc. 12686.

3. Sandburg, *Abraham Lincoln*, 1:325.

4. Ibid.

5. Lamon, *Life of Lincoln*, 324.

6. Ibid., 322.

7. Richards, *Lincoln the Lawyer-Statesman*, 56–58.

8. Duff, *A. Lincoln*, 302–3.

9. Duff, "This Was a Lawyer," 152.

10. Luthin, *Real Lincoln*, 72–73.

11. Power, *Bench and Bar*, 1010. Our only evidence that Harris was involved in the case is the fact that he was listed in the court minutes as co-counsel for Logan.

12. Richey v. McBean, 17 Ill. 63, 65 (1855).

13. Jackson v. People, 18 Ill. 269, 272 (1857).

14. Affidavit, People v. Denton and Denton, *LPAL* doc. 12724.

15. Court Minutes, People v. Denton and Denton, *LPAL* doc. 12677.

16. Affidavit, People v. Denton and Denton, *LPAL* doc. 9981.

17. Affidavit, People v. Denton and Denton, *LPAL* doc. 12724.

18. Affidavit, People v. Denton and Denton, *LPAL* doc. 9981.

19. Court Minutes, People v. Denton and Denton, *LPAL* doc. 12684.

20. Court Minutes, People v. Denton and Denton, *LPAL* doc. 12689.

7. *Various Criminal Cases, 1850–53*

1. Miers, *Lincoln Day by Day*, 2:17.

2. See "People v. William D. Davis: Transcript of the Court File in a Manslaughter Case Which Lincoln Lost," http://almanac-trial.blogspot.com/2016/03/people -v-davistranscript-of-court-file.html.

3. James H. Cheney, et al., Petition for Pardon, People v. Davis, *LPAL* doc. 54728.

4. Lincoln, Letter to Governor Matteson, January 12, 1853, People v. Davis, *LPAL* doc. 54727.

5. Duff, *A. Lincoln*, 274.

6. Palmer, *Bench and Bar of Illinois*, 1:458.

7. Petition and letter for the pardon of John A. L. Crockett, November 22, 1852, Illinois State Archives, http://www.idaillinois.org/cdm/search/collection/isa /searchterm/CROCKETT/order/nosort (July 20, 2015). See "People v. John Crockett: Transcript of the Court File and Pardon Papers in a Manslaughter Case Defended by Lincoln," http://almanac-trial.blogspot.com/2016/03/people-v -crockett-transcript-of-court.html.

8. Ibid.

9. Decree, Lincoln v. Alexander, *LPAL* doc. 53669.

10. Palmer, *Bench and Bar of Illinois*, 1:165.

11. Stowell, et al., *Papers of Lincoln*, 4:275.

12. "An Awful Crime and Speedy Punishment," *Illinois State Register*, May 14, 1853, *LPAL* doc. 132185.

13. "Infamous Outrage and Prompt Retribution," *Peoria (IL) Democratic Press*, May 18, 1853, *LPAL* doc. 132186.

14. Dekle, *Lincoln's Most Famous Case*, 63.

15. Mittimus, People v. Delny, *LPAL* doc. 45695. See "People v. Thomas Delny: Transcript of the Court File of a Rape Case Prosecuted by Lincoln," http:// almanac-trial.blogspot.com/2016/03/people-v-delny-transcript-of-court-file .html.

16. Palmer, *Bench and Bar of Illinois*, 1:643.

17. Court Minutes, People v. Delny, *LPAL* doc. 45697.

18. Abraham Lincoln, Indictment, People v. Delny, *LPAL* doc. 54854.

19. Court Minutes, People v. Delny, *LPAL* doc. 45700.

20. Judge's Docket, People v. Delny, *LPAL* doc. 45703.

21. Court Minutes, People v. Delny, *LPAL* doc. 45700.

22. Subpoena, People v. Delny, *LPAL* doc. 45699. In criminal cases, it was customary to put multiple witnesses on a single subpoena. There were only two subpoenas issued, one for all the prosecution witnesses and one for all the defense witnesses.

23. Subpoena, People v. Delny, *LPAL* doc. 45698.

24. Based on my personal experience.

25. Judge's Docket, People v. Delny, *LPAL* doc. 45703.

26. This was the case in Illinois until 1966. People ex rel. Conn v. Randolph, 35 I11.2d 24, 219 N.E.2d 337 (1966).

27. Krause, "'Infamous Outrage,'" 195–96.

28. Sebastian Wise, Letter to William H. Bissell, February 11, 1859, People v. Delny, *LPAL* doc. 89447.

8. *PEOPLE versus MOSES LOE, May 19, 1853*

1. The following narrative comes from Lincoln's notes of the trial testimony. People v. Loe, *LPAL* doc. 4320.

2. See "People v. Moses Loe: Transcript of a Murder Case Defended by Lincoln," http://almanac-trial.blogspot.com/2016/03/people-v-moses-loe-transcript-of -murder.html.

3. "Murder," *Illinois State Journal*, September 1, 1852, *LPAL* doc. 84272.

4. Untitled article, *Illinois State Journal*, September 1, 1852, *LPAL* doc. 89276.

5. Indictment, People v. Loe, *LPAL* doc. 121633.

6. Affidavit for Change of Venue, People v. Loe, *LPAL* doc. 54856.

7. Endorsement on Indictment, People v. Loe, *LPAL* doc. 121633.

8. Affidavit for Continuance, People v. Loe, *LPAL* doc. 54855.

9. People v. Reddock, 13 Ill.App.3d 296, 305, 300 N.E.2d 31 (1973).

10. Greenleaf, *Evidence*, 3rd ed., 1:175–259.

11. Subpoena, People v. Loe, *LPAL* doc. 121651.

12. Criminal Code § 22, *Statute Laws of Illinois* (1839), 202.

13. Criminal Code § 23, ibid.

14. Criminal Code § 24, ibid.

15. Livingston, *American Book Prices*, 1:80. Today the notes can be viewed online at www.lawpracticeofabrahamlincoln.com. I consulted the relevant books listed as being sold from his law library in an effort to find legal justification for the admission of Gray's hearsay statement to Blankenship.

16. Criminal Code § 25, *Statute Laws of Illinois* (1839), 202.

17. Verdict, People v. Loe, *LPAL* doc. 121654.

18. Court Minutes, People v. Loe, *LPAL* doc. 35257.

19. Campbell v. Smith, *LPAL* case L02072.

20. Lincoln, "Endorsement on Petition for Pardon," August 18, 1857, *Collected Works*, 2:414.

21. Petition for the Pardon of Moses Loe, August 18, 1857, Illinois Digital Archives (hereafter cited as IDA).

9. *PEOPLE versus DAVID LONGNECKER, June 3, 1856*

1. This sequence of events is reconstructed from two sources: "Man Killed," *Decatur Gazette*, April 28, 1854, People v. Longnecker, *LPAL* doc. 138955, and Record of Coroner's Inquest, People v. Longnecker, *LPAL* doc. 31749.

2. Deposition, People v. Hollingsworth, *LPAL* doc. 53771.

3. Affidavit, People v. Hollingsworth, *LPAL* doc. 53741.

4. Affidavit, People v. Hollingsworth, *LPAL* doc. 53742.

5. Affidavit for Change of Venue, People v. Hollingsworth, *LPAL* doc. 53761.

6. Indictment, People v. Hollingsworth, *LPAL* doc. 53753.

7. See, e.g., "Dynamics of Domestic Violence."

8. Deposition, People v. Hollingsworth, *LPAL* doc. 53771.

9. Depositions §§ 1, 2, *Statute Laws of Illinois* (1839), 244.

10. Depositions § 11, ibid.

11. Lupton, "Violence and Murder in Piatt County," 2.

12. Record of Coroner's Inquest, People v. Longnecker, *LPAL* doc. 31749. See "People v. David Longnecker: Transcript of the Court File of a Murder Case Which Lincoln Got Dismissed," http://almanac-trial.blogspot.com/2016/03/people-v-david-longnecker-transcript-of.html.

13. Warrant, People v. Longnecker, *LPAL* doc. 30751.

14. May 16, 1854, *Lincoln Log*.

15. Lincoln, "Speech at Peoria, Illinois," October 16, 1854, *Collected Works*, 2:247–48.

16. Herndon and Weik, *Life of Lincoln*, 301.

17. Affidavit for Continuance, People v. Longnecker, *LPAL* doc. 30765.

18. Minutes, People v. Longnecker, *LPAL* doc. 30743.

19. Questions come from Written Interrogatories, People v. Longnecker, *LPAL* doc. 30782. Answers are from Deposition, People v. Longnecker, *LPAL* doc. 30783.

20. Clark v. Hoxworth, et al., *LPAL* case L01876.

21. Petition, People v. Longnecker, *LPAL* doc. 3633.

22. Ibid.

23. Complaint Affidavit and Warrant, People v. Bosley, *LPAL* doc. 61015. See "People v. Walter Bosley: Transcript of the Court File from a Murder Case Defended by Lincoln," http://almanac-trial.blogspot.com/2016/03/people-v-walter-bosley-transcript-of.html.

24. Lincoln, "Speech at Chicago, Illinois," October 27, 1854, *Collected Works*, 2:283–84.

25. Indictment, People v. Bosley, *LPAL* doc. 127970.

26. Indictment, People v. Herndon, *LPAL* doc. 5690.

27. Court Minutes, Cushman v. Illinois Central Railroad, *LPAL* doc. 33493.

28. Order, Cushman v. Illinois Central Railroad, *LPAL* doc. 40983.

29. Persons v. Harris, *LPAL* case L02014 (the jury found that Lincoln's client owed the plaintiff $72.50); Cox v. Bolton, *LPAL* case L01880 (the jury awarded Lincoln's client $194); Milliken v. Jefferson, *LPAL* case L01966 (the jury found for the defendant, awarding Lincoln's client nothing).

10. Lincoln's Pardon Practice

1. Verdict, Taylor v. Humphries, *LPAL* doc. 66049.

2. Court Minutes, People v. Hibbs, *LPAL* doc. 12880. See "People v. John Hibbs: Transcript of the Court File from a Manslaughter Case Defended by Lincoln," http://almanac-trial.blogspot.com/2016/03/people-v-john-hibbstranscript-of.html.

3. David Davis, Letter, May 8, 1857, People v. Hibbs, *LPAL* doc. 122884.

4. Pardon Petition, People v. Hibbs, *LPAL* doc. 12886.

5. William Henry Bissell, Letter, May 16, 1857, People v. Hibbs, *LPAL* doc. 122885.

6. Walker, *Critical Pronouncing Dictionary*, 382.

7. Stowell et al., *Papers of Lincoln*, 1:156.

8. Lincoln, "Petition for Pardon of Michael Hill," April 2, 1842, *Collected Works*, 1:284n1.

9. Stowell et al., *Papers of Lincoln*, 1:187.

10. Purple, *Compilation of Statutes of Illinois*.

11. Lincoln, "Endorsement: Petition to William H. Bissell for Pardon of David Thompson," April 12, 1858, *Collected Works*, 2:442.

12. People v. Thompson, *LPAL* case L01806. See "People v. David Thompson: Transcript of the Court File from a Murder Case Defended by Lincoln," http://almanac-trial.blogspot.com/2016/03/people-v-david-thompson-transcript-of.html.

13. People v. Barrett, *LPAL* case L01415. See "People v. Barrett: Transcript of the Court File from a Murder Case Plea Bargained by Lincoln," http://almanac-trial.blogspot.com/2016/03/people-v-edward-barrett-transcript-of.html.

14. David Davis, Letter to William H. Bissell, July 11, 1859, *LPAL* doc. 89448.

15. Samuel R. Burns, Letter to Reuben C. Burns, July 15, 1859, People v. Barrett, *LPAL* doc. 89449.

16. This account is drawn from Richter, *Lincoln*, 154–72; Whicker, *Wabash Valley*, 109–13; and "Vermilion Circuit Court—The Railroads, Etc.," *Alton Weekly Courier*, November 9, 1854, *LPAL* doc. 138951.

17. York, "Hooseriana."

18. "Horse Companies," *Williamsport Warren Republican*, November 1, 1860, 3. See "Horse Theft Detective Associations," http://almanac-trial.blogspot.com/2016/03/horse-theft-detective-associations.html.

19. Whicker, *Wabash Valley*, 112.

20. Richter, *Lincoln*, 165.

21. Ward Hill Lamon, Letter to Abraham Lincoln, November 21, 1854, People v. Hill, *LPAL* doc. 65579.

22. "Vermilion Circuit Court—The Railroads, Etc."

23. Court Minutes, People v. High, *LPAL* doc. 48737.

24. Bill of Exceptions, People v. High, *LPAL* doc. 3756.

25. Court Minutes, People v. High, *LPAL* doc. 48741.

26. William McCullough, Letter to Joel A. Matteson, October 13, 1856, People v. High, *LPAL* doc. 53449.

27. Joel A. Matteson, Letter to David Davis, October 17, 1856, People v. High, *LPAL* doc. 133030.

28. David Davis, Letter to Joel A. Matteson, November 5, 1856, People v. High, *LPAL* doc. 53448.

29. Petition for Pardon, People v. High, *LPAL* doc. 48742.

30. Richter, *Lincoln*, 188.

31. Ibid., 188–89.

32. David Davis, Letter to Joel A. Matteson, November 5, 1856, People v. High, *LPAL* doc. 53448.

33. "Horse Companies."

34. Richter, *Lincoln*, 189.
35. Lincoln, "Fragment: Notes for a Law Lecture," [July 1, 1850?], *Collected Works*, 2:81.
36. Joel A. Matteson, Endorsement on Petition for Pardon, November 10, 1856, People v. High, *LPAL* doc. 48742.
37. Illinois Digital Newspaper Collection (hereafter cited as IDNC).
38. "Horse Companies."
39. Williams, *History of Vermilion County*, 1:120; "Political," *Chicago Daily Inter Ocean*, July 23, 1867.
40. Lincoln, Letter to W. H. Bissell, March 22, 1858, IDA.
41. David Davis, Letter to W. H. Bissell, October 24, 1858, IDA.
42. Lincoln, "Endorsement: Recommendation for Pardon of Emanuel Fowler," June 8, 1860, *Collected Works*, 4:73.
43. Buckner S. Morris, Letter to John Wood, August 7, 1860, IDA.
44. Lincoln, "Endorsement: Buckner Morris to John Wood," August 8, 1860, *Collected Works*, 4:92.

11. *PEOPLE versus JANE AND THEODORE ANDERSON*, *November 28, 1856*

1. This recitation of facts is taken from the following news articles in the IDNC: "Murder of George Anderson," *Illinois State Journal*, 8:290, May 22, 1856; "The Anderson Murder Trial," *Illinois State Journal*, 9:131, November 22, 1856; "The Anderson Murder Trial," *Illinois State Journal*, 9:132, November 24, 1856; "The Anderson Murder Trial," *Illinois State Journal*, 9:133, November 25, 1856; "The Anderson Murder Trial," *Illinois State Journal*, 9:134, November 26, 1856; "The Anderson Murder Trial," *Illinois State Journal*, 9:135, November 27, 1856. For an abstract of testimony drawn from these articles, see "People v. Jane & Theodore Anderson: Summaries of Witness Testimony," http://almanac-trial.blogspot .com/p/people-v-jane-theodore-anderson.html.
2. "Sun and Moon Data for One Day," U.S. Naval Observatory, Astronomical Applications Department, http://aa.usno.navy.mil/rstt/onedaytable?ID=AA &year=1856&month=5&day=15&state=IL&place=springfield.
3. "Murder in Springfield," *Illinois State Register*, May 17, 1856, http://www.genealogybank.com.
4. Untitled article, *Illinois State Register*, May 29, 1856, http://www.genealogybank.com.
5. May 20–23, 1856, October 20, 1856, *Lincoln Log*.
6. Chiniquy, *Fifty Years*, 625–29.
7. Court Minutes, People v. Anderson and Anderson, *LPAL* doc. 122617. See "People v. Jane Anderson & Theodore Anderson: Transcript of the Court File from a Murder Case Defended by Lincoln," http://almanac-trial.blogspot.com/2016/03 /people-v-jane-anderson-theodore.html.
8. Benjamin S. Edwards, Letter to Judge David Davis, July 12, 1856, People v. Anderson and Anderson, *LPAL* doc. 133035.
9. Pratt, *Personal Finances of Lincoln*, 39.
10. "Prosecuting Attorneys Elected," *Illinois State Journal*, 9:130, 20 November 1856, IDNC.

11. "The Circuit Court," *Illinois State Journal*, 9:130, 20 November 1856, IDNC.

12. "The Anderson Murder Trial," *Illinois State Journal*, 9:132, November 24, 1856, IDNC.

13. Spiegel, *A. Lincoln, Esquire*, 229–30.

14. Linder, *Reminiscences of Bench and Bar*, 184.

15. November 26–29, 1856, *Lincoln Log*.

16. Linder, *Reminiscences of Bench and Bar*, 185.

17. Ibid., 185–86.

18. "A Ludicrous Mistake," *Cleveland Leader*, December 10, 1856, http://www .genealogybank.com.

19. Linder, *Reminiscences of Bench and Bar*, 186.

20. "Acquitted," *Illinois State Journal*, 9:138, December 1, 1856, IDNC.

21. Fenster, *Case of Abraham Lincoln*, 226.

12. *PEOPLE versus ISAAC WYANT, April 5, 1857*

1. "Murder," *DeWitt (IL) Courier*, October 19, 1855, *LPAL* doc. 133014. The following account is taken from a series of articles published in the *Pantagraph* (Bloomington, IL), *LPAL* docs 53376, 131644, 131645, 131646, 131647, and 133015. See "People v. Isaac Wyant: Testimony Summaries," http://almanac-trial.blogspot .com/p/people-v-isaac-wyant-testimony-summaries_27.html.

2. Ibid.

3. "The Trial of Wyant," *Daily Pantagraph*, April 8, 1857, *LPAL* doc. 131645.

4. Ibid.

5. Ibid.

6. Transcript of Examination, People v. Wyant, *LPAL* doc. 53367. See "People v. Isaac Wyant: Transcript of a Murder Case Prosecuted by Lincoln," http:// almanac-trial.blogspot.com/2016/03/people-v-isaac-wyant-transcript-of.html.

7. *History of DeWitt County*, 87.

8. Transcript of Examination, People v. Wyant, *LPAL* doc. 53367.

9. "The Trial of Isaac Wyant," *Weekly Pantagraph*, April 15, 1857, *LPAL* doc. 53376.

10. Ibid.

11. Murphy, *Chloroform*, 66.

12. "The Trial of Wyant," *Daily Pantagraph*, April 14, 1857, *LPAL* doc. 131648.

13. Emery v. Illinois Central Railroad, *LPAL* case L00500; Allen v. Illinois Central Railroad, *LPAL* case L00662; Spencer v. Illinois Central Railroad, *LPAL* case L00638.

14. Dungey v. Spencer, *LPAL* case L00567.

15. Declaration, Allen v. Illinois Central Railroad, *LPAL* doc. 36420.

16. Declaration, Dungey v. Spencer, *LPAL* doc. 4580.

17. Court Minutes, Dungey v. Spencer, *LPAL* doc. 33951.

18. Court Minutes, People v. Wyant, *LPAL* doc. 53363.

19. Court Minutes, People v. Wyant, *LPAL* doc. 53365.

20. Court Minutes, People v. Wyant, *LPAL* doc. 53364.

21. Court Minutes, People v. Wyant, *LPAL* doc. 53378.

22. Wharton, *Criminal Law*, 1:12–27.

23. Swett, "Leonard Swett," 334–37.

24. Whitney, *Life on the Circuit*, 67, 70.

25. 23 Ill. 283 (1859).

26. Eckley, *Leonard Swett*, 46.

27. Ibid., 158.

28. Palmer, *Bench and Bar of Illinois*, 2:897–98.

29. Baldwin, "Col. Harvey Hogg," 302–9.

30. Miers, *Lincoln Day by Day*, 2:187–92.

31. "Circuit Court," *Daily Pantagraph*, April 1, 1857, *LPAL* doc. 133015.

32. "The Trial of Wyant," *Daily Pantagraph*, April 6, 1857, *LPAL* doc. 131644.

33. "The Trial of Wyant," *Daily Pantagraph*, April 14, 1857, *LPAL* doc. 131648.

34. Ibid.

35. Court Minutes, People v. Wyant, *LPAL* doc. 53383.

36. Lincoln, "To Jesse K. DuBois," April 6, 1857, *Collected Works*, 2:393.

37. Decree, In the Matter of Isaac Wyant, *LPAL* doc. 53384.

38. *History of DeWitt County*, 87.

39. Wilson and Davis, *Herndon's Informants*, 667.

40. Kittredge, *Ingersoll*, 39n1.

41. Swett, "Leonard Swett," 343–44.

42. See, e.g., untitled article, *American Traveler*, August 28, 1857, www.genealogybank.com.

43. "Trial of Robert C. Sloo," 33–68.

13. *PEOPLE versus JOHN BANTZHOUSE, October 2, 1857*

1. "Sangamon Circuit Court," *Illinois State Journal*, 9:256, April 21, 1857, IDNC.

2. "Manslaughter," *Illinois State Journal*, 9:213, February 28, 1857, IDNC.

3. Arrest Warrant, People v. Bantzhouse, *LPAL* doc. 50222.

4. Indictment, People v. Bantzhouse, *LPAL* doc. 21087. For the full text of the indictment and a transcript of the court file, see "People v. John Bantzhouse: Transcript of a Murder Case Defended by Lincoln," http://almanac-trial.blogspot .com/2016/03/people-v-john-bantzhouse-transcript-of.html.

5. Notice of Additional Witnesses, People v. Bantzhouse, *LPAL* doc. 21094.

6. Palmer, *Bench and Bar of Illinois*, 2:194–95; Linder, *Reminiscences of Bench and Bar*, 71–72.

7. "Circuit Court," *Illinois State Register*, August 13, 1857, *LPAL* doc. 130178.

8. "Circuit Court," *Illinois State Register*, August 14, 1857, *LPAL* doc. 130178.

9. "The Brunthouse Murder Case," *Illinois State Journal*, 10:98, October 6, 1857, IDNC.

10. See, e.g., Burlingame, *Abraham Lincoln*, 1:337; Key, "A. Lincoln," 84; Spiegel, *A. Lincoln, Esquire*, 37.

11. Judge's Docket, People v. Bantzhouse, *LPAL* doc. 21096.

12. Habeas Corpus § 1, *Statute Laws of Illinois* (1839), 322.

13. Court Minutes, People v. Bantzhouse, *LPAL* doc. 121606.

14. "The Brunthouse Murder Case," *Illinois State Journal*, 10:98, October 6, 1857, IDNC.

15. 47 N.C. 418 (1855).

16. To a like effect is State v. Tribatt, 32 N.C. 151 (1849). See also Bramlett v. State, 31 Ala. 376 (1848), and State v. Moses, 13 N.C. 452 (1830).

17. People v. Dominguez, 367 Ill. App. 3d 171, 854 N.E.2d 252 (2006); State v. Belien, 379 So.2d 446 (3d D.C.A., Fla., 1980).

18. Lincoln, "Mortgage and Note Drawn for Jacob Ruckel," September 28, 1857, *Collected Works*, 2:422–23.

19. Lincoln, "To Samuel Briggs," September 29, 1857, ibid., 2:423; Lincoln, "To Richard Yates," September 30, 1857, ibid., 2:242.

20. Meyers, *General McClernand*, 42.

14. PEOPLE versus MELISSA GOINGS, October 10, 1857

1. East, "Lincolniana," 80. This account is reconstructed from the testimony of the witnesses as recorded at the coroner's inquest. Coroner's Return, People v. Goings, *LPAL* doc. 57062. See "People v. Melissa Goings: Transcript of a Murder Case Defended by Lincoln," http://almanac-trial.blogspot.com/2016/03/people-v-melissa-goings-transcript-of.html.

2. Josephus Goings, Testimony, People v. Goings, *LPAL* doc. 57081.

3. James Brady, Testimony, People v. Goings, *LPAL* doc. 57083.

4. Greenleaf, *Evidence*, 3rd ed., 1:256.

5. Roswell Hibbs, Testimony, People v. Goings, *LPAL* doc. 57084.

6. East, "Lincolniana," 80.

7. Josephus Goings, Testimony, People v. Goings, *LPAL* doc. 57081.

8. Joshua Van Wilson, Testimony, People v. Goings, *LPAL* doc. 57082.

9. Inquest Verdict, People v. Goings, *LPAL* doc. 57057.

10. Lewis v. People, 23 Ill. App. 28, 32 (2nd Dist., 1886).

11. JP Transcript, People v. Goings, *LPAL* doc. 57066.

12. Court Minutes, People v. Goings, *LPAL* doc. 57068.

13. E.g., Duff, *A. Lincoln*, 348.

14. Court Minutes, People v. Goings, *LPAL* doc. 57070.

15. "Lincoln Statues," http://www.historicmetamora.com/LincolnStatues.htm; "Metamora Courthouse State Historic Site," http://www.villageofmetamora.com/?hiscourt.

16. Myers, "Justice Served."

17. East, "Lincolniana," 83.

18. Ibid.

19. Ibid.

20. Linder, *Reminiscences of Bench and Bar*, 197–200.

15. PEOPLE versus WILLIAM DUFF ARMSTRONG, May 7, 1858

1. J. McCan Davis, "Manuscript: The Armstrong Trial," n.d., Documents of Ida M. Tarbell (hereafter cited as Tarbell Documents).

2. Aten, *History of the 85th Illinois*, 333–34.

3. Dekle, *Lincoln's Most Famous Case*, 74–76.

4. Dirck, *Lincoln the Lawyer*, 117; Burlingame, *Abraham Lincoln*, 1:343.

5. Lincoln, "Appendix II: 1857," *Collected Works*, 8:452.

6. Writ of Attachment, People v. Armstrong, *LPAL* doc. 20697.

7. Miers, *Lincoln Day by Day*, 2:215.

8. J. Henry Shaw, Letter to William H. Herndon, September 6, 1866, in Wilson and Davis, *Herndon's Informants*, 332–34.

9. Caleb Dilworth, Letter to J. McCan Davis, May 18, 1896, Tarbell Documents; William Walker, Letter to William H. Herndon, June 3, 1865, in Wilson and Davis, *Herndon's Informants*, 22–23.

10. Caleb Dilworth, Letter to J. McCan Davis, May 18, 1896, Tarbell Documents.

11. All these accounts have been transcribed and reproduced in Dekle, *Lincoln's Most Famous Case*, 123–49. The accounts of Bailiff John Husted and witness Dr. Charles E. Parker are discounted for reasons that were thoroughly discussed in ibid., 105–8.

12. See, e.g., ibid.

13. Caleb Dilworth, Letter to J. McCan Davis, May 18, 1896, Tarbell Documents.

14. Gridley, *Lincoln's Defense of Duff Armstrong*, 21; Burlingame, *Abraham Lincoln*, 1:344; "Lincoln's Famous Case: Duff Armstrong's Story of His Own Murder Trial," *New York Sun* (June 7, 1896), *LPAL* doc. 133187; Wilson and Davis, *Herndon's Informants*, 334.

15. Sandburg, *Abraham Lincoln*, 2:56.

16. The modern slingshot, of course, is a Y-shaped weapon with an elastic cord used for shooting small missiles such as rocks, marbles, and the like. See, e.g., Koehler, *Slingshot Shooting*.

17. See, e.g., Cobb v. Georgia, 27 Ga. 658 (1859), which uses the terms "slung-shot" and "sling-shot" interchangeably.

18. James H. Norris, Letter to Governor R. Yates, February 22, 1863, IDA.

19. Gridley, *Lincoln's Defense of Duff Armstrong*, 4.

20. Bateman, Selby, and Martin, *Encyclopedia of Illinois and History of Cass County*, 2:690.

21. John T. Brady, Letter to J. McCan Davis, May 23, 1896, Tarbell Documents.

22. Gridley, *Lincoln's Defense of Duff Armstrong*, 21.

23. Philadelphia & Trenton R. Co. v. Stimpson, 39 U.S. 448, 461 (1840).

24. John T. Brady, Letter to J. McCan Davis, May 23, 1896, Tarbell Documents.

25. Bergen, "Personal Recollections," 212.

26. J. McCan Davis, "Manuscript: The Armstrong Trial," n.d., Tarbell Documents.

27. Eggleston, *Graysons*. How Eggleston's piece of fiction came to be accepted as fact has been examined in Dekle, *Lincoln's Most Famous Case*, 30–31.

28. John T. Brady, Letter to J. McCan Davis, May 23, 1896, Tarbell Documents.

29. "Lincoln's Famous Case: Duff Armstrong's Story of His Own Murder Trial," *New York Sun*, June 7, 1896, *LPAL* doc. 133187.

30. J. McCan Davis, "Manuscript: The Armstrong Trial," n.d., Tarbell Documents.

31. Four witnesses bear this out: Duff Armstrong ("Duff Armstrong's Story"); Abram Bergin ("Recollections of Lincoln," 214); John T. Brady (Letter to Davis); and Jury Foreman Milton Logan ("Iowan Juror in Lincoln Case: Milton Logan Remembers Famous Trial," *The Capital*, 1907, Abraham Lincoln's Important Cases: Duff Armstrong Case).

32. "The Famous Armstrong Case: Milton Logan, Only Survivor, Tells How Lincoln Cleared Defendant and Won Case," *Cedar Rapids (IA) Evening Gazette*, June 6, 1906. ("The prosecuting attorney in the case never questioned the issue of the almanac, nor did he refer in any way to the moon shining, or attempt to answer Mr. Lincoln's undisputed argument on this point.")

33. William H. Herndon, Notes of Interview with James Harriott, n.d., in Wilson and Davis, *Herndon's Informants*, 704.

34. John T. Brady, Letter to J. McCan Davis, May 12, 1896, Tarbell Documents.

35. Allen Thurman Lucas, state's attorney for Cass County during the early 1900s, uncovered this information doing research for a play he wrote about the Almanac Trial. The play was performed at the 1929 Beardstown Centennial Celebration and again in 1958 at Beardstown's Lincoln Centennial celebration. In 1929, Lucas played the part of Hugh Fullerton. Allen Thurman Lucas, "Beardstown Centennial Celebration Program," 1929, Abraham Lincoln's Important Cases: Duff Armstrong Case; "Lincolniana Notes," 199–202; Townsend, *Illinois Democracy*, 3:62–63.

36. Erichsen, *Science and Art of Surgery*, 1:369.

37. Ibid.

38. Ibid., 1:376.

39. Jury Instruction, People v. Armstrong, *LPAL*, doc. 20690.

40. The proposed jury instruction, in Lincoln's own hand, survives to this day and may be viewed online at *The Law Practice of Abraham Lincoln* website, http://www.lawpracticeofabrahamlincoln.org.

41. J. Henry Shaw, Letter to William Henry Herndon, September 5, 1866, in Wilson and Davis, *Herndon's Informants*, 333.

42. John T. Brady, Letter to J. McCan Davis, May 23, 1896, Tarbell Documents.

43. See, e.g., Dekle, *Lincoln's Most Famous Case*, 38–39, 100–108.

44. Barton, *Life of Lincoln*, 1:310–18; Beveridge, *Abraham Lincoln*, 2:273–74; J. McCan Davis, "Manuscript: How the Almanac 'Forgery' Was Discovered," n.d., Tarbell Documents.

45. Masters, *Lincoln the Man*, 133.

46. See, e.g., Bartlett, *Life and Public Services of Lincoln*, 113.

16. PEOPLE versus TOM PATTERSON, April 21, 1859

1. This account is reconstructed from Pratt, *Lincoln Defends Tom Patterson*; Duff, *A. Lincoln*, 281–84; Lewin and Hite, "Lincoln's Second-to-Last Murder Case"; and Abraham Smith, Letter to John M. Wood, May 6, 1860, People v. Patterson, *LPAL* doc. 53446.

2. Miers, *Lincoln Day by Day*, 2:231–35.

3. Court Minutes, People v. Patterson, *LPAL* doc. 50151. See "People v. Patterson: Transcript of the Court File from a Manslaughter Case Defended by Lincoln," http://almanac-trial.blogspot.com/2016/03/people-v-thomas-patterson -transcript-of.html.

4. Court Minutes, People v. Patterson, *LPAL* doc. 58132.

5. *Laws of Illinois* (1857), 13.

6. Court Minutes, People v. Patterson, *LPAL* doc. 130677.

7. Defense Requested Jury Instructions, People v. Patterson, *LPAL* doc. 50154.

8. Prosecution Requested Jury Instructions, People v. Patterson, *LPAL* doc. 4297.

9. Wilson and Davis, *Herndon's Informants*, 529, 733.

10. Ibid., 632–33.

11. Ibid., 347.

12. Lamon, *Life of Lincoln*, 322.

13. Dirck, *Lincoln the Lawyer*, 147.

14. Whitney, *Life on the Circuit*, 262.

15. This argument of Lincoln's stands in stark contrast to the argument he made in the Armstrong case, where he ended his speech with an eloquent plea for sympathy.

16. Whitney, *Life on the Circuit*, 131, 262.

17. Ibid., 131.

18. Lincoln, "Endorsement: David Davis to John Wood," August 14, 1860, *Collected Works*, 4:93.

17. *PEOPLE versus SIMEON "PEACHY" QUINN HARRISON, September 3, 1859*

1. T. W. S. Kidd, Letter to Ida M. Tarbell, n.d., Tarbell Papers. Although the letter is indexed as anonymous because the author's signature is illegible, the author identifies himself as the "court crier." In her biography of Lincoln, Tarbell identifies the court crier as T. W. S. Kidd. *Life of Lincoln*, 2:251.

2. Kidd, Letter to Ida M. Tarbell, n.d., Tarbell Papers.

3. Herndon and Weik, *Life of Lincoln*, 264–65.

4. Duff, *A. Lincoln*, 363.

5. Beveridge, *Abraham Lincoln*, 2:253.

6. An actual dying declaration from one of my early cases.

7. Alonzo Rothschild lists a letter he received from Cullom as one of the sources of his account of the Harrison trial. Rothschild, *Honest Abe*, 107n29. Unfortunately, that letter does not exist among the Alonzo Rothschild Papers, in the possession of the University of Illinois at Urbana-Champaign.

8. Bateman, *Abraham Lincoln*, 13–15.

9. Usually, when a case went up on appeal, the lawyers got together and agreed on a stipulated statement of facts for the appellate court.

10. "The Harrison Case," *Illinois State Journal*, 12:69, September 1, 1859, IDNC.

11. Untitled article, *Illinois State Journal*, 12:70, September 2, 1859, IDNC.

12. Stowell, *Papers of Lincoln*, 140n11.

13. "Recent Discovery"; "Harrison Trial Transcript"; Stowell, *Papers of Lincoln*, 4:157–92.

14. Stowell, *Papers of Lincoln*, 4:172.

15. Ibid., 4:174n64, 4:137n1.

16. The first name of this individual is not given in the transcript. David is given as the first name because that name appears in the attorney's notes taken at Harrison's preliminary hearing. People v. Harrison, *LPAL* doc. 75838.

17. "Surrender of Harrison—Examination Set for To-day," *Illinois State Journal*, 12:43, August 2, 1859, IDNC. See "Lincoln's Last Murder Case: The News Reports," http://almanac-trial.blogspot.com/2015/11/lincolns-last-murder-case.html.
18. "The Harrison Case," *Illinois State Register*, August 3, 1859, *LPAL* doc. 78981.
19. Attorney's Notes, People v. Harrison, *LPAL* doc. 75838.
20. "Conclusion of the Examination of Harrison," *Illinois State Register*, August 4, 1859, *LPAL* doc. 93344.
21. "The Harrison Case," *Illinois State Journal*, 12:45, August 4, 1859, IDNC.
22. Miers, *Lincoln Day by Day*, 2:257–58.
23. "Indictment of Harrison," *Illinois State Journal*, 12:66, August 29, 1859, IDNC.
24. "The Harrison Indictment," *Illinois State Register*, August 30, 1859, *LPAL* doc. 93346.
25. "The Register and the Grand Jury," *Illinois State Journal*, 12:68, Edition 2, September 1, 1859, IDNC.
26. Untitled article, *Illinois State Register*, September 1, 1859, *LPAL* doc. 93382.
27. "The Harrison Case," *Illinois State Journal*, 12:45, August 4, 1859, IDNC; "Conclusion of the Examination of Harrison," *Illinois State Register*, August 4, 1859, *LPAL* doc. 93344.
28. "Trial of P. Quinn Harrison, Indicted for the Murder of Greek Crafton," *Illinois State Journal*, 12:70, September 2, 1859, IDNC.
29. Stowell, *Papers of Lincoln*, 4:142–91.
30. "The Harrison Trial—Verdict, Not Guilty," *Illinois State Journal*, 12:72, September 5, 1859, IDNC.
31. "Trial of Sidney Branch," *Illinois State Journal*, 29:1468, September 14, 1859, IDNC.
32. Stowell, *Papers of Lincoln*, 4:141.
33. Ibid., 4:145.
34. Ibid., 4:153–54.
35. Ibid., 4:164–65.
36. Ibid., 4:165, 167.
37. Ibid., 4:169.
38. 16 Ill. 17 (1854).
39. Ibid., 18.
40. Stowell, *Papers of Lincoln*, 4:168–69.
41. Ibid., 175.
42. Greenleaf, *Evidence*, 3rd ed., 1:257–58.
43. "The Harrison Trial," *Illinois State Journal*, 12:71, September 3, 1859, IDNC.
44. Greenleaf, *Evidence*, 3rd ed., 1:253.
45. Ibid., 1:255.
46. "The Harrison Trial," *Illinois State Journal*, 12:71, September 3, 1859, IDNC.
47. Stowell, *Papers of Lincoln*, 4:179.
48. Ibid., 4:180.
49. Ibid.
50. Ibid., 4:178.

51. Philadelphia & Trenton R. Co. v. Stimpson, 39 US 448, 461 (1840).

52. Stowell, *Papers of Lincoln*, 4:189; italics added.

53. Ibid.; italics added.

54. Ibid., 190.

55. Ibid.

56. "The Harrison Trial—Verdict, Not Guilty," *Illinois State Journal*, 12:72, September 5, 1859, IDNC.

57. Whitney, *Life on the Circuit*, 131.

58. "The Harrison Trial—Verdict, Not Guilty," *Illinois State Journal*, 12:72, September 5, 1859, IDNC.

59. Tarbell, *Life of Lincoln*, 2:251.

60. Lincoln, "To P. Quinn Harrison," November 3, 1859, *Collected Works*, 3:492–93.

61. "The Crafton Case Again—Arrest of B. F. Short," *Illinois State Journal*, 12:79, September 13, 1859, IDNC.

62. "The Ely Assault," *Chicago Daily Tribune*, November 29, 1885, 3, https://newspapers.com.

18. The Legacy of Lincoln the Lawyer

1. Oakleaf, *Lincoln as a Criminal Lawyer*, 3–15.

2. Dirck, *Lincoln the Lawyer*, 116.

3. Lincoln, "To John M. Brockman," September 25, 1860, *Collected Works*, 4:121.

4. Duff, *A. Lincoln*, 58.

5. "A lawyer shall not knowingly . . . make a false statement of fact or law to a tribunal or fail to correct a false statement of material fact or law previously made to the tribunal by the lawyer." Rule 3.3(a)(1), ABA, *Model Rules of Professional Conduct*.

6. Whately, *Elements of Rhetoric*, 167.

7. Whitney, *Life on the Circuit*, 130.

8. Wilson and Davis, *Herndon's Informants*, 333.

9. Walsh, *Moonlight*, 2, 35.

10. Offenses against the Persons of Individuals § 48, *Statute Laws of Illinois* (1939), 206.

11. Gridley, *Lincoln's Defense of Armstrong*, 19.

12. John T. Brady, Letter to J. McCan Davis, May 23, 1896, Tarbell Documents.

Bibliography

Newspapers

Alton (IL) Weekly Courier. http://www.lawpracticeofabrahamlincoln.org.
American Traveller (Boston). http://www.genealogybank.com.
Cedar Rapids (IA) Evening Gazette. http://newspaperarchive.com.
Chicago Daily Tribune. https://newspapers.com.
Cleveland Leader. http://www.genealogybank.com.
Chicago Daily Inter Ocean. http://www.genealogybank.com.
DeWitt (IL) Courier. http://www.lawpracticeofabrahamlincoln.org.
Galena (IL) Gazette. http://www.lawpracticeofabrahamlincoln.org.
Illinois State Journal. http://idnc.illinois.edu.
Illinois State Register. http://www.genealogybank.com and
    http://www.lawpracticeofabrahamlincoln.org.
Pantagraph (Bloomington, IL). http://www.lawpracticeofabrahamlincoln.org.
Peoria (IL) Democratic Press. http://www.lawpracticeofabrahamlincoln.org.
Peoria (IL) Register. http://www.lawpracticeofabrahamlincoln.org.
Williamsport (IN) Warren Republican. http://search.findmypast.com.

Papers and Collections

Abraham Lincoln's Important Cases: Duff Armstrong Case. Lincoln Financial
    Foundation Collection. https://archive.org/details/abrahamlincolnsilinc_7.
Abraham Lincoln's Important Cases: Fraim Murder. Lincoln Financial Foundation
    Collection. http://archive.org/details/abrahamlincolnsilinc_10.
Alonzo Rothschild Papers, 1880–1919. http://www.library.illinois.edu/ihx/inventories
    /rothschild.pdf.
The Documents of Ida M. Tarbell. https://dspace.allegheny.edu/handle/10456/13708.
Illinois Digital Archives. http://www.idaillinois.org/ui/custom/default/collection
    /default/resources/custompages/bin/buildSubjectPages.php?subject=10.
Illinois Digital Newspaper Collection. http://idnc.library.illinois.edu/.
The Lincoln Log. http://www.thelincolnlog.org.

Books and Articles

American Bar Association (ABA). 2009. *Model Rules of Professional Conduct.* Chi-
    cago: American Bar Association, Center for Professional Responsibility.

Angle, Paul. *Here I Have Lived: A History of Lincoln's Springfield, 1821–1865.* Springfield, IL: Abraham Lincoln Association, 1935. http://name.umdl.umich.edu /0566798.0001.001.

Archbold, John Frederick. *The New System of Criminal Procedure, Pleading and Evidence in Indictable Cases.* London: Shaw and Sons, 1852.

Aten, Henry J. *History of the 85th Illinois Regiment Illinois Volunteer Infantry.* Hiawatha, KS: Regimental Association, 85th Illinois Volunteers, 1901.

Baggini, Julian, and Peter S. Fosl. *The Philosopher's Toolkit: A Compendium of Philosophical Concepts and Methods.* 2nd ed. Malden, MA: Wiley-Blackwell, 2010.

Baldwin, William M. "Col. Harvey Hogg." In *Transactions of the McLean County Historical Society,* vol. 2, 302–9. Bloomington, IL: Pantagraph Printing and Stationery Co. 1899.

Barr, John McKee. *Loathing Lincoln: An American Tradition from the Civil War to the Present.* Baton Rouge: Louisiana State University Press, 2014.

Bartlett, David W. *The Life and Public Services of Hon. Abraham Lincoln: To Which Is Added a Biographical Sketch of Hon. Hannibal Hamlin.* New York: H. Dayton, Publisher, 1860.

Barton, William E. *The Life of Abraham Lincoln.* 2 vols. Indianapolis: Bobbs-Merrill Company, 1925.

Bateman, Newton. *Abraham Lincoln: An Address.* Galesburg, IL: Cadmus Club, 1899.

Bateman, Newton, Paul Selby, and Josiah Seymour Currey, eds. *Historical Encyclopedia of Illinois and History of Hancock County.* Vol. 2. Chicago: Munsell Publishing Company, 1921.

———. *Historical Encyclopedia of Illinois: Biographical, Memorial, Illustrative.* Vol. 1. Chicago: Munsell Publishing Company, 1920.

Bateman, Newton, Paul Selby, and Charles E. Martin, eds. *Historical Encyclopedia of Illinois and History of Cass County.* Vol. 2. Chicago: Munsell Publishing Company, 1915.

Beam, Alex. *American Crucifixion: The Murder of Joseph Smith and the Fate of the Mormon Church.* New York: Public Affairs, 2014.

Benner, Martha L., and Cullom Davis et al., eds. *The Law Practice of Abraham Lincoln: Complete Documentary Edition.* 2nd ed. Springfield: Illinois Historic Preservation Agency, 2009. http://www.lawpracticeofabrahamlincoln.org/Search.aspx.

Bergen, Abram. "Personal Recollections of Abraham Lincoln as a Lawyer." *American Lawyer* 5 (1897): 212–15.

Beveridge, Albert. *Abraham Lincoln: 1809–1858.* Vol. 2. Boston: Houghton-Mifflin Company, 1928.

Billings, Roger, and Frank J. Williams. *Abraham Lincoln, Esq.: The Legal Career of America's Greatest President.* Lexington: University Press of Kentucky, 2010.

Blackstone, William. *Commentaries on the Laws of England, Book the Fourth.* 13th ed. London: A. Strahan, 1800.

Brooks, Noah. *Abraham Lincoln and the Downfall of American Slavery.* New York: G. P. Putnam's Sons, 1913.

Brown, R. Philip. *Authentic Individualism: A Guide for Reclaiming the Best of America's Heritage.* Lanham, MD: University Press of America, 1996.

Burlingame, Michael. *Abraham Lincoln: A Life*. 2 vols. Baltimore: Johns Hopkins University Press, 2013.

Caton, John Dean. *Early Bench and Bar of Illinois*. Chicago: Chicago Legal News Company, 1893.

Chiniquy, Father Charles. *Fifty Years in the Church of Rome*. New York: Fleming H. Revel Company, 1886.

Clark, William L. *Handbook of Criminal Procedure*. St. Paul, MN: West Publishing Company, 1895.

Conger, John Leonard. *History of the Illinois River Valley*. Vol. 1. Chicago: S. J. Clarke Publishing Company, 1932.

Dekle, George R., Sr. *Abraham Lincoln's Most Famous Case: The Almanac Trial*. Santa Barbara, CA: Praeger, 2014.

———. *Prosecution Principles: A Clinical Handbook*. St. Paul, MN: Thomson-West, 2007.

DiLorenzo, Thomas J. *The Real Lincoln: A New Look at Abraham Lincoln, His Agenda, and an Unnecessary War*. Roseville, CA: Prima Publishing, 2002.

Dirck, Brian. "A. Lincoln, Respectable 'Prairie Lawyer.'" In Billings and Williams, *Abraham Lincoln, Esq.*, 65–80.

———. *Lincoln the Lawyer*. Chicago: University of Illinois Press, 2009.

Duff, John J. *A. Lincoln: Prairie Lawyer*. New York: Rinehart & Company, 1960.

———. "This Was a Lawyer." *Journal of the Illinois State Historical Society* 52, no. 1 (Spring 1959): 146–63. http://www.jstor.org/stable/40189915.

"Dynamics of Domestic Violence." Domestic Abuse Intervention Project, Duluth, MN. January 2002. http://www.ou.edu/judicial/pae/pdf/ii/a/IIAiPowerandControlWheel.pdf.

East, Earnest E. "Lincolniana: The Melissa Goings Murder Case." *Journal of the Illinois State Historical Society* 46, no. 1 (Spring 1953): 79–87.

Eckley, Robert S. *Lincoln's Forgotten Friend, Leonard Swett*. Carbondale: Southern Illinois University Press, 2012.

Eggleston, Edward. *The Graysons: A Story of Illinois*. New York: Century Company, 1887.

Erichsen, John Eric. *The Science and Art of Surgery: Being a Treatise on Surgical Injuries, Diseases, and Operations*. 5th ed. Vol. 1. London: James Walton, Bookseller and Publisher to University College, 1869.

Fenster, Julie M. *The Case of Abraham Lincoln: A Story of Adultery, Murder, and the Making of a Great President*. New York: Palgrave MacMillan, 2009.

Ford, Paul V. "The Crime That Baffled Lincoln." *Grafic: Sunday Chicago Tribune Magazine*, January 28, 1951, 15.

Fraker, Guy C. *Lincoln's Ladder to the Presidency: The Eighth Judicial Circuit*. Carbondale: Southern Illinois University Press, 2012.

Gaetke, Eugene R. "Lessons in Legal Ethics from Reading about the Life of Lincoln." *Kentucky Law Journal* 97, no. 4 (2009): 583–613.

Greenleaf, Simon. *Treatise on the Law of Evidence*. 3rd ed. Vol. 1. Boston: Little, Brown, and Company, 1846.

———. *Treatise on the Law of Evidence*. 14th ed. Vol. 1. Boston: Little, Brown, and Co., 1883.

Gridley, J. N. *Lincoln's Defense of Duff Armstrong: The Story of the Trial and the Celebrated Almanac.* Reprint; Virginia, IL: Illinois State Historical Society, 1910.

"Harrison Trial Transcript." *Lincoln Legal Briefs* 16 (October–December 1990). http://www.papersofabrahamlincoln.org/Briefs/briefs16.htm.

Hay, John, and John Nicolay. *Abraham Lincoln: A History.* 10 vols. New York: Cosimo Classics, 2009.

Herndon, William H., and Jesse W. Weik. *Herndon's Life of Lincoln.* Cleveland: Fine Editions Press, n.d.

Hill, Frederick Trevor. *Lincoln the Lawyer.* New York: Century Co., 1906. Reprint, Whitefish, MT: Kessinger Publishing, 2007.

History of DeWitt County, Illinois, with Illustrations Descriptive of the Scenery. Philadelphia: W. R. Brink and Company, 1882.

Holzer, Harold. "Reassessing Lincoln's Legal Career." In Billings and Williams, *Abraham Lincoln, Esq.*, 5–18.

Key, Janet. "A. Lincoln." *ABA Journal* 80 (February 1994): 82–84.

King, Willard L. "The Case That Made Lincoln." *Lincoln Herald* 84 (1981): 786–90. http://cdm15995.contentdm.oclc.org/cdm/.

Kittredge, Herman. *Ingersoll: A Biographical Appreciation.* New York: Dresden Publishing Company, 1909.

Koehler, Jack H. *Slingshot Shooting: The Poor Man's Shooting Sport.* Marinette, WI: Sportology Publications, 2005.

Krause, Susan. "'Infamous Outrage and Prompt Retribution': The Case of *People v. Delny.*" In *In Tender Consideration: Women, Families, and the Law in Abraham Lincoln's Illinois,* edited by Daniel W. Stowell, 183–203. Urbana: University of Illinois Press, 2002.

Lamon, Ward H. *The Life of Abraham Lincoln from His Birth to His Inauguration as President.* Boston: James R. Osgood and Company, 1872.

Laws of the State of Illinois Passed by the Twentieth General Assembly. Springfield, IL: Lanphier and Walker, 1857.

Lewin, Travis H. D., and Tyler P. Hite. "Lincoln's Second-to-Last Murder Case: People v. Patterson." *American Bar Association,* February 9, 2015. http://apps .americanbar.org/litigation/committees/trialevidence/articles/winter2015-0215 -lincoln-second-to-last-murder-case.html.

Lincoln, Abraham. *The Collected Works of Abraham Lincoln.* Edited by Roy P. Basler. 9 vols. New Brunswick, NJ: Rutgers University Press, 1953–55.

"Lincolniana Notes: 'Duff' Armstrong Trial Re-enacted." *Journal of the Illinois State Historical Society* 51, no. 2 (Summer 1958): 199–202.

Linder, Usher F. *Reminiscences of the Early Bench and Bar of Illinois.* Chicago: Chicago Legal News Company, 1879.

Livingston, Luther S. *American Book Prices: Current.* Vol. 1. New York: Dodd, Meade and Company, 1895.

Lupton, John A. "A. Lincoln Esquire: The Evolution of a Lawyer." In *A. Lincoln, Esquire: A Shrewd, Sophisticated Lawyer in His Time,* edited by Allen D. Spiegel, 18–50. Macon, GA: Mercer University Press, 2002.

———. "Violence and Murder in Piatt County." *Lincoln Legal Briefs* 69 (January–March 2004): 2. http://www.papersofabrahamlincoln.org/Briefs/briefs69.pdf.

Luthin, Reinhard H. *The Real Abraham Lincoln: A Complete One Volume History of His Life and Times.* Englewood Cliffs, NJ: Prentice-Hall, 1960.

Masters, Edgar Lee. *Lincoln the Man.* New York: Dodd, Mead, 1931. Reprint, Columbia, SC: Foundation for American Education, 1997.

Meyers, Christopher C. *Union General John A. McClernand and the Politics of Command.* Jefferson, NC: McFarland and Company, 2012.

Miers, Earl Schenck, ed. *Lincoln Day by Day, 1809–1865.* 3 vols. Washington, DC: Lincoln Sesquicentennial Commission, 1960.

Murphy, Edward William. *Chloroform: Its Properties and Safety in Childbirth.* London: Walton and Maberly, 1855.

Myers, Jean. "Justice Served: Abraham Lincoln and the Melissa Goings Case." *Peoria Magazine* (March–April 2009). http://www.peoriamagazines.com/as/2009/mar-apr/justice-served.

Oakleaf, Joseph Benjamin. *Abraham Lincoln as a Criminal Lawyer.* Rock Island, IL: Augustana Book Concern, 1923.

Oaks, Dallin H., and Marvin S. Hill. *Carthage Conspiracy: The Trial of the Accused Assassins of Joseph Smith.* Urbana: University of Illinois Press, 1979.

"The Only Murderer, Defended by Lincoln, Who Was Hanged for His Crime." *Lincoln Lore*, no. 1459 (September 1959).

Palmer, John M., ed. *The Bench and Bar of Illinois.* 2 vols. Chicago: Lewis Publishing Company, 1899.

Peterson, Merrill D. *Lincoln in American Memory.* New York: Oxford University Press, 1994.

Power, John Carroll. *History of the Early Settlers of Sangamon County, Illinois.* With the assistance of Mrs. S. A. Power. Springfield: Edwin A. Wilson and Company, 1876.

Pratt, Harry E. "Abraham Lincoln's First Murder Trial." *Journal of the Illinois State Historical Society* 37, no. 3 (1944): 242–49. http://www.jstor.org/stable/40188113.

———. *Lincoln Defends Tom Patterson.* Reprint from *Illinois Bar Journal*, October 1940. https://archive.org/details/lincolndefendstoooprat.

———. *Personal Finances of Abraham Lincoln.* Springfield: Abraham Lincoln Association, 1943.

The Public and General Statute Laws of the State of Illinois. Chicago: Stephen F. Gale, 1939.

Purple, N. H., ed. *A Compilation of the Statutes of Illinois of a General Nature.* Chicago: Keen and Lee, 1856.

Ram, James. *A Treatise on Facts as Subjects of Inquiry by a Jury.* 1st American ed. New York: Baker, Voorhis & Company, 1870.

"Recent Discovery." *Lincoln Legal Briefs* 8 (September–December 1988). http://www.papersofabrahamlincoln.org/Briefs/briefs08.htm.

Richards, John T. *Abraham Lincoln the Lawyer-Statesman.* Boston: Houghton Mifflin Company, 1916.

Richter, Donald G. *Lincoln: Twenty Years on the Prairie.* Mattoon, IL: United Graphics, 1999.

Rothschild, Alonzo. *Honest Abe: A Study in Integrity Based on the Early Life of Abraham Lincoln.* Boston: Houghton Mifflin Company, 1917.

Russell, Herbert K. *Edgar Lee Masters: A Biography.* Urbana: University of Illinois Press, 2005.

Sandburg, Carl. *Abraham Lincoln: The Prairie Years.* 2 vols. New York: Harcourt, Brace, and World, 1926.

Schaubs, Michael. "Mountain Men and Life in the Rocky Mountain West." http://www.mman.us/index.htm.

Selby, Paul. *Anecdotal Lincoln: Speeches, Stories, and Yarns of the Immortal Abe.* Chicago: Thompson & Thomas, 1900.

Spiegel, Allen D. *A. Lincoln, Esquire: A Shrewd, Sophisticated Lawyer in His Time.* Macon, GA: Mercer University Press, 2002.

Spiegel, Allen D., and Florence Kavaler. "A. Lincoln, Esquire Defends the Murderer of a Physician." *Journal of Community Health* 30, no. 4 (2005): 309–24. http://link.springer.com/article/10.1007/s10900-005-3708-1.

Steiner, Mark E. "Does Lawyer Lincoln Matter?" In Billings and Williams, *Abraham Lincoln, Esq.*, 45–64.

———. *An Honest Calling: The Law Practice of Abraham Lincoln.* DeKalb: Northern Illinois University Press, 2009.

Stewart, J. R., ed. *A Standard History of Champaign County, Illinois.* Vol. 1. Chicago: Lewis Publishing Company, 1918.

Stowell, Daniel W., et al., eds. *The Papers of Abraham Lincoln: Legal Documents and Cases.* 4 vols. Charlottesville: University of Virginia Press: 2008.

Swett, Leonard Herbert. "Leonard Swett." In *Transactions of the McLean County Historical Society*, vol. 2, 332–65. Bloomington, IL: Pantagraph Printing and Stationery Co. 1899.

Tarbell, Ida M. *The Life of Abraham Lincoln: Drawn from Original Sources.* 2 vols. New York: McClure, Phillips, and Company, 1902.

Townsend, Walter A. *Illinois Democracy: A History of the Party and Its Representative Members—Past and Present.* Vol. 3. Springfield, IL: Democratic Historical Association, 1935.

"The Trial of Robert C. Sloo for the Murder of John E. Hall." *American Journal of Insanity* 15 (1858): 33–68.

Walker, John. *A Critical Pronouncing Dictionary and Expositor of the English Language.* Philadelphia: T. & W. Bradford, 1810.

Walsh, John Evangelist. *Moonlight: Abraham Lincoln and the Almanac Trial.* New York: St. Martin's Press, 2000.

Wharton, Francis. *A Treatise upon the Criminal Law of the United States.* 5th ed. Vol. 1. Philadelphia: Kay and Brother, 1861.

Whately, Richard. *Elements of Rhetoric: Comprising an Analysis of the Laws of Moral Evidence and Persuasion with Rules for Argumentative Composition and Elocution.* New York: Harper and Brothers Publishers, n.d. Reprint, Whitefish, MT: Kessinger Publishing, 2005.

Whicker, J. Wesley. *Historical Sketches of the Wabash Valley.* Attica, IN: J. Wesley Whicker, 1916.

Whitney, Henry Clay. *Life on the Circuit with Lincoln*. Boston: Estes and Lauriat, Publishers, 1892.

Williams, Jack Moore. *History of Vermilion County Illinois*. 2 vols. Topeka, KS: Historical Book Publishing Company, 1920.

Wilson, Douglas L., and Rodney O. Davis, eds. *Herndon's Informants: Letters, Interviews, and Statements about Abraham Lincoln*. Urbana: University of Illinois Press, 1998.

Woldman, Albert A. *Lawyer Lincoln*. New York: Carroll and Graf Publishers, 2001.

York, Jack. "Hooseriana," *Indianapolis Star*. December 19, 1948, 103.

Index

Italicized page numbers indicate figures.

GEORGE R. DEKLE, SR., retired in 2016 from a ten-year career as a legal skills professor at Levin College of Law, University of Florida. Before that, he spent thirty years as an assistant state attorney in the Third Judicial Circuit of Florida (which bore a striking resemblance to Lincoln's Eighth Circuit), where he investigated and prosecuted hundreds of homicide cases. Dekle has written several books on trial advocacy and legal history, including *The Last Murder: The Investigation, Prosecution, and Execution of Ted Bundy*; *Abraham Lincoln's Most Famous Case: The Almanac Trial*; and *Prosecution Principles: A Clinical Handbook*; and has coauthored *The Lindbergh Kidnapping Case: A Critical Analysis of the Trial of Bruno Richard Hauptmann* and *Cross-Examination Handbook: Persuasion, Strategies, and Techniques*.